Portrait of a Jew

OTHER BOOKS BY ALBERT MEMMI

The Pillar of Salt

Strangers

Albert Memmi

PORTRAIT
OF A
JEW

Translated from the French by Elisabeth Abbott

The Orion Press · New York

*To the comrades of my youth,
today Chalotzim.
To Jean-Paul Sartre, a free man.*

Contents

preface

"Could I be descended from a Berber tribe
when the Berbers themselves failed to
recognize me as one of their own? I was Jewish,
not Moslem; a townsman, not a highlander.
And even if I had borne the painter's name,
I would not have been acknowledged by the
Italians. No, I'm African, not European.
In the long run, I would always be forced to
return to Alexandre Mordekhai Benillouche,
a native in a colonial country, a Jew in an
anti-Semitic universe, an African in a world
dominated by Europe."

ALBERT MEMMI (THE PILLAR OF SALT)

Preface

As this book is to a great extent a self-portrait, it would be well for me to give at least a brief account of myself. I was born in Tunisia, in Tunis, a few steps from that city's large ghetto. My father, a harness-maker, was somewhat pious, naturally somewhat so, as were all those men of his trade and his station in life. My childhood was marked by the rhythms of the weekly Sabbath and the cycle of Jewish holidays. At a fairly early age, after first attending Yeshiva and then the Alliance Israelite, I became associated with various Jewish youth movements—scouts, cultural groups, political groups—so that, though I had profound doubts about religion, I did not stray from Jewry. On the contrary, I found it secured and even deepened a certain continuity for me. For a number of years I pursued a course of studies that dispensed Jewish culture both traditional and reformed, open to the most immediate problems and yet solidly anchored to the past. I took up collections, among the flat graves in the Jewish cemetery or in front of old synagogues, on behalf of various community works, for the poor, for Polish refugees, for German refugees. Without too much embarrassment, illegally or not, I went from door to door trying stubbornly to convince my co-religionists of the beauty, importance and necessity of the Zionist movement at a period when that movement appeared to be nothing but an adventure. I even thought of going to Israel, or rather, to the romantic, pioneer Palestine of those days. In other words, I was sufficiently involved in all Jewish activities for my emotions, my mind and my life to become identified with the lot of all Jews over a fairly long period.

A moment came, however, which actually had its roots in the French lycée, when that intense ardor seemed to stifle me, and the rest of the world suddenly became more important. That was the period of the war in Spain, of the French *Front Populaire,* and of my own departure for the university. While the physical break with the clan and the community, then with the city, and the contact with non-Jews whom I admired and liked, did not make me forget I was a Jew, it did cause me to consider that aspect of myself as part of a nobler and more urgent problem. The solution to that large body of ills from which all men suffered would in a way automatically solve my personal difficulties. Exchanging one enthusiasm for another, I came to consider anyone who did not think in universal terms as narrow-minded and petty.

It is necessary to bear in mind what that extraordinary period meant to our generation. We believed, finally, that for the first time humanity had perceived the light that could and must disperse darkness once and for all: oppressive measures, differences that separated us from each other, would be shattered, they were already being shattered. . . . Paradoxically, that universal light bore the clearly defined face of Europe—and more specifically, of France; but that did not trouble us; on the contrary, we were doubly grateful to the privileged for relinquishing their privileges and so identifying themselves with freedom and progress. After all, it was they who had invented the remedies after the ills: equality after domination, socialism after exploitation, science, techniques and promises of abundance. And by the time I left Tunis to continue my studies—soon to be interrupted, however— I thought no more about Palestine but only of returning to my native land, a universalist and non-denominational, reconciled to everything and everybody, Tunisians, French and Italians, Moslems and Christians, colonizers and colonized. . . . "The Jewish problem" had been diluted with the honey of that universal embrace which, though not yet fully realized, was so near, so obvious, because so necessary.

We know what came of it: the sequel belongs to world history: it was war. Our youthful hopes of universalism and brotherly love were destroyed. The Europe we admired, respected and loved assumed strange faces: even France, democratic and fraternal, borrowed the face of Vichy. Afterwards they explained that Vichy was not their only face, nor even the true one, that behind that mask, clandestine and noble. . . . So greatly did I hope it was true that I almost believed it, but I was no longer so enthusiastic or naïve. On the whole, it was better to make allowances for a dual personality and hope for a change of roles which was always possible on the revolving stage of history. In any case, I had learned the harsh lesson that *my* destiny did not necessarily coincide with the destiny of Europe. And when peace came and, after numerous vicissitudes, I returned to Tunisia, I envisioned, for the first time but of my own accord and without anxiety, that separate destiny.

What it was to be, I had no idea when suddenly the

event presented itself. My Moslem fellow-citizens, having made the same discoveries, were beginning to develop their own history. Sensitive to mass enthusiasms when I considered them legitimate, I naturally shared in theirs: the Tunisians aspired to become a nation; in a world composed essentially of nations and oppressed minorities, what could be fairer?

This time, however, I did not altogether overlook the fact that I was a Jew. Moreover, mistrust, hesitancy, blunders forced me to remember it constantly. But, I was assured, Jews would certainly have their place in the future nation; had they not suffered the same lot and the same insults as other Tunisians? Why would they not benefit from the same liberation? I wanted to believe this. In any case, how could I, who applauded so wildly the struggle for freedom of other peoples, have refused to help the Tunisians in whose midst I had lived since birth and who, in so many ways, were my own people? In short, I did not believe I had any right to think of a separate Jewish destiny. Thus, having ceased to be a universalist, I gradually became, in some ways, a Tunisian nationalist . . . though I failed to see that, on my part, there was still a great deal of hidden, abstract universalism in it, and perhaps even escapism.

Justice done to the Tunisians, I quickly found myself faced with that strange destiny which was still unchanged. Events that followed would force me to recognize that its singularity was still unimpaired, that it decidedly could not be overpowered by any other. To take only one example: the young states, formerly under colonial rule, were in urgent need of all sorts of personnel: technicians, administrators, intellectuals. That formidable vacuum could be partially filled by Tunisian Jews. But, as I had feared, the new states preferred to do without them. I hasten to add that it was difficult to picture a fifty percent Jewish personnel at the head of the new state; such a situation would have raised dangerous problems of domestic, and perhaps foreign, policies. But it was soon equally apparent that our distinctness as Jews was by no means resolved by our new status as citizens. Neither for non-Jews, nor for that matter, for Jews. When the war over Suez broke out, the Tunisian newspaper to which I was contributing and which I had helped to found, printed on the front page: "Whoever sheds the blood of Egypt, sheds our blood!" At that time the hearts of all Jews beat as one for the Israeli Army: their sons and their grandsons were there and the sons and grandsons of their friends. I did not approve of that expedition, but how could one reconcile those two conflicting loyalties! When the Tunisian Constitution appeared, it established the Moslem religion among its essential provisions. For a number of reasons that have nothing to do with my subject, I did not find that too shocking; but why would I, who had rebelled against my own religion, accept, under compulsion, the Moslem religion which was now official? Each step, in short, had to be carefully reviewed and put in order.

It will be said that this is no different from the situation of Jews in Europe, in a Catholic country, for example. Of course, I know that! I have now been around the world enough to realize that precisely the same situation exists everywhere. But does that make it any the less difficult? The end of colonization in Tunisia and Morocco has almost restored the condition of those Jews to the level of the condition of all Jews, a notable and decisive step forward. But where has the common Jewish lot ever been simple and without trouble?

In short, I must admit that I had only postponed attacking my problem seriously, it was time for me to tackle it directly and, if possible, finally. Not that I regret or repudiate anything leading up to this; neither my Jewish childhood and adolescence, my Western and

French culture and experiences which played such an essential part in my development, nor the aid and backing I gave to the just cause of the Tunisians. Isn't this confusing diversity a part of the situation I shall try to describe?

This book has, as you see, a special importance for me, and I hope that those readers who honor me by following my argument will give it special attention. In a way, it completes and concludes everything I have written in the past. I have recapitulated and carried to its logical conclusion everything connected with one major aspect of my life.

I now come to the other aspect of myself: I am a Jew. An equally essential aspect since it is obviously impossible for me to evade it, whether I choose clarity and courage or diversion and flight. Whether or not I decide to learn who I am, to understand myself and to understand other men in their relation to me, in order to live day by day or to face my destiny, it is impossible for me seriously to ignore it. Though I may prefer self-forgetfulness and abstraction, others do not forget and constantly, clumsily, make it their business to remind me of myself. In any case, the basis remains the same and I prepare myself to come to grips with the situation before me. I refuse to spend my life brooding over my situation as a Jew. Since the issue cannot be dodged, it seemed to me preferable to see it through, at least once.

First and foremost, I want to draw *my own portrait,* but only my portrait as a Jew; it is the *fate* of a Jew as I have lived it and as I still frequently live it.

Second aim, there is scarcely a writer who does not hope, through the special quality of his work, to strike a universal note. My path in life is reminiscent of so many other paths, my life as a Jew has been the same as the lives of so many other Jews, that I believe this portrait becomes not only my own.

Some of the portraits would obviously have to be retouched; we would have to bring out certain features, tone down others. But these differences are unimportant; the innumerable variations that we can imagine without disturbing the general outline. I believe that there exists a universal Jewish fate: and with this portrait I confess I have tried to describe it.

If I have chosen to confine myself to the use of the first person, it is neither from excessive modesty nor from boldness. Because I speak only for myself, I can guarantee the sincerity and the accuracy of my remarks and also avoid those useless quarrels, that grim resistance of bad conscience or of bad faith. I hope the reader will find in this picture more than a self-portrait; but if, in spite of all, he decides to see in it merely a confession, I agree to it. Let us then say that I am keeping a personal record, a balance sheet.

This is then also a book *about* Jews. How dare I write such a book when there are already so many intelligent, well-documented volumes on this subject, many of them even very well disposed towards Jews?

All the same, it seemed to me necessary that this task should be undertaken by a Jew; that it should be undertaken from within, from an intimate involvement with the Jewish fate. I thought that only my first plan would warrant the second—that the portrait of myself as a Jew was the best means of arriving at a portrait of the Jew.

"Certain women," writes Simone de Beauvoir in *The Second Sex*, "are still in the best position to interpret the situation of Woman . . . We know the feminine world more intimately than men, because we have our roots in it, we grasp more quickly what it means to be a woman."

This does not mean that no Jewish writer has ever attempted the same thing. The subject should be taken up again, I thought, and under certain specific conditions: a Jew would have to agree to tell all, to hold nothing back —and he must succeed in doing so. However, that has not always been possible. In the vulnerable and dangerous existence of the Jew throughout history, the slightest disclosure has played into the hands of his assailant. His sharp concern for self-protection has outweighed his concern for truth. It is true that a particular Jew may not have lived the Jewish fate as threats, anguish and shame; therefore, not paralyzed by fear and scruples, he could speak freely. But, by a cruel paradox, in that case his testimony ceased to reveal the Jewish fate.

In short, a man had to have lived his Jewish life completely and, at the same time not to have feared it, not to have experienced it as a mental and spiritual ankylosis. That type of man is beginning to appear; as yet he is scarcely visible, but it no longer requires too great an effort to imagine him, to call him into being. It is certainly no coincidence that we should catch a glimpse of the liberation of the Jew at the precise moment when we are drawing up this careful record with no concern but that of the truth. It is not chance that young national literatures are born on the eve of the emancipation of nations. It is not chance that literature written by women is only recently coming to fruition. If social freedom helps to hasten the advent of inner freedom, the end of inner oppression also ushers in the end of social oppression.

Throughout these pages I must therefore remember that promise: if this portrait is to have that new, and in a way decisive, value, it must be ruthless; that is, it must be both thorough and uncompromising. It is not merely a matter of a turn of mind as Descartes shows, nor only of logic and reason, but also of flesh and blood, of passions;

my passions and the passions of other men. It must be a coherent record which follows each characteristic to the end and relates one characteristic to the other; which gives each characteristic its proper place and therefore brings out its true significance. It must also dare to consider all things, to take everything into account, everything that constitutes my reality as a Jew, not only those things that might reassure me, but also what I would have preferred not to discover—my friends' illusions and my own, my misconceptions and the misconceptions of other men as regards me.

I know only too well how hard it is to get the truth out of oneself, especially when it must be made public. What a temptation to disclose only what other men are able to hear and what you can bear to let them know! Moreover, never so much as here is my word in danger of boomeranging, never has the word run so much danger of being transformed into action. I know what awaits me: "So you admit your weaknesses!" my enemies will sneer. "So you are giving them ammunition against the Jews," my friends, Jews and Gentiles, will say.

However, I must end this struggle with my fears, with those false calculations of prudence and those postures of respect which, I confess, I still feel. I shall often have to struggle with myself, to trick, to bully myself in order to get at the deepest truth. And on that condition only— I must repeat—can this record attain its goal. Otherwise, what would I do but add a plea that would be of no use to anyone? It is only because I shall tell *everything* that I shall be able to impose my conclusions.

part one

THE
MISFORTUNE OF
BEING A JEW

"And among these nations shalt thou have no repose, and there shall be no rest for the sole of thy foot; but the LORD shall give thee there a trembling heart, and failing of eyes, and languishing of soul. And thy life shall hang in doubt before thee; and thou shalt fear night and day, and shalt have no assurance of thy life. In the morning thou shalt say: 'Would it were even!' And at even thou shalt say: 'Would it were morning!' for the fear of thy heart which thou shalt fear, and for the sight of thine eyes which thou shalt see."

DEUTERONOMY 28: 65-67

The Malaise

1

I do not believe I have ever rejoiced in being a Jew. When I think of myself as a Jew, I am immediately conscious of a vague spiritual malaise, warm, persistent, always the same, that comes over me. The first thing that strikes me when I think of myself as a Jew is that I do not like to consider myself in that light. I can already hear the protests: and would I not like to protest myself?

"I've never been ashamed of it! I have never made a secret of it!"

Never? Really? As though the one precluded the other: as though by accepting anxiety and misfortune, even proudly, they miraculously ceased to be anxiety and misfortune! How well I now know that reserve of the oppressed, that refusal to admit his wretchedness!

For a long time I myself delighted in stressing the few privileged moments in Jewish life, in going into raptures over the touching affection of family life, the miraculous pauses of great ceremonies, Friday evening, the white tablecloth, the candles, the flowers; or more simply over those little pleasures of the Jew—a less repressed sexuality, a delight in comfortable living on earth, the joy of eating on festivals, with meat obligatory even on the tables of the poorest. . . . But, I also quickly discovered, I felt keenly how wonderfully preserved and protected those moments seemed to us in the midst of the uncertainty and the turmoil of our life. On Friday evening, we liked to say, every Jew is a prince in Israel and it is true that one of the best memories of my childhood is the picture of my father seated on the sofa, a jasmin flower behind his ear and a glass of wine in his hand, bathed, rested, in good humor. . . . And only two hours before, in the dank hole that served as his shop, he had been struggling to earn our daily bread amid scorn and contempt. The Jewish family saved the Jew, but like an oasis in a desert. That is a frequent theme in our literature, one I have not failed to use myself, and the ambiguity of my Tunisian memories is widely echoed from Central Europe, as in the tale by Shalom Abramowitsch:

"Schmulik, the ragpicker, lives like a dog for six days in the week. But on the eve of Sabbath, everything changes. Then the house is thoroughly cleaned and whitewashed, the table is set with a glistening white cloth; on it are placed two loaves of *challah*, a delight to the eyes; candles are lit in the brass candlesticks that have been highly polished in honor of the Sabbath; and a delicious odor rises from good food hidden under a cover in the warming-pan of the stove. . . . All week the mother has been as black as coal; today her face shines under a white headdress and a breath of grace has breathed upon her.

" 'Good Sabbath,' says Schmulik as he comes in. He looks lovingly at his wife and children, and his face beams.

"The ragpicker is no longer a dog; today he has a new soul. It is the Sabbath. Schmulik is the son of a king. All week long he runs here and there and wears himself out, but when Sabbath comes he pauses and rests. And there is no more sadness and there is no more sighing."

In contrast to the afternoon of the peddler, the artisan, the shopkeeper or even the Jewish businessmen, what revenge indeed, what frank triumph over humiliation or simply over the artifices, the efforts to conceal oneself, to dissimulate, to endure! For, after all, why be so astonished at those fleeting glimpses of happiness, if they are not essentially fugitive and in danger?

To reassure myself, to exorcise my deep-seated distress, I used to remind myself of our letters of nobility: the unusual duration of Jewish history, the extraordinary originality of Hebraic thought, its astounding impact on the world. . . . That pedantic reasoning, like our revolts of wounded pride, served only, as I fully realize, to foster a misinterpretation: was it really a question of the intrinsic value of Jewish culture? Though this culture were the foremost in the world, the richest and the most ancient, it would be beside the point if it had little effect on the daily life of the Jew. In vain I kept telling myself: Remember who you are! That marvelous past, that extraordinary contribution. I saw in general only indifferent, empty or skeptical eyes. For that matter, do the Jews themselves really know who they are? On that score, in truth, the ignorance or forgetfulness of Jews equals the indifference of non-Jews.

Dare I say fortunately? If the Jews had their whole culture constantly in mind, that view would be absolutely unbearable for them. For a culture is not only a collection of theories and values, of ideas and glory; it is also history and tradition, it is a long adventure with echoes and reverberations on the present and on the future. As I have said, I was for a long time associated with Jewish youth movements, where I was systematically instructed in that tradition. Ah, yes! Jewish tradition is consoling! Jewish history is reassuring! Curiously enough (I now see why) we strove to convince ourselves that Jewish thought is fundamentally optimistic. We insisted on the joyous character of Jewish ceremonies; we contrasted the contentment and even the jubilation of the Jewish religion with the sadness of Catholicism. And, in a certain way, this contrast is true. Christian ideology is in great part an ideology of misfortune. It reminds us incessantly that sickness and death lie in wait for us, that sooner or later they will catch up with us and destroy us. But today I wonder whether, paradoxically, the meaning of that painful reminder is not less dramatic than the bitter satisfaction of the Jew. An ideology is always, at least in some respect, a system of compensation; and to visualize its exact significance we must return it to its place in the lives of men who are living it. The Catholic religion pulls the Christian by the sleeve and reminds him: "Don't forget. You are perishable flesh. Time is passing swiftly and the day of reckoning is drawing near!" But this is intended to shake the thoughtlessness, heedlessness and pride of the Christian. The Jewish religion tells the Jew: "Look at the incredible succession of miracles God has wrought for you in order to protect you! Whatever misfortunes, whatever your faults, you are assured of His benevolence. Rejoice! Give thanks to God fervently, gratefully and joyfully!" There is indeed optimism in the Jewish tradition, but an optimism beyond despair. It is the optimism of the psychiatrist after his patient's abortive suicide; since the bottom has been reached, now only better can come. This attitude has almost become a mental habit of the Jew. After each family catastrophe, my mother used to thank God in this way: "Blessed be Thou, our eternal God, who hath preserved us from a greater misfortune." When Anne Frank's parents discover in their garret a thief who, moreover, will be their denouncer, what do they do? Do they tell themselves that perhaps this thief may denounce them? No, the father concludes that it might have been worse and therefore they have reason to rejoice!

What was, what still is, Jewish history but a continual alert, punctuated by ghastly catastrophes? Jewish anniversaries are frequently euphoric: they mark the end of a tragedy, life renewed, salvation after torment. We rejoice gravely at Purim, we celebrate, we shoot off fireworks, we receive and give presents, money, toys. Yes, indeed! We barely escaped one of the most complete exterminations in our history: it all but succeeded—saved by the charm of a woman, Esther! Popular imagination goes so far as to confuse the person of Haman with that of Hitler: the oldest instigator of our collective slaughter with the most recent. Thus, in the ghetto of Tunis, we bear aloft the traditional effigy of the Persian minister decked out with the little mustache of the Nazi dictator. Passover celebrated the end of a terrible enslavement, the frantic flight before the Egyptian army. What would have happened if God or the tide had not drowned our pursuers in the Red Sea? Hannukah, the festival of lights, is also the reminder of a deliverance which the Maccabean leaders paid for with their lives. Those are joys, to be sure, but how ambiguous! On what a background of sorrow and anguish! I shall not stress the ceremonies of ordinary mourning (that would be too easy) as, for instance, the national catastrophe of the ninth of April. On that day fate dealt a double blow: twice, on the same calendar date, a hundred years apart, Jerusalem was destroyed. The anecdote is perhaps false, but highly significant!

There was a moment, certainly, when Jewish history was a history, like any other, with shame and repentance, humiliations and arrogance, a national history, after all, with murder committed and not always suffered, a period in which the Jew was the agent of history and not always the victim. There are, of course, some elements of pure triumph, the amusing festival of the law, Simhath Torah, or perhaps Sukkoth, the feast of tabernacles, which is, however, more questionable. But what is the proportion of these joys compared to the tragedies?

Enough, however, of this problem of exegesis to which I shall return in a later chapter. For far too long our history has swung back and forth between a long series of persecutions, followed by rebellions occurring more and more rarely, which in turn were followed by oppressions. Martyrdom has become the sole collective habit the Jewish people have retained in their memory. Whatever the historic or geographic particularities of their unfortunate scattered groups, their trials seldom vary and serve only to nourish that apparently fixed sense of their destiny. History often acts as an alibi to peoples, and it is frequently necessary to break through a fog of dreams and deformed memories to get at the truth: Jewish history does not even permit that compensation. The events were too frightful, too consistently black for the calendar not to remind us of the price paid for our safety. I can clearly foresee that a day will come when the atrocious Nazi period will be celebrated by some ceremony: we shall rejoice that not all of us passed through the crematory furnaces, where only one Jew out of three was sent. One can foresee the quality, the gravity of that somber joy; with time it will come to resemble the Passover of the bitter herbs.

That, in any case, is the way the Jewish tradition appears to me, a Jew of today, the way I have lived it. My delight in Jewish history has never been more than a gloomy delight, the reminder of an endless succession of disasters, flights, pogroms, emigrations, humiliations, injustices. This is not merely an impression: I have only to open a book of Jewish history, a Dubnow or a Graetz. What is called Jewish history is but one long contemplation of Jewish misfortune.

TWO

The Jewish fate, as I have lived it, is first of all one of misfortune. That is the basic fact, the point of departure and an essential element of this portrait. Are there no happy Jews? I am tempted to answer: no. But let me be prudent and make myself clear: no, not *as Jews*. No, in truth, I know scarcely any Jew who rejoices in being one. There are Jews who, perhaps, are happy in spite of their Judaism. But because of it, in relation to it—no! Adjusting to it, eluding it, forgetting it, if one can. The moment you face it, the moment it arises, it inevitably becomes a strain, another shock, an honorary obligation if you insist, but in every way a burden. There are brief moments when one can take a somber pride in it, discover the substance of a philosophy, draw from it the motivating force of a life dedicated to glory. A man may be successful in everything he does; but at the same time he cannot fail to find in his success the deep-seated flavor of misfortune. Every writer who has ever written on this subject, who has dared to violate that disinclination of the oppressed to disclose the cause of his oppression, has confessed that it is a misfortune to be a Jew; as it is a misfortune to be a woman, a Negro or a proletarian and also as it is a misfortune to be a native in a colony. Each writer has a different name for it: malaise, restlessness, insecurity, anxiety, anguish. But all of them know that particular tension in themselves, that familiar gnawing.

"When a Jew has no worries, he invents some," the novelist Wassermann confessed in *Mein Weg als Deutscher und Jude*. "His ultimate incentive was a feeling of anxiety," Boris Pasternak noted in *Doctor Zhivago*. Ein-

stein, the scholar: "the insecurity of the individual Jew."
The philosopher, Jankelevitch (*Evidences*, December,
1950) : "That sense of strangeness is the daily experience
of every Jew." Jules Isaac, the historian ("Genèse de
l'antisémitisme" in *Christ Social*, Jan.-Feb., 1958) : ". . . a
constant sign: the precariousness, the uncertainty and the
anxiety of tomorrow."

An elderly middle-class Jewish Frenchman (or French
Jew as he preferred to call himself) protested that theory,
but when I assured him that I was not trying to influence
him to doubt France or Judaism or even his future as a
French Jew, he ended by giving me an excellent definition.

"Yes, I always feel I am in a front seat, that I am in the
wrong place. Let us say I am constantly in a state of alert.
But," he added, "that really did not begin until the war!
It took the silence of other men, their passivity, their
collusion, and all of a sudden our solitude in the presence
of the Nazis. Before that I did not feel especially Jewish.
I almost never thought of it."

In this way the malaise would be dated: suddenly it
becomes an accident. Having had a beginning, it might
just as well not have existed. At this point, I must admit,
I suspect, if not the sincerity of my informants, at least
some reconstruction of their memory in these sudden
facts that disrupt all the fundamental ideas of Jewish
life. The overwhelming nightmare must have made them
forget the familiar malaise, the countless little daily irritations. And, indeed, there must be few, if any, who have
discovered in a flash that they were Jews. They point
complacently to the experience of the Zionist leader,
Herzl, who became aware of himself only when suddenly
faced with the racial demonstrations of the Paris mob.

And, in *The World as I See It*, Albert Einstein noted:
"When I came to Germany fifteen years ago I discovered,

for the first time, that I was a Jew, and I owe this discovery more to Gentiles than Jews."

However, if Herzl had been so completely a stranger to Jewish misfortune how could he have dashed off his book *The Jewish State*, which is at once pathetic and explicit, lyrical and constructed with attention to the smallest details? And the date of Einstein's birth coincides within a few months with the founding of the Anti-Semitic League! When he was twenty, Germany rang with accusations of ritual murder, even in the Reichstag! A few years later, anti-Semitism was at its height in Austria, Poland, Hungary; in Russia, Jews were massacred, in France there was the Dreyfus case! And of all those tragedies Einstein claims to have known nothing! Is it possible that man of genius would not have guessed that those events concerned him even a little? But perhaps his astonishment must be otherwise interpreted; we shall come back to this later.

Is it not curious and, conversely, revealing, that each successive generation has had its historic mishap, its unexpected and incredible anti-Semitic tragedy, before which it claims to have lived in unconscious happiness and without which it would have lived in peace in a peaceful world? For Herzl it was the Dreyfus case, for Einstein German anti-Semitism, for us World War II. But here let us call a halt. History ceases to take the blame and soon shies away; that retrospective astonishment, whose candor I question, cannot be pushed very far. The farther one retreats into the past, the more striking and obvious the misfortune of the Jew becomes. Any reassuring doubt as to history's treatment of the Jew is possible only since Jewish existence has been legalized. Now that we are considered the equals of other peoples, we can pretend that we are their equals in reality. Whence our disillusion when we understand that legality is only one of the aspects of reality. Before, how could we even doubt it? We were the oppressed by right of law, rootless human beings, and everything that happened to us was deemed inevitable. It was so throughout all the Middle Ages, and again quite recently in Central Europe, in Russia, in the Arab countries. Even today in numerous lands, North Africa for example, the problem of whether one can hide the fact that one is a Jew is plainly ridiculous.

Isn't it necessary rather to believe that we at first reject, for a long period, this inopportune fact? Then, that it imposes itself progressively, punctuated by more or less revealing episodes that weaken a precarious equilibrium a little more each day, until at last the blow falls, until the eyes dare not see what lies before them? That the so-called revelation is never more than an established fact we have at last recognized? I have also written that I did not discover I was a Jew until I went to Paris. Now, I had lived in an undeniably Jewish environment; I had even gone through the war and the German occupation of Tunisia without coming to terms with myself in that respect. And paradoxically certain memories of my life as a Jew, among those I have not succeeded in digesting, belong to that period: the one, for example, that marked my first classes at the Sorbonne. We had just listened to a well-known professor, a Jew and, moreover, undersized and sickly and a meticulous splitter of metaphysical hairs. One of my companions immediately diagnosed him as "the typical little Jew."

So, even there! Even among my equals, the one place in the whole world, so it seemed to me, where I should have been accepted as the equal of all! It was a false alarm, however, and the battle could not be joined. With my hands trembling, and swallowing hard, I answered sharply: "I must warn you that I, too, am a Jew!" He looked at me and smiled: "My wife too, imagine that!" But already that quivering inner trigger that prepares me for battle, bitterness and anger, humiliation and revolt, had been released. Why such a commotion, such a mobilization of force, in the face of incidents that are, after all, futile, if not because the crystallization had begun so long ago? Because I need only turn my head to see the memories rise up, form in line, add to their numbers. I mentioned some of them in *The Pillar of Salt:* my father's sudden panic the moment the city began to stir, the lighted cigarette thrown on the head of Bissor, the arrival of Polish refugees, desperate, silent "sleepwalkers" or insufferably churlish and unjustly harassing to those of us who gave them shelter. How could I forget the strong impression the strange face of one of those refugees made on me? Jacobovitch was a little man, bitter to the point of cruelty, always in a rage, always rebelling against his woes, scolding, ironical, challenging his stupid Jewish destiny, our stubborn persistence in living, God's persistence in saving us, in other words, in torturing us —until the day when the Germans landed in Tunis. Then Jacobovitch, who had fled from them across all Europe, apparently changing tactics, suddenly became their interpreter, a quasi-official personage, respected and feared. Until that other day when, no less suddenly, I learned that he had been shot: persistent Jewish destiny indeed.

One way or another the day always comes when you discover that you are a Jew, just as you discover that you are mortal, not because of the collective and abstract promise of death, but because of your own individual condemnation. Did I not know, or did I prefer not to know, that I myself was destined to end in oblivion? One day, indeed, I stopped fighting desperately against that ghastly conviction: I ended by understanding, almost by conceding, that I would probably be maimed in an automobile accident, or injured by an illness, that this hand, this foot would rot, would dry up. That time I was really overcome and I stared at my hands, I ran my hand over my face. Sooner or later, be the discovery slow or sudden, hesitant or an overwhelming, decisive intuition, a man becomes aware that he is a Jew. Sooner or later each Jew discovers his little Jew, the little Jews he sees around him and the *little Jew* who, according to other men, is within him. And that realization comes to him no matter what his life, his successes or his failures, no matter what he is or what he thinks he has become, and notwithstanding his pretenses, the masks he wears or even his profound metamorphosis. Perhaps he has not even clearly formulated the questions before the replies are suggested to him: willy-nilly he is obliged to infer the problems from them. That moment always comes when you stop not thinking about it, when you understand what it means, over and above the legal and categorical boundaries, what it implies for the details and the direction of life, and you end by admitting: so then, I am a Jew. I am a Jew to myself, I am a Jew to other men. It is a fact, definite, compact, important for me and for others. From this, perhaps, comes the frequent impression of rediscovering oneself, of revelation, of unexpectedness at once inexplicable and inevitable, which I would like to call the illusion of a second birth.

"You cannot explain to others what it is to be a Jew nowadays. It is as though you suddenly discovered you had syphilis, as it was to have syphilis in other times when there was no known treatment for it." (Clara Malraux, *La Lutte Inégale*.)

THREE

So finally, if one is not always aware from birth of being a Jew, one always becomes so, each in his own way, which adds to the confusion and perplexity. Once he has discovered that he is a Jew, every man reacts as best he can, which again gives that impression at first sight of the diversity and dispersion of Jewish destiny. One man thinks he has managed to make other men forget him and at the same time to stop thinking about himself to a certain extent. Secretly, he hopes that someday he will stop thinking about himself altogether and in so doing that he will lose forever the haunting spiritual malaise that torments him. Another man will boast defiantly, call attention to himself, declare he is "proud to be a Jew." One man will try to control, to assuage, to take the edge off his Jewishness—and will spend his life deceiving himself; still another will resign himself to accepting it as one would accept a neurosis, will consider himself Jew, but will cut himself off from other men, withdrawing into a little word of his own, seek protection in abstraction and flight . . .

But is it not clear that the way in which each individual reacts to the misfortune of being a Jew is another step and, as it were, adds another trait which calls attention to and specifies the general characteristic? Is it not clear that the basis is the same and the malaise general? That the distracted and the forgetful, the aggressive and the obsessed, those who evade and those who proudly proclaim their pride, are all fighting the same anxiety? The realization that it is a misfortune to be a Jew is more or less dramatized, more or less a shock: it cannot be evaded, it can only be lived through as drama. From the moment the misfortune is recognized, being a Jew is *ipso facto* an inescapable fatality. The moment it is acknowledged you cannot ignore it, you are obliged to regulate your conduct by it in short, you cannot be a Jew and not think about it.

These, then, are what we may call the three states of the Jewish consciousness; the Jewish misfortune is certain and absolute: I cannot help discovering it. I cannot help living it. I can also do little to correct it. The result is that a man never lives his Jewishness naturally, spontaneously. The European, white and adult, sane and civilized as they say, a Christian in a Christian land, may question his religion, his nationality and his culture and even condemn them. In the majority of cases, however, he relapses into a somnolent torpor, born of long familiarity, and settles back happily among the traditions and collective customs of his people. I doubt whether the Jew as a Jew would ever succeed in doing that, for Jewishness is always uneasy. I can hardly think of any Jew who is natural and sure of himself. Ashamed or bragging, persecuted or proud, Jewishness can never be anything but tormented.

Here we must mention an illusory viewpoint based, I know, on generosity. This time it is a parallel illusion of the non-Jew. Because the Jew who is eager to be forgotten, to be like his fellowmen, never speaks of the road he has traveled in discovering himself, non-Jews, to whom such a thought seldom occurs, are inclined to believe that he attaches no importance to it. They are therefore surprised and embarrassed when they discover this hidden aspect of a Jewish friend or comrade. I recall the astonishment, often the irritation, of Europeans when they were told the real sentiments of most colonized peoples, when they learned that the natives have always felt they were either too little or too much colonized. As the Europeans did not look upon the natives in that light, they liked to think they were not suffering under colonization. But when, confronted with insistent and corroborative evidence, they saw the truth and could no longer deny it, they condemned the native: he was wrong to take that attitude. He "exaggerated," he was "too sensitive," he was "out of his mind."

"Very well," I, too, have often been told, "you suffer because you are a Jew. I believe you because you say so. But you are wrong to feel that way."

After denying that the situation exists, they say it is a "mistake;" after refusing to believe in the Jew's anxiety, they declare it is unfounded. In the end they even lose their tempers and retort sharply: "You think of yourself too much! Come now! You enjoy pitying yourselves! Have a little pity for others!"

One of the best arguments I have heard accused me of selfish complacency.

"You are not the only victim—if there are any victims at all!" they told me. "Look at the Negroes, at the Spanish Republicans, at all the displaced persons. And what about the gypsies! What social outcasts they are!"

A fine argument indeed! They are going to chop off your leg (and sometimes your head) but just look at that poor man in the bed next to you, they say. They cut off both his legs and he was so brave. Aren't you ashamed! A little more and they would blame you for not singing while they dismember you!

Far from thinking I am the only one in this situation, I believe, on the contrary, that racial discrimination is more widespread than anything else in the world. I note, with horror, that most individuals, most peoples, are basically inclined to xenophobia. Far from believing I am the sole victim in a world of peace and justice, I think, unfortunately, that the statement should be reversed: the Jewish tragedy is part of a much broader human category—the category of oppression and misfortune.

But, I repeat, I do not understand how the misfortune of others can be reassuring and comforting. All the misfortune in the world gives me no consolation at all for my own. It does not console me for anything. All the injustice in the world cannot make me accept the injustice I suffer. On the contrary, it feeds my anger, it whips up my fury against the shame and the outrage. Because I am a Jew, am I to console myself with the thought of anti-Negro racism or racial difficulties in the colonies? What my would-be comforters suggest to me is that since, after all, xenophobia does exist, it is up to me to suffer patiently the insult to the Jews! I understand perfectly. There are, in short, two attitudes: either one accepts all the suffering or one rejects it all. Well, I reject it *in totum* as I reject in detail each face of oppression.

Hostility

ONE

To tell the truth, I find this discussion of Jewish anxiety irritating, poorly conducted and futile. Some people persist in denying the facts: the Jew is no more anxious than the non-Jew, they say, and the anxious Jew would have been anxious even were he not a Jew. To others, anxiety is a mark of the Jewish nature, hereditary, a matter of chromosomes, or deriving from a more mysterious, perhaps miraculous cause. The two adversaries, so at odds on this point, agree curiously enough on another: anxiety is a fatality, whether it is constitutional or mystical. At the same time, if both of them are right in some respects, in others they are both completely wrong: the question is at once simpler and more serious.

Very few among us that I have seen, for example, were able to lie still in the sun, stretched out on the grass or dreaming in a chair as I have seen, with envy, non-Jews do. We could never keep still. Every week-end we jumped into a car and drove about one hundred kilometers, lunched abominably wherever we happened to be; then, time out for a cigarette and off we rushed again on the pretext of having coffee thirty kilometers away or of re-visiting such and such a famous site, on which we cast a distracted glance, only to notice finally that night was falling and it was time to go home, in other words, to get back in the car and rush off again. Of course, I reminded myself that we are a Mediterranean people, accustomed to long palavers and to living in public, that we needed human warmth, but our Moslem neighbors supplied the negative proof of our malady. The truth is that we were never even partially at ease unless we were on the move; not because we enjoyed exercise, but because movement took us from the place we were in to some other place which was better only because we had not yet reached it—and which we hastened to leave the moment we arrived. I found the same restlessness, perhaps even worse, among the Jews of Europe.

"When I take a walk with Ellen or Dina or Mosche," writes Arthur Koestler in *Thieves in the Night*, "and we stop for a rest, they either squat on their haunches with knees pulled up, or lie on their stomachs kicking the earth with their toes; and always after a minute or two they become fidgety and change position. Living on the land has washed a good deal of restlessness out of our blood . . . Arieh is an exception; but then Arieh is simple-minded."

Non-Jewish writers who know us well, our friends as well as our enemies, are hardly ever mistaken on this point. Henry Miller, whose first wife was a Jewess, Louis-Ferdinand Celine, who hates us so, both use the same picturesque language to call attention to the Jew's perpetual restlessness. And it is that same itch, I am sure, which to the distrust and annoyance of our fellow-citizens, drives us constantly to be doing something, no matter what, as if we were obliged to keep constantly feeding an insatiable inner flame. I am now convinced that the frequent intellectual and economic successes of young Jews result in part from that self-consuming, aimless agitation. In a novel that enjoyed a certain success some years ago, the author asked of his Jewish hero: "What Makes Sammy Run?" But Sammy was, apparently, not running towards anything: he was running away from himself.

Is that trait of the Jewish character which, after all, must be considered a fact, so shrouded in darkness that to illumine it we must explain it by an even more obscure mystery? Is it really necessary to trace the explanation back to more profound, more hidden sources, to talk of atavism and of curses? Is it really useful to say, like Koestler: ". . . but there is still something atavistic in us constantly on the alert."

Let us suppose that the long oppression, the long accumulation of staggering blows may have affected, thanks to an unknown mechanism, the nervous system of all Jews. Freud hints at it, but he could not explain it. But, then, mystery for mystery hypothesis for hypothesis. However, what time has done, why cannot time likewise undo? Koestler notes in the same book; speaking of young Israelites:

"Our collective unconscious must be crowded with the hosts and ghosts of Legionaries, Inquisitors, Crusaders, Landsknechts and Cossacks But our Tarzans, I believe, have got rid of them. Theirs the dreamless aseptic sleep without the fear and the vision . . ."

A strange atavism that would cease after one generation and as soon as living conditions change!

For my part, when I consider that endless procession of centuries throughout which the Jews were persecuted—have they ever ceased to be?—when I think of that geographic, historic and cultural instability of which every day I learn new phases (and am affected by them in my turn), when I think of the restlessness of my people from the beginning of their history down to my present life, including those around me, in the bosom of my family, and all of it continuous and inevitable, why would I not be worried, distressed about myself, about my future and my relations with other men? It would have been a miracle, incredible, utterly incomprehensible, if such constant and prolonged insecurity, handed down from generation to generation, had not resulted in a complete inner restlessness.

I remember our unanimous refusal, our suspicious revolt, when, in a recent census in Tunisia, the authorities proposed distinguishing Jews from Moslems and Christians. When one understood the importance of the denominational factor, its fundamental significance, in that country, it was clear that the mere division into denominations would be inadequate and even fallacious. But our anxiety outweighed any scientific and practical considerations. Why that mistrust, that defensive attitude, always on the alert? Why not admit quite simply that we were afraid?

Afraid of what? Look! All is serene, scarcely a cloud in the national and international skies. What are you afraid of?

Do I myself really know? For the moment it is only a vague fear, the apprehension of a threat. The threat is not immediate, it is barely probable, you say? Well, let us say the threat of a threat and let it go at that. Experience has too often taught us that there are no negligible threats for us, that anything can happen. If, instinctively, we refused to allow the census to designate us as Jews, it was because to us that meant being card-indexed, and indexes can always be used for other purposes. The arrival of the Nazis had already shown us that the threat was not wholly imaginary, our dread not altogether neurotic, our fear not always unfounded. To be on the safe side, therefore, I prefer to give only such information about myself as is strictly required. Certain countries, Switzerland for example, ask you to s.ate your religion when you apply for a visa (I have never yet understood why!). For a long time I refused firmly on the grounds that it was a question of decency, of honesty, of principle: I was no longer sure enough of my bel efs to attach importance to them; moreover, the state of my soul was nobody's business. I am well aware that my refusal had nothing to do with modesty or the soundness of my religion, legal or real, but with an *a priori* suspicion of everything that unmasks me. It was simply a matter of that anxious query that has now become second nature to me: why do those people want that information? What are they going to do with it? If I am not forced to give it, it is much wiser not to.

Need we look further to understand the present exodus (certainly surprising even viewed from outside) from North Africa to Paris, Marseilles and Tel-Aviv? Still too fresh in the memories of those emigrants are somber stories of throats cut, of hangirgs, of terrifying and totally unfounded accusations, immediately followed by atrocious punishments and plunderings ordered by (or covered by) the tyrannical Beys of Tunis. My childhood was made hideous by ghastly stories told by my parents and my grandparents; and I must confess that for a long time I hated to pass the walls of the Bardo palace where, it was said, many Jewish heads had been cut off. Historians now tell us that there were relatively few serious incidents; but the Jews of my father's generation spoke of the Moslem period in fear and trembling. They remembered it as an era of darkness, of tyrannical and widespread oppression. Then the Moslems came into power again! In vain we told our frightened people that the present generation was different, that the past was over and done with.

In vain the new leaders of the young nation reassured us in speech after speech. The Jews listened skeptically or hopefully; then, taking no chances, they went off and settled in France or in Israel. Whether they will be better off there, it is too early to say, but their memories of the past are still too vivid, they are still too deeply affected to bear even the thought of that threat.

This is not a question of biology or of metaphysics, nor is it a question of social essentiality or of actual essentiality. There are no more essential Jews than essential proletarians or than peoples predestined to be colonized. It is not my Jewish nature that secretes anxiety, but a continually fostered anxiety that has left its mark on my Jewish physiognomy. There are too many real reasons, both slight and weighty, but all objective, for my anxiety; reasons that would make any man in the world anxious. But anxiety is only one facet of the misfortune of being a Jew, its realistic aspect. Placed by itself and unconnected with hostility, it would still be inexplicable, or mysterious, which is not much better. There is no malaise on the one hand; then comes the discovery of this formidable world; anxiety and then the threat; anxiety, a trait of character that sometimes encounters a hostile reality. I have said that psychologically a man could scarcely help discovering he was a Jew; but that is because socially, of course, he already was one! All at once the Jew is presented with the full tragedy of being a Jew, all at once he is faced with the disaster of living in a world of threats and suffering provoked by that misfortune.

TWO

I admit that it is no longer easy for me to speak properly of that hostility. Not because I have not thought about it deeply, discussed it, argued the question, written about it! As adolescents we used to spend as many hours discussing it as we did in running after girls. How many violent sessions in strange places: laundries, icy cellars, backshops or in the open air under a tree, indifferent to cold and wind and even to the sweetness of summer evenings! How eagerly we sought the answers, walking each other home several times in succession, arguing excitedly as if we were on the point of finding the solution at last! I do not know what other young men in the world discussed around campfires or during long winter nights, but the subject that interested us, the one we argued passionately was the nature of anti-Semitism. Was the origin of the monster religious or economic, or primarily religious and then economic, the one relieving the other, keeping the other alive? Or was it simply a wretched diversion to distract nations from their internal difficulties, a hideous game suggested by rulers to make their people forget their reverses, their blunders and their swindling? Or perhaps all of these things together, inextricably interwoven? And later on, in how many groups, how many conferences, did we discuss this subject! There is hardly ever a meeting of Jews, whether interested in music or in stamps, that does not end by touching on that haunting theme; there is scarcely a Jew who does not have his own explanation on the tip of his tongue.

Why shouldn't I confess it? Today, confronted with that din of explanations, that economic, political, psychoanalytical, historical turmoil, I feel exhausted, depressed. Not out of disdain for knowledge and for the motive involved. Like everyone else, I have tried to shed all possible light on the nature and the sources of that continued aggression, to enumerate the elements that nourish it, to arrange them in their order of importance, to discover the cause, past and present, its genesis and its history. All that is very important and I shall come back to it later on. I still continue to listen avidly to any suggestions, I will change my ideas, my classifications, even my indignation and my hopes, according to the conversations I hold and the books I read. And yet I feel that no explanation of this hostility, which is so responsible for my misfortune, so complex, so involved, a living thing of multiple heads that speaks with a thousand grimacing faces, can ever exhaust the subject, can ever reassure me. Today I cannot bear to have an explanation so much as suggested to me, nor can I take comfort in it, if it does not condemn that hostility and utterly destroy it. That is, perhaps, an admission of weakness on my part; of ignorance and of anxiety disguised as impatience. Perhaps it is because I live it too deeply and feel that it is shameful. For I live it as soon as the talks turn derisive. I thought I had said everything in a few words: anti-Semitism, racism, mystification, economy—and I find I have said almost nothing. The further I go, the more I realize that I still have something to discover and that the perspective changes. And, finally, to be fair, I must tell *everything* about myself and about other men: it is my task to explain my whole life in this book, all my life as a Jew, and to do so as clearly as possible.

It must be plain however, that if, for the moment, I leave the explanation open, I do not admit any doubt that there is one. I myself cannot doubt the existence everywhere of constant hostility, virtually unweakened in its heavy tyranny. It is the only fact that matters to me, though it crushes me. Like the spiritual malaise that is so alive in me, so obvious in all the Jews around me, hostility is the common denominator of our life. In other words, the misfortune of the Jew concerns all Jews, who are called Jews largely because of that gloomy peculiarity.

THREE

As I was putting the finishing touches to this text, the recent wave of anti-Semitism broke out in Germany and swept over the whole world. I shall not use it as proof, it would be too easy! Nor do I wish to exaggerate its importance. It confirms, unfortunately, my opinion that this is the point from which I must start, from that solid mass of fact, whether it is possible to explain it or not, to understand it or not.

People have sometimes tried to reassure me: "In such and such a country," they say, "there is no hostility towards Jews!" The trouble is those countries change according to the nationality of the speaker and it is always a country other than his own: England when the speaker is French, France when he is American. "Switzerland," they assured me vehemently only the other day, "an old and genuine democracy; bourgeois to be sure, but quite rich; sure of itself, therefore liberal; Protestant and virtuous. How could it be racist?"

I make no comment on the value of that logical description. However, while I was on vacation near Geneva last year, I happened to read in a local paper one of those editorials in which the journalist amuses himself by taking his fellow-citizens to task. Beating the collective breast, he criticized his country, "land of perfect equality," for never having tolerated a Jew as a Federal counselor, for never having promoted an officer to high rank if he was a Jew: in short for cheerfully permitting a diffuse but obvious racism.

I should like to think that those old countries are the only ones still affected by this ancient evil, that a long racist tradition . . . But, no! Were I to go to the ends of the earth, I know I would find the same miasmas there. Since I have known this, my dreams of distant and fabulous lands are permanently ruined.

"From Venezuela I went to Peru," writes Max Fuks, a great Jewish traveler ("*Le Tour du monde d'un Lavarède juif*" in *La Terre retrouvée*, Nov. 1958). "I had been warned that it was very difficult for a Jew to obtain a Peruvian visa.

"In New Caledonia I looked for Jews and I found a few . . . the white minority is somewhat anti-Semitic, and my friends did not dare to say they were Jews . . .

". . . what is not well enough known, what I myself did not know, is how anti-Semitic Canada is. It is an anti-Semitism that is chiefly religious at bottom. To Canadians, and French Canadians in particular, Jews are still the people who murdered 'Our Lord.' "

It is, of course, impossible for me to enter most of the Arab countries. For some time it has been wiser for me not to go too near their borders: as a passenger on a ship calling at Alexandria or Beirut, I cannot be altogether at ease. John Hawkins, another Jewish explorer, relates that, wishing to make a tour of the world in a sailboat, he was refused permission to pass through the Suez Canal and was obliged to sail around the Cape of Good Hope as men did before the isthmus was cut. It is not easy, as one can see, for a Jew to be an explorer or a world traveler. In every land, in short, the misfortune of the Jew stares one in the face. Unless it is carefully hidden; unless a man disappears as a Jew—if he is able to do that! For it is not always possible if, for example, your name is Levy or Cohen or Abraham; or if your passport is stamped "Jew," as it is in certain countries of the East; or if you are a citizen of free and powerful America! To avoid any annoying ambiguity, many American companies have agreed to make available to Arab countries the list of their Jewish passengers, employees and clients, thus making it easier to turn them down.

The argument about the absence of hostility where Jews are nonexistent, is often amusingly naïve! Certain countries are definitely not anti-Semitic—because they do not have any Jewish citizens. Like China, for instance, India, or even some innocent little piece of earth in the midst of a racially biased country. "I spend all my vacations in such and such a village," people tell me triumphantly. "The villagers there have never seen any Jews, they don't know what a Jew is."

A poor consolation, indeed! But suppose they did, what then? For that matter, you find the same argument surprisingly enough in anti-Semitic form. Mr. Deasy, one of James Joyce's characters in *Ulysses* explains why Ireland has never persecuted Jews: "Because she never let them in!" In short, there is no hostility where there are no Jews. And what would happen if I were suddenly to appear in their world? I can hear them: they would advise me to arrange *never* to exist; as I am a Jew I must avoid living openly as such. I have no doubt that is what my friends succeeded in doing on their holidays; they lived for years by passing themselves off as other than they are, by keeping their real identity secret. But suppose all that is distasteful to me. What if it is as difficult for me to force myself constantly to hide my real self as it is for me to endure a certain hostility? For, as everyone must realize, this situation is not an absence of hostility, but a miserable compromise on the part of the Jew with that potential hostility he always fears and which is certain to break out if he begins to live like other people; it is, in short, a banal means of escape.

" 'You must be well-dressed if you want Paraguayan society to accept you.' said my relative.

" 'But I don't want it to,' I replied.

"Monsieur Mélamède raised his head: 'It is essential.'

" 'We will help you, we are greatly respected here,' my relative assured me and she added: 'No one knows we are Jews. We let them think we are Turks. When they speak of my husband they say: the factory of Monsieur Mélamède, *el Turco*, the Turk.'

" 'From now on, you, too, are a Turk,' said my cousin.

"I look out through the open window and I long for

the sky. The palm trees sway gently after the rain."
(Jacques Lanzmann, *Le Rat d'Amerique*.)

After all I am forced to admit that this hostility,
whether latent or expressed, whether violent or restrained, exists today in every land where it is possible for
me to live. In the United States a great American newspaper, the New York *Herald Tribune,* tells me there are
forty publications that specialize in stirring up racism
and anti-Semitism, a total of a million copies. Vercors, a
pro-Soviet writer, says that the USSR has taken a heavy
toll of Yiddish writers and has deported an enormous
number of Jews. In France there is currently a *numerus
clausus,* and Jewish newspapers are camouflaged to disguise their ownership. All social groups in a country are
more or less affected, each in its own way, each applying
to the disease the tone of its own particular invalid. There
is a hostility of merchants and a hostility of the liberal
professions, a hostility of the military and a hostility of
the clergy. If I am a lawyer, I have to realize that I
shall probably never be president of the Bar; if I am
a doctor, that a barely discreet *numerus clausus* will work
against me; if I am a soldier, that certain posts and
certain regiments are permanently closed to me. I am
reminded of my friend Berdah's experience. He joined
the African army as a volunteer but, though a superb
horseman with several prizes to his credit, he was not permitted to enter the cavalry. He had to die in the engi-
neers; it is less honorable, I suppose, to be blown up by a
mine, and military nobility cannot be shared with a Jew.
And finally, there is a hostility of the rich and a hostility
of the poor, a hostility of small shopkeepers and a hostility of wage earners. Yes, and there is also an anti-
Semitism of the workingman. That was one of my most
painful discoveries (was it really a discovery?) : to be
forced to admit that, in spite of all our ideological hopes,
there is a definite racism among the poor and the op-

pressed. "It is impossible for laborers to be racists," we had been assured. "What interest would they have in it? Besides, just as in those villages-without-Jews, the Jew is unknown in laborers' groups." Nevertheless, that absurd racism in which "they would have no interest," does exist; and when workers discover a Jew among their fellow-workers, they are amazed. They showed the same amazement, though it was not to their interest and politically stupid, when they came in direct contact with Algerians. I have been told there is even anti-Semitism among the blacks in Dakar's shanty-town. The truth is that anti-Semitism is not simply a matter of class or of economy. The assurances of democrats and non-Jews of good will can be traced to a curious half-magical, half-tactical attitude. By dint of talking about the ideal democracy and future proletarianism, they finally succeed, by a stretch of imagination that goes beyond present reality, in settling themselves in that perfect democracy, that lucid and virtuous proletarianism, that ideal church. By dint of wishing and asserting what they wish for, they end by believing it is so.

Unfortunately I cannot indulge in the luxury of talking myself out of this reality that crushes me. I can hope that one day priests will attain the heights of their faith, that they will absorb its holiness and become saints; that some day, perhaps, they will lay aside all anti-Semitism, among other disastrous delusions. I hope ardently that moral and social progress may one day sweep away all oppressions, all iniquities and, among them, anti-Semitism. Meanwhile, as a Jew living today, I must make the best of democracy and church, army and proletariat as they exist today.

Non-Jews of good will are sometimes misled by the fact that the hostility is not always overt and legal. But because the action against the Jew is not out in the open, does that mean it is not effective? It is enough to abstain when the decision is really one of the most elementary justice—and frequently cleverer to do so. An engineer with a great national concern, whose name I am not at liberty to mention, explained to me how this unofficial anti-Semitism works. The company in question does not hesitate to call on Jews if it needs them, but it refrains from doing so as much as possible. By this means it is free to protest if charges are brought against it and thus wins both ways. It is also true that the Jewish misfortune is not always unbearable all the time in the same place: it does not always show several faces simultaneously. And there again I understand the bewilderment of my non-Jewish friends. But to me, to my restless vigilance, it is only an obvious and continual succession of tragedies that rise up again and again out of the human jungle, now at one point, now at another, and I know that the respite will only be brief, that the evil has struck somewhere else and is ready to raise its ugly head again. For one hundred and fifty years, I am told, a process of assimilation has been going on in France. Perhaps! But what about Vichy? Vichy was not French, my friends retort. Indeed! So be it. But how can a Jew, living in France, shut his ears to the cries of pain and anguish from other Jews in the world, cries that have never ceased during those hundred and fifty years? In 1881: the assassination of Czar Alexander causes an exodus from Russia to America. 1903: pogrom in Kichinev, 15,000 Russian Jews settle in France. 1908 to 1925: 15,000 Levantine Jews flee the revolt of the Young Turks. After that came the flight of German, Czech and Polish Jews from the Nazis. And this persecution has never ceased since the days of Abraham, the Patriarch, flung into the fiery furnace of Chaldea; the enslavement in Egypt; the building of the Pyramids and the slaughter of newborn babes; the European ghettos and pogroms, the humiliating, stifling conditions in Moslem lands. Always, somewhere in the world, Jews are being oppressed, endangered or killed. The Jewish misfortune may abate, it may become almost bearable like a quiescent malady that a stabbing pain calls periodically to mind. But as for me, I feel it always there, barely masked by more urgent historical anxieties or by good manners and social conventions. I know that when I leave a drawing room where, at the moment, my hosts treat me as one of themselves, I run the risk of recovering my heterogeneity. What difference does it make since I am not there to suffer from it? Naturally! Until the day when the good manners crack, when I catch a glimpse, insinuated or overt, of what others really think of me—which I well know, but which I have a tendency to act as if I have forgotten . . . Why, therefore, would I not always be on the watch, even though I tried, even though I pretended to have no interest in what happens to other Jews in other parts of the world? Even though I live in a land where the evil has not been seriously manifest for a long time? And how could that vigilance and that anxiety, that false ease or that strained effort, corroborated, sustained and consolidated by that tremendous historic and geographic experience, daily established, secular, religious, civil, military, fail to leave its mark on me? How could it fail to form, like an old neurosis, one of the surest, strongest and deepest layers of my so-called Jewish nature?

The Problem

When I announced my intention of writing this book, I was greeted by a storm of protests from both my Jewish and my non-Jewish friends.

"You are going to stir up monsters that are only asking to be roused," they told me. "The best thing for this subject is silence!"

I am not convinced of that. I am not sure that ignorance and blindness may not be more harmful. I believe, on the contrary, that one must call a spade a spade—and I have decided to do so. I also believe that those particular monsters shun the light and it is better to call them out, to expose them, and have done with it. I have also been accused of cruelty, injustice and, at the least, tactlessness, particularly towards non-Jews of good will.

"After all, you seem to be accusing everybody. You generalize all the time! Do you suspect all of us of latent xenophobia and racism?"

I am well aware that this reminder, and my insistence on it, may appear excessive and disagreeable; particularly at a time when we are trying to forget the past and make sure the future will never be like it. But if that good will, which is after all fairly new, is not a pretence or a whim, it is better to take a frank look at the present and its cruelty, for there is cruelty even today. I force myself to weigh my words: I do not think I am being either unjust or trivial, nor am I generalizing in a moment of thoughtlessness or anger. The matter is unfortunately far more serious: I believe firmly that anti-Semitism is profoundly widespread and real; I fear we must start with this generalization, for it is among the half-truths of the nation in which I live.

When you tell me indignantly: "We are not xenophobes! We are not racists!" I do not doubt your good faith. Your revolt even pleases me: so then, there are men who would never harm a Jew because he is a Jew. But to be frank: how many of you are there? What can you do, you men of good will? Must I be even more frank? Do you imagine that you represent the whole or even the majority of your people? And what do you actually do but stand aloof, refrain from doing anything? Is not that, in the final analysis, the advice you are giving me: discretion, silence, forgetfulness? We had exactly the same friendly quarrel when I drew the portrait of the colonized natives. "I have lived ten years in the colonies," someone will tell me, "I never treated a native scornfully! I do not have any of the sentiments you attribute to the colonizer." There again, I have known men whose equity, benevolence and courage are beyond dispute; but has that changed the general aspect of the colonial situation? Has the recent significance in relations between colonizer and colonized been transformed? Has the current picture of the European colonial taken on a different coloring, a different form? Has the plight of the colonized native been perceptibly ameliorated? Many non-Jews, you tell me, have no anti-Semitic sentiments, have never contributed to the Jewish misfortune. Better still, entire groups, companies, various social units, are apparently unaware of any hostility toward the Jew; it does not enter into their plans. All that, however, scarcely helps me if society in general remains hostile to me, if I continue to live in a structurally hostile universe. Some men, it is true, make a sincere effort not to treat women as inferior beings, to talk to them as they would to men, and are fully as indignant over woman's position in the world as she is herself. But for all that, does not woman still occupy an inferior position, is she not still oppressed? I do not believe, in short, that the generosity of a few men, feigned or real, spontaneous or calculated, can change the essential substance of my situation.

The truth is that anti-Semitism, like all oppressive relationships, goes beyond will power and good will, breaks out cruelly in individuals. Jews or non-Jews, we are faced, almost from birth, and throughout our whole lives, with that abject and disturbing but indisputable fact that has now become familiar, even chronic. That fact is almost a part of our institutions, our collective customs and our culture, like certain huge, ugly old monuments, which no one thinks of destroying, so much do their age and their bulk seem to defy the powers of the wreckers; but, after all, as they obstruct only the view of their immediate neighbors, in other words the view of only a few people, they do not seriously annoy the large part of the nation. And, finally, we run the risk of not understanding the Jewish misfortune, of minimizing it, of denaturing it, if we forget that it is first and foremost a collective and world-wide phenomenon. And not only a collective phenomenon to non-Jews but (I shall return to this later) a fundamental relationship between the Jewish group and the non-Jewish group; in other words it affects and colors all relations between Jews as a whole and non-Jews as a whole everywhere.

Of course, I do not feel that every non-Jew is hostile and menacing! In the face of certain individual facts, when I am with a university colleague, for example, or in the midst of a group of writers, I can forget the misfortune of being a Jew. I forget myself to the precise degree in which I forget them, and I forget them to the extent that they make me forget who I am. But at any moment, the whole fine edifice may topple: a mistake, a carelessly spoken word, an action, a more or less unconscious gesture, and all is lost. The entire relationship is again suspect: I doubt them, they doubt me. Of course I can have loyal non-Jewish comrades, affectionate friends, even a non-Jewish wife. Nevertheless, non-Jews as a whole constitute that universe of hostility and exclusion. This I feel strongly. I believe that all non-Jews are part of a society that renders the life of the Jew unlivable as a Jew. Is that feeling so wide of the mark, so unexpected? Is it not shared to a certain extent by non-Jews themselves? Why, for instance, do they become irritated when they are reminded of the horrors suffered by Jews and other oppressed races? Is it only because they are surfeited with too much reading, too much hearing about it? To be sure, even the most shocking scandals will end by irritating us if they last too long. But after the war, once past the first stunned surprise and the first demonstrations, people turned a deaf ear all too quickly to those stories of massacres, deportations and plunderings as they would to an obscenity. Wasn't that a defensive reaction against an insidious worry, a fleeting sense of responsibility?

I am distressed that this truth is so harsh, but it is real, brutal and dramatic. Just as all men, each and every one of us, are responsible for that social order that makes women servants or dolls, that permits great numbers of women to be turned into prostitutes, so every non-Jew, directly or indirectly, shares the responsibility for the Jewish misfortune; every non-Jew, willingly or unwillingly, shares the responsibility for oppressing the Jew. The fact that we do not have colonial possessions or that we refrain from frequenting prostitutes does not relieve us of our responsibility. We would also have to repudiate a society built solely for men, which assigns to women a position restricted in advance. We would have to overthrow a society that condemns the Jew to such a destiny. And since, after all, we can contribute but feebly to that overthrow, I confess that I consider the situation nearly hopeless.

TWO

That statement is at once harsher than it seems and at the same time less harsh. Will anyone believe me if I say that I hoped to write this book with a minimum of accusations against those who accuse us? Some other time, perhaps, I shall describe at greater length the difficulties the non-Jew experiences in the presence of the Jew, as I have done for the colonizer and the colonized. I know it is hard to break away from those roles. What to say to the Jew, for instance, and what not to say to him, to avoid hurting him? The tyrannical relation that chains the oppressed to the oppressor is greater than either of them: its generality, its ancientness, both recommend it to, and impose it on, the oppressor. In bourgeois structures, the bourgeois and his son are offered such privileges that it would be surprising if they did not take advantage of them. The same situation prevails in colonial structures. I realize that, on the whole, a responsibility so general and so inevitable becomes in a way weakened. It is practically impossible to blame any one individual when the guilty are so numerous. I sometimes will ask myself with a sort of desperate forbearance:

What can the non-Jew do, even with the best of good will, in the face of a phenomenon that is so far beyond the strength and the span of one man's life? He may, of course, disapprove or approve and at the same time contribute to that phenomenon, but he does not invent it, he is merely a party to a crime that is committed and perpetrated without him. This fact goes far in explaining the undeniable tolerance the anti-Semite enjoys as long as he behaves himself, that is, as long as he does not disturb the peace of other men. Though they may vaguely disapprove, people are inclined to shrug their shoulders at a passion which, though somewhat vulgar, is so general, so commonplace and perhaps, after all, slightly justified.

Now, however, we come to the gloomy reverse side of that forbearance, the sinister face of that negative good nature. Moreover, I do not consider the rabid anti-Semite an unusual being, a pervert, a kind of absolute evil, an immoral monster on whose shoulders one can calmly unload the sins of racism and xenophobia of an entire society. I think, on the contrary, that the anti-Semite is the natural product, the fruit of that society and can only be explained through it. Psychologists maintain that the anti-Semite has a special personality, narrow, rigid, sclerosed, phobic. They are probably right. In any case, it is useful to show why one man is an anti-Semite and another man is not; why one is extremely anti-Semitic, while another is only partially so. Perhaps if we knew the answer we could throw light on and correct certain statements. But why does a narrow and rigid personality find revenge and compensation in hating the Jew? Is it not because society so conveniently, so generously, suggests it to him? How can one clear up, correct, suppress that powerful suggestion? Society as a whole calls the Jew to account, insistently and continuously; with bitter incidents to be sure, but on a chronic basis. There is no rupture, no real break between the anti-Semite and his people, but a gradation, an exasperation, a systematization. Just as there is a simple gradation and not a difference in nature between the good employer and the bad, and perhaps, ultimately, the slave-trader. The anti-Semite, in short, is always the anti-Semite of a given society: he is only repeating statements, whispered or barely expressed, but he speaks them aloud in a snarling, sadistic tone, more or less badgering, more or less trenchant. The drunkard on holidays who shouts in the middle of the street: "Kill the Jews!" is often expressing the secret thoughts of the passersby who laugh but think to themselves that some day they too will get drunk and run wild. History has too often taught us that, given a favorable occasion, those whisperers and those laughers can one day become at least the accomplices of murderers. I mean, in short, that there is nothing original about anti-Semitism. Its curses, its accusations, its aggressions merely express the surprise, the rage and the will to murder of all non-Jewish society. Anti-Semitism openly borrows the language, the images and the obsessive themes from the society in which it lives. And when anti-Semites go so far as to commit murder, that is because they believe they have almost been given permission to do so. Finally, perhaps the anti-Semite is a sick man, but every society has its own sick men, its own mad men. To make the rejection of the Jew the sole object of overt anti-Semitism strikes me as too convenient, too demagogic and too false.

That is why I cannot be satisfied to shrug off the anti-Semites' statements and questions: I know they are not his alone. There are degrees of brutality and rejection, but I know that the fundamental question is always there, in the background, more or less clamorous, more or less urgent. To my half-innocent friends, to the tolerant ones, I am always tempted to repeat what the Jews of Algiers say with a bitter smile: "Racism is like the trolley from Saint-Eugène: it runs through the whole town, the beautiful sections and the ugly ones, it goes very fast . . . but it always leads to the cemetery." At one end of racism there is always the same question, at the other end, there is always assassination. "Let every brave Frenchman kill a Jew and the French will be free again," advises an anti-Semitic tract I have before me as I correct this text. When I hear the ritualistic phrase: "I am not a racist but . . ." I know that the racism-trolley has started, that the questioning has begun, that sooner or later, my life is in danger.

Let no one tell me: now there you are expressing a personal opinion, one that derives from your own experience; that great collective outcry you persist in describing exists, perhaps, in those distant, and frankly rather backward, countries where you were born, in those Oriental ghettos, so poor and so terribly vulnerable, where Jews had no choice but to submit *en masse* to the hostility of other groups. I thought so myself, until my first trip to Europe. It is not the same thing, of course, to have lived in a North African *meliah,* in an East European ghetto or in a large, anonymous city. It is one thing to have had socially outcast parents whose Judaism was intensified and increased by poverty and humiliation, and quite another to have had parents whose money and culture compensate for many worries. And finally it is not the same thing when one has been aware of being a Jew from birth or when one "discovers" it from the whispered words of strangers and even of one's own people. But I have always found the same question that non-Jews ask the Jew; or, what amounts to the same thing, the same question which the existence of the Jew poses to non-Jews. "Since the day of the promise," notes J. Nantet, a particularly benevolent Christian in *Les Juifs et Les Nations,* "Israel has never ceased to be a problem to other peoples. It lives among them like a stranger." The fumbling efforts of the Jew to reply vary, of course, according to temperament and personal experience. One man will try persistently to accept his Jewishness, that is, to get along with the world and with himself; another will make an effort to cast it off as one rips off a piece of one's skin . . . But at the heart of all those efforts I thought I had found a common motive, one that governs them all: the same desperate search for an answer to the same question. For too long I was an exceedingly passionate, exceedingly bitter internationalist, then a nationalist with the same violent enthusiasm, then just as passionately a skeptic and a humanist. Today I know that the passion is always the same, the quest always the same.

"For as long as he could remember, he had never ceased to wonder why, having arms and legs like everyone else, and a way of life common to all, one could be different from the others, liked only by a few and, moreover, loved by no one. He could not understand a situation in which, if you were worse than other people, you could not make an effort to improve yourself. What did it mean to be a Jew? What was the purpose of it? What was the reward or justification of this important challenge, which brought nothing but grief?" (Boris Pasternak, *Doctor Zhivago*.)

How can I avoid trying to answer this question that bears on my very existence, concerns my very being? Not that I find it clear or legitimate; not that I always foresee the replies, nor do they seem to me easy to grasp. On the contrary, I sometimes fear they may be beyond my power. But, constantly urged by others to reply, how could I fail to ask myself that question? The result is that all my life has been warped, deformed, by this futile effort. I say, in short, that I am a problem, that in our societies the Jew is of necessity considered a problematical being; he is driven to become a problematical being. A problem to other men, why would I not be a problem to myself?

The Separation

What is this question and what is this problem? I realized that I was being called to account even before I knew why; I found myself accused before I knew of what I was being accused. Would I ever know precisely? However, faced with an accusation that is vague, one may as well resign oneself. Then, too, there are times when the obscurity of a situation adds to its hopelessness: I have long struggled painfully, desperately, to distinguish the indistinct voices of that immense clamor, and I have made no progress. That, I believe, is the meaning of Franz Kafka's revolt: a Jew blindly facing his fate as a Jew, a confrontation raised to the dimensions of a metaphysical drama. The darkness of the Jewish fate is a symbol of the darkness of man's fate. The defeat of Kafka's efforts to understand himself, to grasp what was wanted of him, what he wanted of himself, the increasing suppression that followed his frenzied anguish, all led him in the end to offer his stifled mind voluntarily to the tormentor. In Christian lands, as one knows, one can always fall back on the theme of deicide: the Jews killed Jesus and that is why they suffer. No doubt this story contributes to their misfortune, but when I examine it closely, I have difficulty in keeping a straight face. How can an anecdote, so vague in details, so uncertain in motive, a tragedy that must have taken place two thousand years ago, still be used to crush a people who have as little connection with those judges of bygone ages as has the supposed victim with his defenders of today? I suspect something very different in that persistent effort to keep the pot constantly boiling with the old hatred of the Jews in the name of a murder presumably committed two thousand years ago. At present there is much talk of the recent good will the Catholic Church is showing: last year, wishing to make a fine gesture, a well-known priest stood up in the pulpit at Notre-Dame to correct the traditional interpretation of the "deicide." "It is not altogether the fault of the Jews," he explained solemnly, "but all men are to blame—Jews included." What excuses, what justifications the Church always needs to enable it to cling so firmly to the misery of the Jews! We must look beyond the accusation and the letter of the anti-Semite's speech!

I could almost affirm that the way in which I have experienced that accusation, in which it has distorted my features and poisoned my soul, cannot be wholly attributed to the reasons I have cited; these reasons are much too confused. With a somewhat cruel irony we might give a new interpretation to the old adage: the accusation is incumbent upon the accuser; after all, he is the only one who knows what he is talking about. Is he not the key to the problem? Is he not the one who starts it, upholds it, keeps it going? If he chooses, he may make his disclosures by degrees, keep certain details to himself, wait for the case to come up; he can refuse to explain publicly and content himself with insinuations, with whisperings; at the most, if he wishes, he can refuse to talk and halt proceedings. And what of the accused? What becomes of the defendant? Actually his role appears to be passive or at the very least subordinate. Every lawyer will tell you: Wait! Let your opponent take the initiative, it is easier to defend yourself afterwards. And meanwhile? Meanwhile, the defendant will wait, he will worry, he will suffer, he will wear himself out, he may even die without having really understood what was wanted of him. Carried to the extreme, the paradox would come out as follows: in any description of the accused, one should not pay too much attention to what the accuser says. And, all things considered, in drawing my portrait of a Jew, I could almost ignore the remarks of the anti-Semite.

That, of course, would not be altogether possible. The anti-Semite has played an important part in enlightening me on my Jewishness, and I shall have occasion to revert to this point frequently. I have been obliged to interpret his impassioned, fragmentary speech, sometimes stammering with hatred, other times wrapped in the tissue of politeness; I have had to guess at it, to fill it out, to correct it incessantly. As a result it is seldom the precise meaning, the true meaning, if it has one, that worries me, but its presence, its very existence, that obsesses me. To be a Jew is first and foremost to find oneself called to account, to feel oneself continuously accused, explicitly or implicitly, clearly or obscurely. Little by little and in snatches, the explanations will come through the intermediary of school, street, profession, but first there is that constant hostility, that noxious haze in which the Jew is born, lives and dies.

"Our children" writes Adolf Rudnicki, a Pole of the new Poland (in an article in *Les Temps Modernes*, Sept.-Oct. 1958), "are growing up surrounded by mysteries.

They do not know what they are accused of, but they know they are being accused of something, that they must not mention it to their parents, because the parents can do nothing about it. Frequently the children are convinced that the mystery concerns only their parents and not themselves.

"One day I tried to persuade my little boy of eight to go and play with the neighbor's children. He refused. It took me a long time to get the reason out of him. In the end, he told me he could not go there, because his little friends knew.

" 'What do they know?' I asked.

" 'You know, Papa.'

" 'I don't know.' I was beginning to guess.

" 'My friends know.'

" 'What?'

" 'That I am one.'

" 'That you are what?'

" 'That I'm a "Joos." '

" 'What is a "Joos?" ' I had not the slightest desire to laugh.

" 'But you know: "Joos." '

"His playmates had nicknamed him 'Jew,' he himself had mispronounced the word, but he already knew. So, for me, that problem was settled. But there are men who live in constant expectation, in constant dread of the day when they will have to explain to their children."

Like those Polish children, at an early age, I felt that I was being *pointed out* in a certain manner that was not the same used towards other children. Moreover that designation held a definite note of blame. Rightly or wrongly? Wrongly! Wrongly! Of course, when I came to think it over the whole thing sickened me. However, let us make a distinction: I found it unjustifiable and unjust that I was considered blameworthy, but I could not prevent the others from blaming me. And, even if I were perfectly sure of myself and my family and so placid that nothing could disturb me, the fact remains that, through that designation and that blame, I would discover myself, I would ascertain that I was *separated,* set apart from other men.

I must add, unfortunately, that in spite of myself, this worried me considerably. Confronted with myself, I was by no means sure of my complete innocence. There is a certain independence between the clear motives of an accusation and the feeling of being accused; between the reality of the offense and the blame one takes for it. The blame has the vagueness, the formlessness and the unfairness of a nebulous halo effect. Let us not forget in passing that if I want to rid myself of this whole question, I shall not only have to confound my accuser, but I shall also have to dissipate the fog in other men—and in myself. The result, in any event, is that constant ambiguous feeling that scarcely ever leaves me no matter where I am: I am both of this world and not of it; I long passionately to be of it and I never hope to be completely. Better still, I distrust that integration. With this opinion of me how far will groups or masses, small circle or nation, tolerate my participation? The very question, the anxiety, rob me of my spontaneity, prevent me from living naturally as others do. To be a Jew is also that: to be a Jew is to be set apart from other men, it is also to be set apart from oneself.

Someone said the other day that a great many psychologists, psychoanalysts and psychiatrists are themselves neurotics and, far from being harmful to the exercise of their profession, it is, on the contrary, perhaps helpful.

"I myself am not a neurotic," remarked a distinguished specialist. "But I am a Jew and that is quite enough."

It was not chance after all that Freud was a Jew; that the famous nucleus of the psychoanalytical school was composed of Jews; as are also a great many theoreticians and practitioners of mental health, in other words, specialists in separation, healers of *dis*harmony, of the non-harmony of the human being with other men and with himself. How could a Jew help looking at himself with astonishment, with suspicion? That is the natural result of being called to account: the victim himself inevitably continues the process; he begins to draw away from other men of his own accord, to be his own eyes and his own judge. I have rarely ever made up that terrible distance, that split in my nature I thus acquired.

It seemed to me necessary to distinguish, at least by method, that quarantine of the Jew from the pretexts and justifications invoked to explain his exclusion. When one considers the Jewish fate, as a rule one immediately leaps on the problem of difference. And at once a difficult question arises: is the Jew really different? Is that not an illusion, a calumny? And, according to the reply, everything may fluctuate, the Jew seems about to disappear between the observer's fingers. If the Jew is not different, in short, there would not be any possible significance to the separation. The Jew is wrong to think he is set apart from others . . . he is almost wrong to think he exists. Nevertheless whether he is *really* different or not, he feels excluded and he is excluded. The point is that difference is a problem and separation a fact; and under any circumstance it is better to start from a fact than from a problem. In my opinion, a Jew need not know the exact wording of the question he is asked, nor that he may have answered, to feel and to find himself excluded.

As I have said, I was born in a relatively homogeneous Jewish milieu. It is difficult for me to know whether I was aware of the difference fairly early in life or whether I always recognized it. I am inclined to think I did not: in any case I did not live it. On thinking it over, I claim that since on the whole we lived among Jews, in primary school, then to a lesser degree in high school and even in the city, I must have had at least a sense of communion with Jews as opposed to my attitude towards non-Jews. But did I feel that I was different from the others, from the non-Jews? Probably. But I am almost certain, be it only through the non-evidence of my memory, that the one group clearly outweighed the other: my feeling was more of belonging to my group than of being rejected by the others. I did not belong in the other group; that was all there was to it. Besides I had no clear concept of the others, or of myself. They were simply the others; I belonged to my people. It was some time before I realized that the others rejected me. I did not really understand what anti-Semitism was; only little by little did I become aware of it and, not until later, when I went to Europe where outsiders mingled freely with the Jewish community and I came in contact with non-Jews, did I fully realize their rejection of us.

For a long time I attributed my poverty and my social or professional difficulties solely to the ordinary difficulties connected with social and professional life. We were poor, but there were so many other poor people in Tunis! The Jewish quarter where we lived was no poorer than the Arab quarter that surrounded it, and there were wealthy families in both populations. It took me some time to discover, or rather to admit, what I vaguely sensed, that my difficulties were also the worries and the difficulties of a Jew, that they had, in short, a special dimension, a special coloring, the Jewish coloring and the Jewish dimension. So, too, for a long time I was unaware of the colonial influence in my life, though it was always there, in an almost systematic fashion. Of course there was always that vague unrest, that diffused hostility I felt as I walked through the Arab quarter that pressed so closely around the Jewish quarter where I was born. But it was more an absence of communication, a lack, a non-good will in the glances of the people I met on my way to school; they were not my people, I was not one of them.

Aside from that vague unrest, I had no particular concept of myself as a Jew. Difference is probably a long apprenticeship, a confused experience, a neverending discovery, a vague concept constantly knocked about by everyone, even by the Jew himself. How, for instance, would a Jewish child conceive of himself as a Jew? What would that mean? The several characteristics that are perhaps more common in Jews than in non-Jews do not seem distinctively Jewish to me. I noted one day that I had a horror of bloodshed. Did that mean that I immediately knew, that I was aware of it as a Jew? That my aversion characterized me as a member of a group with which I shared the same repulsion? Not at all. It simply meant that, on several occasions, I had noticed my consternation at the sight of that warm, sticky liquid, a sure sign of possible catastrophes vaguely associated with death. At first, I thought it was a personal trait, perhaps shared by other men but as the only thing we had in common. Later on, further meanings of that aversion were suggested to me, but they only added to the obscurity. My own people told me that it was a sign of humanity, of morality, a rejection of violence; the enemies of the Jews called it a shameful weakness, in line with other taints, such as cowardice. In either case it was a mere detail in the ensemble of traits characteristic of a group to which I belonged. I admit therefore that this horror of bloodshed was not mine personally, that it was related to and related me to far broader categories. Even so, did I easily accept that trait as a Jewish characteristic? Actually, when I realized the degrading connotation that accompanied it, I immediately tried to explain it, to put it back in a universal and humane perspective.

I acknowledged certain facts. It seems true that the Jew rarely owns weapons, at any rate less so than other men, in spite of the danger that threatens him more often, and more cruelly. It seems true that he loathes to shed blood or to see blood shed though other men are so generous with his own. Agreed! But, I added promptly, is that really peculiar to the Jewish temperament? Is it not rather the inevitable result of a given situation? The Jew has always paid more dearly than other men for the slightest retort, the slightest divergence. To be sure, he finds in his ethnic-religious tradition material to support such a condemnation of bloodshed, but there are so many things in a tradition! Why has that command assumed such importance, such severity? Here, in point of fact, we come up against a long collective pattern of behavior, or rather of inaction. But does the Jew not share that resigned passivity, that timid behavior, with many of the weak throughout history? It is not, I concluded, a specifically Jewish trait but a trait of the oppressed (which is by no means unique, on the contrary, as I know today).

Difference, in short, seems to me to have been just another stage. To know its nature and extent, we would have to hear the accusation and discuss it. Difference, derived from the accusation, is fluid and complex like the latter; born and bred in confrontation, it is also constantly disrupted by it. Separation, on the contrary, is connected with obscure hostility, with what one might call the Kafkaian stage of the accusation. As it is not directly derived from the substance of the accusation, it is considered an important but relatively simple fact and of an important nature.

THREE

There again, however, for practical purposes, the distinction is difficult; the Jewish misfortune can certainly
be understood only by analysis. The farther one goes in
the itinerary of the life of the Jew, the more obvious the
connection of separation and differences between Jews
and non-Jews becomes. From separation to difference the
distance is short. Today I no longer doubt that if I am
separated, and in a way treated separately, it is also because I do not enter fully into the life of my fellow-
citizens, that, whether I like it or not, events and institutions separate me from them. In spite of the protests of
those many strange Jews who both proclaim their sin-
gular existence and yet insist they are perfectly integrated, who deny all hostility, for example, I know very
well that there is an obvious dialectic between those two
terms: separation begets and nourishes difference; difference emphasizes and seems to make separation legitimate. Separated, the Jew cannot help feeling that he is
different, and, finally, other men end up considering him
as different. Shall I confess that I am not even sure
today that this is completely unreasonable? That I sense
in a certain way that the non-Jew is frequently ill at ease
in the presence of the Jew? I can understand, if not
justify, his impatience before that troublesome witness,
who has been there for centuries and centuries.

Many anti-Semites harbor a confused admiration for
such a stubborn will to survive—in spite of innumerable
blows, of separation, of being different—as well as an
anxious resentment against this exasperating ghost who
jogs their memory, for better or for worse, out of respect for the ancient common law and for such frequent
betrayal of that law. The mere presence of that ghost,
even silent or indistinct, accuses them of so many crimes.

Why then do I insist so strongly on showing that

separation and difference do not coincide? I would ask my reader to be a little patient and promise him that further on he will see the necessity of this distinction. The drama of Jew versus non-Jew is played, unfortunately, on a register infinitely greater than that of language and accusation. Calling the Jew to account is not the same thing as exchanges of arguments between Jews and non-Jews or even of thought and logic. At the same time, the logical refutation of difference, to which my friends usually confine themselves, is far from adequate. Even should they demolish all the anti-Semitic *arguments*, the basis of the problem, I believe, would still remain. The Jew would continue to be treated separately and to feel separated.

Is this despair as well as a preliminary admission that there is no possible solution? Not at all; it is simply the belief that the difficulties of the Jew are not a matter of a point of view; that the solution of the Jewish misfortune is not a matter of simple persuasion. It concerns a misfortune of importance of which language is only a part, a translation and a partial weapon. It concerns, writes the Jewish historian, Leon Poliakov, in *De Mahomet aux marranes,* "a persecution, in the heart of Western society, which was closely tied to the supreme values of that society, for it has been carried out in their name; to blame the persecutors, to call Christianity to account is, to borrow an expression of François Mauriac, to call that society and its values to account."

To remedy that situation would probably require a transformation, an overthrow of that condition, and perhaps of that whole society, and not merely an elucidation. But I shall come back to this point.

What then is the use, someone will ask me, of all this flow of words, all this discussion, all these pages blackened, if you tell us that words are relatively ineffectual? That is at least a logical despair; but nothing more. It is true that if one could sum up the results of so much talk about the "Jewish problem," one would be dismayed. And if reasoning were all that was needed, everything would have been settled long ago: God knows the Jews have been at it for centuries—propounding, devising and revising their arguments. This balance sheet of insolvency finally would prove to them only that they must look elsewhere. But, in this, there is neither despair nor disdain of logic; for if logic did nothing more than show that the issue is not of a logical nature, it would have played its part.

The Difference

With so much said, I must now try to answer the question: Am I or am I not different? Does the difference exist? This is one of
those turning points where I must remember my promise: I must try to see clearly no
matter what it may cost me. This problem
has been too persistent an irritation; I cannot be satisfied to shrug it off, to evade it.
Am I so nervous because of the constant
threat those accusations present? Certainly
mine is the normal agitation of any defendant, the anxiety of any victim. But
there is something else: this unrest in me, of
which I have spoken, and which unnerves
me, makes me think that perhaps I am not
wholly a victim. How often on hearing a
suggestion, or on reading a phrase, of that
tenor, do I protest angrily, while at the
same time a voice deep within me asks
faintly: "And yet, is that altogether untrue?
Isn't that Jewish financier you are defending a suspicious figure? And what about

that trait they say is characteristic of you? . . ." I promptly silence the voice, I allay my growing anxiety, I point out the ambiguity in that reasoning. I am not defending the financier, I am challenging the people who explain his dishonesty on the ground that he is a Jew. Although for a brief moment I hesitated, wondering whether there might not be some truth in what the anti-Semite said, I must now put an end to this hesitation, and clear up the matter once and for all.

In so doing I fully realize to what I am committing myself. But why do I fight so against myself under pretext of scruples and accuracy? I know well that strange devil of objectivity which is only another form of my masochism. Am I not about to lay myself open to abuse, to allow myself to be gradually weakened by the unshakable conviction of my enemies? Even worse, by joining issue in this discussion, I bind myself to abide by its conclusions; otherwise it would be useless to begin the discussion. But, in that case, would I not run the risk of grievously shocking my own people? That has happened to me too often; and, I can assure you, it is far from pleasant when your own people are already oppressed. Must one add to their troubles in the name of stern and abstract truth? Well, it is a "poor search for truth that stops at the doors of your chapel!" And then I am helped to this decision by my conviction that truth is, in the last analysis, beneficial to the victims. As victims, in the present corrupt state, what more can they lose? To say nothing, to leave everything obscure is as good as admitting that the anti-Semite is right *de facto*. He himself claims that he is legally right, since he continues to triumph, since his words carry weight. Therefore, either I allow him to continue to assert his authority and even apparently to triumph, or I open the record: in the end, I have no choice.

It will not be easy. It is remarkable that on this problem of the difference between Jew and non-Jew, everyone, except the avowed anti-Semite, stumbles. It would be a simple matter if I could answer yes or no. Preferably no: the anti-Semite would be wrong and that would be that. In fact, as I have said, I am troubled and doubly so. I am well aware that I cannot be so trenchantly dogmatic. Moreover, those differences, real or supposed, are regarded by everyone as a taint, an evil, and often a defect. In short, everyone admits that difference works to the advantage of the accuser, that it furnishes him with an important argument.

The anti-Semite knows this so well that he makes it his chief weapon of attack. In defining the Jew as different from his fellow-citizens, he at the same time exposes him to their mistrust and vindictiveness. He hopes to stir them up against him and thus obtain a quick and un-founded condemnation. It is true that in so doing he echoes the too-frequently blind wisdom of nations, which feel an unquestionable suspicion of difference that is deeper and more tenacious than any impulse towards universal brotherhood. This, the oppressors as well as the oppressed must admit, is found in every nation, and every group. In my romantic youth I was shocked by the smiling disdain, the calm condescension I discovered in that expression "Goyem" by which the poor inhabitants of the ghetto designated all non-Jews. This was a question of a primitive and general feeling that has no need of justification or argument. Children, as we know, show a spontaneous aggressiveness when con-fronted with a strange piece of clothing, an unusual haircut. I still carry on my forehead a permanent scar in memory of a ridiculous hat an ill-fated gift of a tasteless uncle, as the result of which, under the pretext of playing, I was thrown violently to the ground. Jean-Jacques Rousseau's turban and greatcoat aroused the villager's hatred more surely than did his ideas about God and society—contrary to what that proud and naïve philosopher thought. Montesquieu's "How can one be a Persian?" expresses not only astonishment, but also mistrust and anxiety. It is not necessary to know what the Jew's difference is fundamentally, or how it is harmful; on the contrary, it causes more annoyance and anxiety by what it seems to conceal than by what it reveals. It was a Nazi measure, more diabolical than one realizes, to have pasted a distinctive mark on the backs of Jews. And by that measure they thus reverted to the rites of initiation practiced in the Middle Ages, the pound of flesh of Catholic countries, or the black or blue bonnet of the Moslems.

The concrete symbol suggests and embodies difference, the lure towards who-knows-what shady background on which it is best not to throw too much light. That, in short, is why the accuser does not need to develop his argument, if he has one. He need only point out the disgrace to call forth promptly the malaise. And, to be sure, difference is, in a certain way, turmoil and negation of the established order. When you see how strange the other man is, you almost wonder about yourself. To reassure yourself, to be confirmed in your opinion, you would have to reject and deny the other; it is either he or I. If I am right, he must be wrong; if my way is good, his must be bad. This explains the extraordinarily frantic ferocity of certain devout people towards scandal: they do not so much decry the evil in itself, as the fact that it calls them personally to account; and this abnormality jeopardizes their standards.

Given that enormous handicap, one can readily understand the obvious embarrassment, the paralysis of the friends of Jews: all things considered, they are beaten at the start. They do not want to know whether the record is good or bad; they prefer to ignore it; they avoid being drawn into the discussion. What is the use of opening that controversy? Nothing but harm can come of it. If there is a difference, the Jew could only suffer cruelly from it; the mere presumption is enough to crush him. For that matter, certain of those friends think, in the bottom of their hearts, the Jew would then be in the wrong. And I must confess that I myself have had a great deal of trouble in getting out of that very dilemma. For a long time, in spite of my efforts, the discovery that other people were different began to disturb me, no matter what detours and disguises that disturbance took. My first reaction, as regards myself, was to deny everything that seemed to distinguish me from others. How I wished I could treat everything the anti-Semite said as slanderous vagaries, a spate of words, wild ravings! How comfortable it would have sometimes been to be invisible and nameless.

But the final result is that the debate would always be left open. The accuser accuses, judges and condemns *a priori,* almost certain of the approval of the crowd; the Jew and his friends prefer not to listen and not to argue. There is not even any real encounter and therefore never a conclusion; one side attacks and the other retreats.

TWO

Now that I am convinced that my record is not so bad, I am willing to risk examining it. How can one know, for that matter, if the case has never been fully tried? Naturally I do not count the discussions opened when I am not present. From time to time a writer, a contemporary dramatist, tries his hand, almost in good faith, at the trial of the Jew. It happened just recently, before an enormous throng, with the blessing and in the presence of the Catholic Church. The question, admittedly, was the trial of Jesus; but actually it was the trial of the Jew, the alleged aggressor of Jesus. All those efforts are of no avail; they are vitiated at the very foundation, for I scarcely know how to find my bearings in those courts.

Almost always a wretched extra plays the part, an alias someone or other, a poor devil who gives the answers they expect from him, disguises himself as best he can, and tries painfully, wretchedly, to avoid the maximum penalty.

If I were summoned before such a jury, I would decide first of all to appear and not dodge the confrontation. Times have changed, as I have said; a new Jew is about to be born, as are also a new woman and a new Negro. The men of my generation no longer tolerate so easily the traditional Jewish fate, which means that, in our hearts, we have set our revolt in motion. Thus, far from soliciting the indulgence of the court . . . I would begin the argument by unveiling and challenging the implicit principle that governs the whole discussion: is difference bad in itself and to be condemned? I would denounce and reject this strange accord between my friends and my enemies. For if the Jew's enemy accuses him of being different, the Jew's friend would spare him that misfortune; both agree on this point: it is intolerable to be different. Now, in what name do they condemn difference? In the name of one of the most common and the most obscure, the most unfair and the most incoherent of prejudices—which collapses the moment it is rationally examined. If a man permits himself to judge other men and to reject them, he is, by implication, setting himself up as a criterion of the beautiful, the good and the true. He is implying, more or less consciously, that it is churlish, reprehensible and absurd to be different from him. Condemnation is then inevitable. But who does not see, the moment he reflects on it, that the formula can be completely reversed? Is this not, in fact, what is happening? Each man is condemning all other men in the name of his own qualities which, in others, are considered defects. The Northerner calls the Southerner effusive, indiscreet, vulgar: the man from the South finds the Northerner egotistic, cold, surly.

But the case that concerns us is worse; in a situation where one group is oppressed, condemnation of difference can no longer work both ways. The weight of oppression is such that it always reacts to the detriment of the oppressed and to the profit of the oppressor. Difference being bad, it is inevitable that the oppressed is automatically charged with it: he is the one who is different, he is the evil one, the ridiculous the guilty man. In this way, difference is related to the accusation. So far, the case of the Jew has always been conducted according to the values of the non-Jew; the Jew has never presented his own values in defense, or, if he has, so feebly, so timidly that he can scarcely be heard. Furthermore, both the Jew and his friends have practically accepted the values of the accusation, they have accepted the problem as it is posed by the anti-Semite, they recognize his code and the sanctions it imposes. It is this, among other things, that has made the case of the Jew so difficult, so dangerous. If one accepts this starting point, the situation is hopeless; at the most one can hope for extenuating circumstances; but the Jew is almost certain to be condemned.

As I have already shown, one never really shakes off oppression except by revolt. That is why I would have contested the very principle of this case, of which I admit neither the evidence nor the legitimacy. All revolutionists instinctively contest the legitimacy of the court, as it is constituted; that is to say, they reject the rules of the game. Montaigne recognized this implicit right for women: "Women are quite right to rebel against the rules of life current in the world, all the more so because men have made them." That is what Julien Sorel did in *The Red and the Black,* what many fighters of the Commune did; and, closer to our day, it is the struggle of the colonized natives. "I do not recognize the competence of your court!" is the constant leit motiv in the records of those cases. To me, those rules are the opinions, judgments and viewpoints of the majority of the people among whom I live. I am well aware that I cannot deal with this terrible problem of the majority so hastily; it must be developed separately and in more detail. I simply mention it in passing: majority rules and laws are respectable only to the degree in which they express the greatest justice and the greatest rationality. If they become oppressive, unjust and humiliating, I can and I must object to them and fight them. I refuse to grant any man the right to set up his mores and his habits as an absolute criterion and bed of Procrustes for other men. Comparison does not imply any previous claim of one of the two partners. In other words, I do not consider the values of the majority *ipso facto* superior to mine. They are different, perhaps, and that is all. The day I understood this, I also understood that I had no need to deny any difference in myself, any particularization. I refuse to pay this price, this foolish disguise, this unnatural game for my hopes of forgiveness and universal brotherhood—if even they too are not a joke.

THREE

Do I consider myself different? Yes, I do and I admit it calmly: on a great many points the Jew is different from the non-Jew. Having exorcised the difference, I see no reason why I should try to attenuate it as I have forced myself to do for so long. On the contrary, I am now convinced that this hesitation, these anxious reticences in the face of such blatant evidence, are one of the typical signs of Jewish oppression. The first reaction of the oppressed is always to deny difference. He insists that he does not see what separates him from his oppressor. That is the best way he can find to draw closer to his oppressor, to lighten his oppression. To that end he is ready for any sacrifice, even to repudiating himself for the benefit of his oppressor, whose person and values are held up to him as superior and steadfast, a height to which the oppressed aspires. To me there is nothing more intolerable, more humiliating than the memory of certain Jewish appeals to non-Jews: "We are all alike, aren't we?" On the lips of the oppressed that statement of equality and brotherhood always has the same note, humble, unconvinced and desperate. When I hear a Jew deny any difference, I cannot help suspecting him either of lying or of fooling himself. Does a French or an English socialist, exponent of international union, need to deny the characteristics of his people? On the contrary, he takes pleasure in them, he boasts of them; he has not the slightest doubt of the value of the dowry he brings to the marriage of nations. But the Jew is convinced that he must masquerade as anything but a Jew, if he wants to make this marriage. Is it not obvious, under those conditions, that the enterprise is generally doomed to failure or at least to appear equivocal and suspect? No, from now on, we must get it into our heads and state positively that to be different is neither good nor bad in itself. True justice, true tolerance, universal brotherhood do not demand negation of differences between men, but a recognition and perhaps an appreciation of them; let us not ask more for the moment. From now on we must cease to hide before the tribunal of history which is always open; on the contrary we must say exactly who we are. "In the nineteenth century," Nahum Goldmann, a Jewish leader, recently said, "we had to fight for the right to be equal; in the twentieth century we have to fight for the right to be different."

The plan strikes me as excellent; I shall merely add that we are already different, and we always have been, even when we were clamoring for equality. We have not always acknowledged it, because we considered it a weakness and a hindrance to the equality we demanded. Now, however, I am convinced that difference is the condition

requisite to all dignity and to all liberation. To be aware
of oneself is to be aware of oneself as different. To be is
to be different. We are always "the other man" to someone, to all other men. That does not justify *a priori* any
presupposition of worth. If "the other man" condemns us,
we can always pay him back with the same abuse or irony.
As May Britt, the Swedish actress who married Sammy
Davis, Jr., a Jewish Negro, said so pertinently: "They
blame him for being colored! I am colored too: I am
white." Nor—let me point out in passing—does this
justify going them one better on our part or on that of any
oppressed person: to be a Jew is to possess virtues and
deficiencies, unquestionable deficiencies, unfortunately!
"Why should we not have our thieves and our murderers?" the Jewish author, Manes Sperber, said to me
angrily. "Why should we not have the right to have them
like everyone else!"

That strong distinction between the existence of difference and its value, and the condemnation it arouses,
ought likewise to free the defenders of the Jew. It is from
a moral conviction, a generous attitude and a logical
loyalty to themselves, I know, that they categorically deny
any difference. And I am distressed to have to thwart people who wish me well. But I cannot help seeing the impasse into which their generous persistence in trying to
make the faces and destinies of all men the same, is leading both them and us. I have had the same discussion
hundreds of times. How well I remember that impassioned and almost painful controversy, incessantly renewed at each meeting, with an admirable woman we
called the Duchess because of her stately gestures and
more especially because of the extraordinary nobility of
her life. A German, coming from a racist, bourgeois
milieu, she had experienced a complete conversion with
the result that she went to the opposite extreme in every
respect, or at least what seemed the opposite to her. Hav-

ing decided to devote herself wholeheartedly to this new life, to rid herself of all prejudices, all barriers between human beings, she closed her mind to everything else. Thus, she had adopted a young man from Madagascar and married him to a European girl. But, though "the Duchess" was a professor of philosophy and psychology, she denied desperately any specific characteristics as the cause, obvious though they were, when her adopted son had conjugal difficulties. Sometimes, carried away by her arguments, she even went so far as to deny everything—Jewish misfortune and hostility, separation and difference. It was a complete blindness to reality, as frequent among progressives as among traditionalists. But more often she would decide to believe what suited her mood: she acknowledged that there was a certain rejection of the Jew, but she maintained that neither separation nor difference was the result. I told her this seemed completely contradictory. On other occasions, she reversed the procedure, admitting a certain exclusion (though I greatly exaggerated it). But a real difference? By no means! In the end she lost her temper and hurled friendly insults at me.

"You're helping the anti-Semites!" she cried. "You're carrying grist to their mill! It's definitely a mania with you! I knew a Jewish professor who wanted to write a thesis on Gobineau! On Gobineau of all people! You confirm the very things of which they accuse you: that you are a race apart . . . Besides, often you set yourselves apart; you really live apart!"

So there we had the famous reproach of the Jew's exclusiveness! And there we were in a fine mess of logic, if I may say so: we were exclusive, but not set apart . . .

But let us be serious: I am convinced, I will come to it a few pages further on, that a great many so-called Jewish traits are imaginary. I shall even show that a certain mental picture of the Jew, ideal and negative, is extremely useful to the anti-Semite: it gives him an excuse for excluding the Jew, for the persecutions he inflicts on him. But is that all there is to the affirmation of difference? Nothing but alibi and provocation? Is difference only a word and a more or less suspect illusion? To be honest, I do not think so.

It is, however, an illusion so strongly held that it has convinced great numbers of people, including the victim himself, an illusion we are obliged to argue constantly— to combat, of course—but which we never manage to ignore. But at least as an idea, as a matter of conscience, what vigor, what deep-rootedness! Is difference an actual part of the accusation? Is it, first of all, nothing but a case? Of course. An iniquitous case? Certainly. But such an important case, of such long duration, and one that concerns so many men as accusers, so many men as accused, so many partisans and so many enemies, that it ultimately involves a crowd of busy magistrates, prosecutors and lawyers, as well as an enormous volume of written documents! I find myself called to account by so many different people and defended by so many others, there are so many arguments, so many pleas, documents, whole volumes that, on days when I am discouraged, I feel I shall never be able to understand, to comprehend it all, to form a definitive opinion. If difference is only a word, how terribly that word is made flesh! If it is only an illusion, what weight, what power of collective bewitchment it has! One knows other illusions that involve innumerable priests, the building of temples, directing the movements of vast crowds. Are those really false ideas?

"Let us catch our breath," the Duchess said to me when I told her that. "You are almost lyrical about it! How passionately you defend a lost cause! To sum up: what have you proved? That the matter is more serious, that the word causes you more suffering than I thought, but after all we are still dealing with semantics!"

"You interrupted me too soon: I mean that at this precise point we are not dealing with a semantic matter. At this point, indeed, difference is far more than a word: this word and this thought—if that were all they were—would already have the appearance, the concreteness and the power of a social fact. They would also have the efficacy and the consequences of that social fact. The Jew encounters them from childhood, throughout his whole adolescence, his whole life, as an integral characteristic of the society in which he lives. The non-Jew meets them in his education, in the family, in school, in church, in his culture, and in his traditions. Such a social convention, so constant, so insistent, so multiple, compels both Jews and non-Jews to make a decision. The Jew accepts it or refuses it, or better still, accepts and refuses it at the same time. What effect do you think this has on his physiognomy, his behavior, his very existence? It is this: *the Jew is one of the most perfect examples of a defendant in our day.* To speak only of our day, is this not a very real, very concrete result? He thinks and acts like a defendant: he is convinced that he is accused and conducts his life accordingly. Looked upon as different, treated as different, he considers himself different. That is one of the most pertinent comments of what might be called a philosophy of points of view: a sustained point of view ends by becoming his very flesh. The permanent accusation brought against the Jew is an integral part of his unhappy condition."

"Yes, I know," said the Duchess. "It is the evil eye all over again, that is why it fascinates you . . ."

"The evil eye is nothing . . . But let's not talk about that! The other parallel and equally concrete result is the repercussion of that accusation on the non-Jew. He, too, makes his decision with regard to that proposition and that case. He, too, must accept or reject the condition forced on the Jew; he, too, more often, both accepts it and rejects it in varying degrees. By agreeing to it, he partly contributes to it; by denying it, either directly or indirectly, he runs up against the accuser. Inevitably he ends by doubting the legitimacy of established values and customs. That is why the non-Jew's attitude towards the Jew is, in the last analysis, significant, I believe, of his own relations with humanity and with the world."

"Let us admit that we are no longer dealing with a linguistic matter. Even though false, I admit that an accusation would inevitably end by causing certain confusions in mind and conduct, but that is all. I still do not see what *real* differences separate Jews from non-Jews."

"Then what do you call real? Are not those confusions very real? Do they not have visible and foreseeable consequences? But I understand: you ask whether there are other differences, other consequences than the confusions born of accusation? Well, yes! We must go one step further. Here I leave the philosophies of points of view; they have taken us only halfway. Whatever the corrosive acuity of that point of view, the Jew is not merely the product of other men's views. He is not only the man who is looked upon as a Jew. If he were only that, he would be nothing more than pure negativity, anxieties and confusions, wounds and scars. Though he is unquestionably malaise and misfortune, he is also much more than that. His negativity is much richer, unfortunately, than a set of responses to the views of other men: he is actually *treated* negatively by other men. He puts up with small irritations, not just with outrages. In many ways his life is always limited, restrained, curtailed. Like the colonized native, the proletarian, and most certainly in his own guise, he is a concrete negativity. He is truly insolvent in his private life both as a citizen and as an historical man. I emphasized at length this notion of insolvency in *Portrait of a Colonized Native;* it is fundamental in any oppression and I shall revert to it again. Had he only this aspect of suffering, we would have no trouble in recognizing the Jew. But he is not only that: he is also history and traditions, institutions and customs. He is brimming over with positive traits, he is also broad and rich positivity. In short, the Jew is far above the poor, shabby, cantankerous fellow the anti-Semite pictures. If only the anti-Semite knew what Jewishness really means and hides.

And here someone will accuse me of siding with the anti-Semite.

I repeat: if the anti-Semite had seen clearly on certain points, I would quietly say he was right. But I am not siding with the anti-Semite; I explain him, I include him and I understand him. I believe, thus, that certain differences exist between Jews and non-Jews, but I do not believe they are always the differences most frequently mentioned, nor do I believe they have the meaning attributed to them. The Jewish fate goes far beyond the relation of Jew to non-Jew, even though they are closely connected. The Jewish fate is the views of other men and the incarnation of those views; it is accusation and response to the accusation; it is the determination of the Jew and the determination of the non-Jew, that is to say, their behavior, their collective habits and their institutions. It is at once viewpoints and concrete situations; in a word, there is a Jewish fate.

The Accusation

ONE

I began to be aware of myself, however, only as the result of the accusation; through those images of the Jew that other men suggested to me, imposed on me, imperceptibly, feature by feature. Before I discovered who I was, before I became aware of my actual situation, I had to face myself. But everything—their absurd calumnies as well as their legitimate demands, the effective part I play in society as well as the fantastic role they impute to me—is, for different reasons, terribly real and objective. Everything has its import and its consequences. I mean, in short, that by approaching my general fate as a Jew through the intermediary of those images, I at last discovered and lived an important aspect of it.

Very early in life, like everyone else, I heard many strange and extremely disturbing tales. To know that I was about to enter, that I was already moving deeper into the shadows of the Jewish misfortune,

I had only to pay attention to the blunt commonplaces of everyday language, to be surprised by what they revealed. To make money, people said in my presence—jokingly, of course—you have to kill an old Jew. To explain petty annoyances or the direst calamities, they blamed the Jews. The word "Jew" was, it seemed, a natural synonym for avarice and double-dealing, for hardness of heart. Even in my schooldays, some of the men I admired and respected joined in that chorus. In my youth, as a future member of the teaching profession, I worshipped artists and thinkers, those restless minds and those righters of wrongs who came to meet my adolescent discoveries, my anxieties and my indignations. However, when those heroes of mine wished to hold the ignominy of their villains up to shame they seldom forgot to point out that the villains were Jews, if they were; or if they were not Jews, they accused them of "acting like a Jew." "What a Jew!" exclaimed Molière to vilify a non-Jewish character. It is true that on the same occasion he said: "What a Turk!" but I scarcely found it reassuring at that period to be classed with the Turk, that bloody executioner and perfidious marauder of the seas. Shakespeare's Jews are cruel and sordid usurers. *The Merchant of Venice* is—it seems to me obvious—an anti-Semitic play.

In the course of a polemic with his Jewish contemporaries, Voltaire's irony in his *Philosophical Dictionary* ill disguises his disdain and hatred of them:

"You will find in them only an ignorant and barbarous people who have for ages combined the most sordid avarice with the most detestable superstition and the most invincible hatred for all peoples who tolerate them and enrich them: however, one should not burn them."

Gide! Gide whom I admired so much for his meticulous efforts to give an honest picture of himself, including even his weaknesses, Gide of all men, admitted that he was anti-Semitic. How I have tried to "understand" him, to put back in the "context" certain of his sentences, as for example from his *Journals:* "So, in spite of our friendship and the confidence I had in him, he did not hesitate to deliver me into the hands of a shark, because the latter was of his race . . . That story somewhat dashed my feelings for Blum and has greatly helped to feed my anti-Semitism!"

But the context only enlightens me further:

"I detested his manner of accosting me when I chanced to meet him in a theater lobby after years of silence, the way he had of putting his arms around my neck and asking: 'And how is Madeleine?' "

This was definitely a most banal aversion to Jews, as numerous texts fully confirmed. The novelist, Jean Davray, who had felt the same enthusiasm for Gide and then the same consternation, says that he went to the Master to reproach him and that the latter was deeply moved and explained it away. But Gide was not precisely the man to be satisfied with an approximation and when he wrote "his race" and "my anti-Semitism" it was not a slip of the pen. Some time ago, a controversy arose over the many definitions insulting to the Jew in *Larousse,* the most popular French dictionary; the dispute is long overdue and very limited; actually all dictionaries have, from time immemorial, offered their readers similar definitions. But if only those insults were confined to dictionaries! A great many children's books, among those most widely distributed and most harmless in appearance, sow and foster scorn and hatred of the Jew. I shall not attempt here to make an inventory of everything in the cultural itinerary of a young Jew: a fat volume of citations would not suffice to hold it. Recently, while choosing books for my little boy, I came upon several of those cheering discoveries again. This is how the Jew is portrayed by Sir Walter Scott in *Ivanhoe* (Green Series, especially edited for children, if you please). (And since it is Sir Walter Scott the description is therefore handed on to little Anglo-Saxons as well) : (p. 54) Inhuman, (p. 31) Liar, (p. 26) Hypocrite and throughout the book "Usurer, thou art covetous" . . . A great many little French children are familiar with *Le Petit Trott* by André Lichtenberger. What is the story about? A wicked man tries to seduce Little Trott's young mother while his father is away. Little Trott hates the intruder with all his might, shows his hatred and succeeds in dissuading his mother. His father finally returns, makes a terrible scene and order is restored. A trite story with a moral as is fitting for a child's book. But the seducer's name is Mr. Aaron; he is rich and miserly, obsequious and sly, etc. Moreover, so that there may be no misunderstanding in the famous explanations at the end, the father calls him "Jew!" The father is an Army officer, he had been away on duty. The parallel is obvious: on the one hand, money and avarice, leisure and the will to do evil; on the other, the father's honor and the close family harmony, so necessary to Little Trott's peace of mind. But did the author give a moment's thought to the peace of mind of our little Jewish readers?

This is the image of himself as a Jew that my little eight-year-old boy is receiving from his first books. It will practically never be contradicted; on the contrary, it will be confirmed and constantly embellished. Our children are luckier than we were: thanks to the movies, they will see the Jewish characters of Dickens in the flesh and will not forget them so easily. Do not tell me that they also show as many Christian cheats and cowards. They are cheats and cowards on the one hand and Christians on the other, like everyone else. There is no relation between their double-dealing and their faith. Moreover, the heroes are equally Christian. The Jewish character is money-grasping and cruel because he is a Jew. Usury, ruse and wickedness are traits that serve to differentiate the Jew from other characters in the book. In short, the little Jewish reader cannot help feeling, as I did, that he is accused. Sooner or later he cannot help asking himself the same questions: must rejection and hatred of the Jew be part of the ideal of every decent man? Am I therefore one of those ignoble characters whom all those marvelous men portray so well and whose portrayal I generally applaud?

For a long time I was able to shake off this fascination only by refusing to dwell on those trying passages, by turning a deaf ear to them. That is what many Jews do all their lives. They have succeeded so well in overlooking certain subjects that their eyes and their ears are almost selective. An accusation? they say, what accusation? They have never seen anything, they have never heard anything. How wonderfully in harmony those people are with their surroundings. When my little boy was still a baby, he had a very effective weapon against our scoldings: he used to shut his eyes and make us disappear. Those statements about myself, however, which I did not enjoy, which revolted me, became weightier and more voluminous until they seemed almost a necessity; before I tackled them, before I tried to separate the false from the true, I was obliged to take them into account. Furthermore, even if I managed to separate them successfully, I knew that I would have to continue to take them into account, since they would always be there, at my side, like blind hatred and stupidity on the forehead of a bull. In any event, I had to build my life around them. Yes, the conscious life of the Jew really begins with an accusation and a problem and that problem decides each move, whether ruse or resignation, surrender or revolt.

TWO

Is it necessary to draw up the complete list of the traits that make up the full-length portrait of the Jew-as-others-see-him? I do not even know whether it is possible. There would have to be definite outlines, whereas, in spite of the wealth of material, or because of it, the picture is vague, many sided, and varies according to the speaker, the group, the country and the era. Everyone seems to have his Jew or, better still, several of them, unstable and contradictory. The expression "I have a Jewish friend" means "I feel friendly towards a man who happens to be a Jew," but frequently too: "Just see how well I can overlook his origins and his execrable background," in other words, the salvation of that particular Jew and rejection of all the others. Every Jew receives at least once in his life that awkward and banal declaration of friendship: "You are not like the others!" It is ill-timed support, a balm so bitter and so ambiguous that it irritates as much as it comforts. Each time I have tried to collect all the traits I am supposed to have, I quickly find myself confronted with an incredible jumble of them, accumulated apparently without any attention to coherence or even to verisimilitude.

Certain fanatics, a few pseudo-scientists or even some real ones, have tried to straighten out this confusion by reducing the portrait to a few characteristics, or a few combinations of characteristics. We then find ourselves faced with three or four awkward figures, miserable creatures with heavy features, all of them grotesquely simplified, but all based on a central idea which gives support to and orients the whole. There are people, as we know, who claim to recognize the Jew by certain biological characteristics which explain, call forth and involve a special psychology. For others, the Jew is primarily a combination of economic habits, formed and strengthened throughout the centuries, and these habits govern his entire way of life. One also finds the Jew-destiny, metaphysical or mystical, or even the Jew simply as a sociological survival, accidental residue, historical fossil, as an eminent historian has recently called him . . . We shall see what those constellations are worth, whether they even approximately account for the reality of the Jew. We shall have to investigate in particular whether the underlying intentions really have that objective character of pure science they claim. It is well to note also that the hierarchy of those traits, the interest in certain combinations, has varied widely throughout history. Thus, the violent light of racism recently turned on the biology of the Jew has not always been so intense. We know now that racial prejudices, though by no means a new development in the history of the human race, have never had the importance in the past that they have acquired since slavery. On the contrary, numerous texts bear witness that the Negroes were proud of their wives' beautiful black skins. It was the slave-traders and their clerks who discovered the use they could make of differences in the color of the skin and in the form of the lips. Since then, the Negroes have been ashamed of their physiology and of themselves. And since biological anti-Semitism, the Jews have begun to be conscious of their noses.

I know, however, that method is not absolutely to be proscribed, if one persists in trying to analyze, other than by an honest description, a subject as complex as a living man, and I have stated that I would keep to the present figure of the Jew: I would thus accept the manner in which the contemporary phase of the examination is presented. I must first examine, seriously and systematically, two current propositions: the biological figure and the economic figure. There is, however, a final objection: is it possible for me to study my own people with the critical eye of a stranger? Only too possible: I am perfectly at home in that traditional exercise; because one must always be on the alert to forestall an attack, we have become accustomed to putting ourselves in the place of the aggressor, to seeing ourselves through his eyes. Jewish humor is frequently only an attempt to stand off and look at oneself objectively, the better to understand oneself. For that matter, the biological figure has been sufficiently vulgarized and I shall have no great difficulty in harvesting that biological confusion which non-Jews claim is characterisitc of me. Because I am a Jew, my eyes should be close together, I should have a hooked nose ("a sheep's nose"), pointed at the end like a bird's beak or curved indefinitely, full, thick lips, enormous protruding ears, bad breath, a shrunken hand, damp palms, fingers curved like claws, flat feet, a sickly and undersized or a fat body (the proportion is uncertain—short, in any case). I must have dark hair or red hair, I must be "Oriental" in type, etc., etc. . . . I could go on; I have certainly omitted some features.

At this point I again await the usual impatient protest from non-Jews of good will.

"Who believes in all that nonsense?" the Duchess used to say. "That is a description of the Jew by the most obtuse, the most virulent, the most rabid anti-Semite!"

Now, I persist in believing that the matter is more serious, more complicated and, at bottom, more obnoxious than people, and particularly my friends, say. For after all, in me, in the majority of Jews, not to say in all of us, the confusion seems to me obvious. It is true I have often rejoiced that I do not have a hooked nose or thick lips. It is true that, when people told me, "You don't look like a Jew," in spite of myself, my revolt at that equivocal compliment was mixed with the bitterness of an ambiguous pleasure, just as a woman violated may experience a shameful and hated pleasure. It is true that I looked at my body anxiously, questioningly. Am I even sure, scientifically, that, as a Jew, I do not have special biological characteristics? Frankly, I do not know; I still often ask myself that question. And are non-Jews, even the best of them, really as innocent, as surprised as they say? Leave aside the outright bigots—though they shout aloud their hatred and their prejudices and proclaim them in public, before their children and in newspapers that are sold everywhere and are read by thousands upon thousands of readers. During the Vichy era there was a widely read book called *Fifteen Ways to Recognize the Jew;* and before the war the popular newspaper *Gringoire* launched the expression "sheep's nose." In 1958, in a resumé of the most recent researches, the International Bulletin of Social Sciences of UNESCO concludes that persons questioned in West Germany fully agreed that the Jew was characterized by his hooked nose. The same Bulletin notes the existence in England and in the United States of an important racism with a biological basis. Unfortunately, I do not need official publications to know that a similar racism exists in France.

But do many of those good people who shrug their shoulders when they hear that regular, cumulative description, restrain themselves from saying or from thinking: "He looks like a Jew"? Do not many of those people, who are revolted when they see that grotesque figure clearly and forcefully depicted, nevertheless refer to it, involuntarily perhaps, so long as it remains discreetly in the background? How many times have I heard from the lips of a man I believed to be almost a saint, a certain suggestion that plunged me into childish consternation? How many times have I noted, among the best people, a certain allusion to what I believed to be definitely outdated? An old hypothesis in a new form, apparently scientific, apparently neutral? Specific maladies or immunities, for example:

"All the same, this special alimentation for centuries,

perhaps . . . Circumcision? Isn't is possible that the removal of the foreskin. . . ?"

I know very well that most often such remarks are only the result of fleeting impressions, routine thoughts, a play on words, which do not pretend to go farther.

"I am as ugly as a Jew," writes the philo-Semite Henry Miller in *Tropic of Cancer,* and in a sudden aboutface Anatole France in *Penguin Island* notes: "He criticized him for his zealousness, his hooked nose, his vanity, his taste for study, his thick lips and his exemplary conduct."

I know, too, that if called on for a straightforward answer the majority would be confused; they would deny the importance of those approximations or in any case they would be incapable of defining them more clearly. But should I tell them that those denials of principle, that vagueness, or that blundering do not satisfy me, that they do not solve anything? That their modesty or their generosity, their delicacy or their tactful solicitude do not console me if that is all there is to it; for in that case they leave intact my distress and my doubts. At this stage I demand of myself, I call on my best friends, to be merciless. I hope, on the other hand, they will help me to bring the whole problem out in the open, to throw light on everything: *even at the risk of discovering a real place in biology.* For after all, what if the Jew really has a certain biological aspect? If such were the case, I would acknowledge that it had a place, but this time its exact place. Let them therefore pour out everything they have in their hearts whether hidden or on the surface. Let them formulate those residues, let them reveal everything that seems to constitute or helps to constitute the biological figure of the Jew.

Am I closing in on them? I am closing in on myself. I subject myself to this odious confrontation. Once more, if I want to end this miserable examination, I must carry it to the end, at least for my own sake.

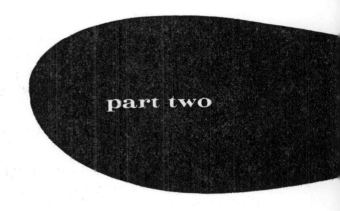

part two

THE MYTHICAL
JEW

"Certain Jews share responsibility, not only for being put in the ghetto and exaggerating the consequences therefrom, but also for delaying their true emancipation and for some of the blows that followed."

J. NANTET, PUBLICIST (CHRISTIAN)

". . . Anti-Semitism presents an almost universal character. . . . Can one constantly take a stand against the entire universe? Don't the Jews themselves bear a part of the responsibility? Are we completely innocent?"

W. RABINOVITCH, PUBLICIST (JEWISH)

Am I a Biological Figure?

ONE

I examine myself closely, I study myself in the mirror, I touch myself: what does that studious inspection teach me? To be frank, I do not recognize my supposed portrait, not the protuding ears . . . The lips, perhaps? No, not especially, not fuller than in many other human beings who are said to have sensual lips. Besides even if I should have certain so-called characteristic features, that would not be conclusive; I would have to have several of them, enough anyway to constitute a whole. Am I then something very rare? The Jew-not-like-the-others, biologically at least? I do not think so: my personal history and that of my family represent the average in my native land. . . .

"That you yourself cannot be accused of looking like a Jew does not change anything," someone will immediately say. "That you, individually, do not answer that description proves nothing. This is a description of the *majority* of Jews; it concerns a general truth." (Do not forget this aspect of the accusation; it concerns a collective case.)

"No, that is not true either. I study the people around me: neither my parents, my friends, nor my close relatives bear out that hypothesis. To be sure, one of them may happen to have a 'revealing' nose or lips that are suspect, but would I have seen that if I did not already know who he was? Moreover, are those lips or that prominent nose more frequent among Jews than among non-Jews? After all, I seldom run across that general truth. . . ."

"All the same, it seems to me . . ."

"Wait, I know what you are going to say: I will even come to your aid: to be precise, and completely honest, I must remind you that I was born in Tunis, in Tunisia. Now, I have never seen protruding ears or eyes set abnormally close together in Tunisia . . ."

"Ah, you see!"

"What do I see? What you should see, on the contrary, from those details, is that the biological figure of the Jew, if there is such a thing, is largely a matter of geography. I suspected in advance that this description did not concern me; it has been suggested by the inhabitants of Western Europe. It is highly probable that the model who inspired it—if there is a model—did not resemble me at all. When people say in my presence: 'Such and such a person is, or is not, the Jewish type,' I quickly ask: 'Which type?' And I am amused at the speaker's embarrassment. The other day I was told the following story: a French Jew, traveling through China and wishing to fulfill his religious duties, found a synagogue and entered it. He was about to pray when he noticed that he was being stared at anxiously and defiantly by the Chinese Jews. A moment later that Chinese rabbi approached and asked him what he wanted. He answered that he had come to pray.

" 'But,' the rabbi asked skeptically, 'are you a Jew?'

" 'Yes, of course,' the man replied.

" 'Strange,' exclaimed the rabbi, raising his hand to his slit eyes. 'Strange,' he added, 'you don't look at all like one.' "

In fact, as Sartre also notes, each country has it own Jews. The Sephardim are usually roughly distinguished from the Ashkenazim by saying that the former are Mediterraneans and the latter from the north. But that dualist classification is too wide of the mark, though it explodes the anti-Semites' robot portrait since the Ashkenazim are inclined to be Slavic in type, coloring, eyes and light hair. Also there are Chinese Jews and Negro Jews, Berber Jews and Hindu Jews and even Aztec Jews —"Many Jews of today are the pure Inca type. I have seen splendid young girls in the youth movements in Peru. Their heads were like those on the bas-reliefs of Arequipa." (Max Fuks, *op. cit.*).

Today with the increase in travel and the abundance of records, there can no longer be any doubt that the biological concept of the Jew is purely relative and is rapidly disintegrating. That is indeed the unanimous conclusion of scientists when they are not engrossed in serving other gods than scientific objectivity.

On that particular point, an effort has been made to solve a strange and unfortunately necessary puzzle; cranial dimensions, color of the hair, shape of the nose, blood groups, the Rh factor; and all of it in beautiful comparative tables, with precise measurements and percentages . . . The differences among Jews, our scholars conclude gravely, are quite considerable. "The Jews vary," writes the scholarly biologist Julian Huxley, in *We Europeans*, "as much, if not more than any people in Europe." That is in truth an understatement: Jews vary among themselves much more than any other people in the world. Not to be paradoxical, one may say that they vary among themselves infinitely more than the majority of their accusers do. But did I really have to wait for those results? Was I blind not to have seen to what extent I differ from the Jews of Germany or of Russia? My knowledge of Jewish history should have shown me that a separate Jewish race is an absurd concept: constant migrations, deportations, invasions and intermingling of populations all prove the fallacy of that contention. But I seem to be making fun of this, and I'm wrong. Scientific guarantees are probably not useless to everyone; all the same, I am annoyed when obliged to answer to such nonsense which I know was not based on reason. The classic and unitary description of the Jew is, I fear, merely a description by a near-sighted European who cannot see further than his nose and who denies, derides and despises anything he does not see. It would have been too easy to make an experiment in the opposite sense. The other evening, in a group of Parisian Jews, I indulged in a sort of counter-proof. Setting aside where I was and what I knew, I looked around me and opened my eyes wide. The conclusion was obvious; had I been led in with eyes bandaged and not told where I was going, I would never have guessed that I was among Jews. In Paris, I am quite incapable of distinguishing who is a Jew and who is not. Would it therefore be imprudent to conclude that there is no such thing as a *universal Jewish biological figure?*

"What is a Jew? I am going to tell you something. When I was in Abyssinia, our group tried to rejoin the local patriots through the brush. It was raining in torrents, we were lost . . . At last I saw someone under a tree; a tall jet-black Abyssinian, armed to the teeth. My comrade who knew a few words of their language, asked him the way. He did not answer. Irritated, I said to my comrade: 'Let that old fool alone and let's go on.' The Abyssinian finally opened his mouth to say, in Hebrew:

'Ah, I see you speak my language.' What is a Jew? When I saw that motley crowd on the streets of Tel-Aviv, I often wondered!" (Avner in *"Un Temps pour Tuer, un Temps pour bâtir"* in *France-Observateur*, Nov. 1959).

In this controversy between the devil's advocate and the anti-Semite, there is, however, but a limited triumph.

"Your Ethiopians and your Chinese do not impress me at all," he might say; "most Jews are in Europe and in the Mediterranean countries, or in America. And among us, even to our myopic eyes, as you say, they are visible. So drop the few Aztec examples, if you please, and the problematical Hindus in their distant land, and let us come back to Paris. Do you believe Jews are not recognized by their non-Jewish fellow-citizens? That Parisian Jews do not recognize each other? That is the real problem."

TWO

"You ask, in short, whether the Jew is *recognizable* within a restricted human group, if not throughout the world? If the answer is 'yes,' the Jew would be a *regional* and not a universal biological figure. The French Jew would be recognizable by the Frenchman, the Chinese Jew by the Chinese, etc."

"Exactly."

"That is not, perhaps, impossible. The anti-Semite (and not only he) claims to recognize Jews infallibly at a hundred paces, by their color. I have seen too many mistakes to take that infallibility seriously. One of my Jewish friends, married to a French Catholic in good standing, told me: 'When my husband and I explain that we are a mixed marriage, people never fail to take him for the Jew. I must say that my husband is short and dark; whereas I have broad shoulders and I am blonde. We often laugh over that misunderstanding.' But let us

suppose there is some truth in the anti-Semite's claim
that he never fails to recognize a Jew. After all, hatred,
like love, sharpens the lucidity, if only through the attention brought to bear on the object. It is not impossible
that anti-Semitic persons should identify Jewish faces
more rapidly than others. It is not impossible, generally
speaking, that Jews and non-Jews of the same locality or
belonging to one same group should have less difficulty
in recognizing each other. How would that recognition
work? What, in short, would be that regional difference
thus indentified and how can we characterize it?

"Let us say that I am in a group of Jews in Tunis. Do
I, a Tunisian, recognize the Jews of Tunis? Well, I admit
I do. But let us not forget what we are trying to find out:
whether, within a given group, in an unlimited geographical region, the Jew is biologically recognizable.
Now, is it really because of their biological description
that I recognized the Tunisian Jews? Do other Tunisians
recognize Tunisian Jews because their ears are set in a
certain way, or because they have a mouth of a certain
shape? This time, in all seriousness, I hesitate. It does not
seem to me at all obvious that I can distinguish the Jews
biologically from the Moslems for example, or even from
a great many French, Italian, Greek and Maltese Europeans. The Moslems are more often dark-skinned, perhaps. But that is more a feature of sub-groups, peasants
or Bedouins living out of doors. City people, men of the
Souks, are as pale as Jews, with that ugly yellowish pallor
that comes from a defective alimentation and lack of
light, paradoxical as that may seem in a country of brilliant sunshine. And I have never seen people who reminded me so much of our *fellahs* as certain Sicilian
peasants in the heart of Sicily: put a Djallaba on them
and they could pass for *fellahs* in a film on North Africa."

"And yet you would recognize them both?"

"Yes, generally. But not because of any physical characteristics. By their dress, for example, statistically at least: in a group of Moslems one finds a number of *chechias,* no hats, a few *burnous.* By their language: accents, intonations, different vocabularies. By their habits: I know in advance that I would hardly ever meet any Jews in a certain group, etc. As my wife says: 'It is not true that a Jew can recognize another Jew; but he can make a good guess.' "

Inversely, when I went to the south of Tunisia, where differences in dress and language were slight, at least to my eyes, I was completely unable to find my bearings in front of the same tanned skins of those workingmen crouched there for centuries, the same large eyes of the women made larger by black kohl. More than once, looking for the old synagogue there, I was surprised to be addressed by Jews of that region who recognized me as a Jew and were delighted to meet a co-religionist. Biologically, in short, the Jews resemble their fellow-citizens much more than they differ from them; on this point, all simple observations seem to agree.

And now, I am going to confess. I knew individually so many of my co-religionists, I had so many points in common with them, so many memories, so many experiences attached to that little community that I did not need any particular traits to recognize them. No traits, for that matter, taken separately, can give me any definite information. On the contrary, in the accelerated evolution in which Tunisia has been living these past years, each trait may be deceptive. Dress was revealing, to be sure, but it was part of the social class, the age, the degree of culture, the progressive secularization and Europeanization, and all that was in full swing and constantly clouding the issue. I was amused to see that it became harder to differentiate as one approached the extremes: in the still traditional South and among Westernized intellectuals. A few blunders taught me at my expense that biology was no criterion and that there was no difference in clothing and language. To avoid falling into the same errors, I was obliged to pay attention to other nuances and to carry my investigation further. It is clear, in any case, that the problem of recognition goes *far* beyond the problem of biology. If the biological plays a role, that role is slight compared to the role of other factors. It is, moreover, so intermingled with them, it has been so re-interpreted, that by itself it would be negligible. For men to recognize each other by their physical attributes, they would have to study each other without speaking, without moving and in the nude; in other words, without clothing, speech or movement. Then what would remain? Corpses. And even with unclad human corpses, we would not find pure biology, for life would have left its traces, it would have marked, refashioned the flesh; the cut of the hair, the beard, the care a man takes of himself or the lack of care, nails, skin, hair, teeth, deliberate or accidental scars, magical or medical, circumcision, the callousness of the hands, the development of certain parts of the body, professional deformations, the harmonious remolding as the result of sports. . . . For the pure human biological factor to exist man would have to cease to be human. He would have to be reduced to an abstraction, a terribly abstract concrete. When he eats, makes love, sleeps, the human animal is already human, already socially, historically and geographically placed. The biological is, after all, nothing but material of the human being; and it is not the biological that makes the man, it is the man who utilizes his biology, puts his stamp on it and makes it significant. In short, in our effort to describe the human being by his biology, we are promptly thrown back on psychology, history and culture.

THREE

"Then, neither a universal biological figure, nor a regional ethnic variety would differentiate the Jew biologically from the non-Jews. Is that what you are trying to show? It is too much. In trying to prove too much, you increase my suspicions. You yourself have acknowledged that the biological factor plays an important role in the Jewish malaise, in the non-Jew's suspicion, in the anti-Semite's hatred and even in the anxiety of the philo-Semite. Is there no basis for all that agitation? You say yourself that everything has a meaning, even delirium. And here I am sure I am not dreaming: I insist on believing that, in many cases, the Jew is recognizable and biologically so, if you please. Less clearly than they say, less frequently, if you wish, but *Jewish types* do exist. On this point I have had furious discussions with one of my close friends, an anti-racist, a layman, a humanist, etc., who denied that evidence violently until he married a Polish Jewess. He told me that when he saw his wife's relatives gathered together, he had to admit that there is a type of Polish Jew. When German Jews arrived in France, following the Hitler persecutions, we knew immediately who they were, I assure you, and it was not a matter of dress nor of . . ."

"Of what? Go on, finish. You meant, nor of language. You stopped because that was precisely what it was: a matter of language, therefore of culture and of deductions that they might be people who spoke German, since you knew that an influx of German Jews had recently arrived. If they had spoken French without an accent, if they had looked like Frenchmen, in dress, behavior, haircut, glasses, and had rigorously abstained from making any reference to their past; in short, if they had managed to conceal their cultural, historical and social background, would you have recognized them? You hesitate?"

"A little, but I am not convinced: even if you took away the gold-framed glasses, Germans would still be blonder than we are, they would more often have blue eyes, squarer heads and jaws."

"I shall continue along your line; you will see, once again, that I am not trying to deny *a priori* any biological differentiation. But I want to discover the exact position, therefore also the ambiguities, in my estimation of the Jewish situation. Obviously there are biological anxieties behind the non-Jew's suspicions, judgments and his rejection of the Jew; and Jewish suffering is deeply conscious of it. But is the meaning of biological difference, when it exists, very accurate? Does it authorize the conclusions and the feelings that usually flow from it? In Tunisia we had the same experience you had, though perhaps more pointed; we too had our Jewish refugees from Germany. I grant you that we recognized them easily, and even more certainly than you did. They spoke Yiddish, they liked to go about in groups, they specialized in certain professions, they were, in general, technical artisans. But I admit, too, that they were blond, whereas we were dark, that they had light eyes, whereas ours were dark (not always: my bootmaker, a German from Berlin, was darker than I and had no distinguishing features. But let us keep to statistics . . .). In short, we could not be mistaken when we saw, on the day of Yom Kippur, the different people in our respective synagogues.

"But, now I ask you to make an additional effort. What did you recognize in your German Jews? Did you recognize that they were Jews or simply that they were Germans? That slightly washed-out blondness, those cold blue eyes, that soft fine hair, that pink skin, translucent and slightly porcine—were those Jewish features or simply the features of immigrants, of men from another

land, who surprised us because they did not correspond
to the average of our autochthonous population? You
see, I do not obstinately ceny that Jews can be distinguished biologically from the population of a country. But I claim that the difference is not specifically
Jewish. Any influx of foreigners, any fairly massive immigration, may also differ from the original population.
Since the Russian revolution the figure of the White
Russian has played a prominent part in French literature. Our German immigrants happened to be Jews;
from that it was but a step to the conclusion that they
had an obvious Jewish phys que. A fine example of false
evidence! If the only Jews the French had known were
Chinese Jews driven from their homeland, they would
have come to the conclusion that the Chinese type was
the Jewish type. The connection is purely incidental and
by no means requisite. One day, after a conference in a
northern city, I was invited to a banquet where, I was
assured, I would eat only Jewish food. To my surprise
and delight they served me a succession of dishes I had
never tasted in my life. To those Jews of Central Europe,
Jewish dishes consist of *gef-illte Fisch, Meerrettich* and
Pickel fleisch. To us, Jews of the Mediterranean, the Sabbath was celebrated with *couscous,* meat balls and beans
with black spinach sauce. And each of us firmly believed
that those alimentary rites were authentically expressive
of the Jewish soul. In fact, they expressed it so well that,
before the last historic upheaval which flung the survi-
vors of one community thousands of miles into the arms
of another, we were all ignorant, often completely ignorant, of all those multiple souls. German Jews, in other
words, did not constitute an original Jewish biological
figure, but simply a biological figure of a foreigner. Settling in France, they would, perhaps, enrich by a nuance
the biological palette of France, but that new ethnic variety was a *false Jewish figure.* In an excellent book,

entitled *Et Cie,* the author, Jean Richard Bloch, described two Jewish industrialists who had come from the East to settle in France. What physical picture did he draw but the picture of two Alsatians of a very common type (also among non-Jews) but in whom I myself did not recognize anything at all Jewish. After all, to determine whether the Jew exists biologically, the true comparison must be made, you will perceive, between autochthonous Jews and non-Jews of the same country. Otherwise there is an ambiguity; otherwise we are comparing Germans and Frenchmen, not non-Jews and Jews. The resemblance among your friend's Polish in-laws would lead us to suppose that there is at least a Polish type, and not a type of Polish Jew. Your friend would have been right to change his mind if he could have seen his wife's relatives in Poland among other Poles and not among Frenchmen. That is the only decisive test, the crucial test, since it compares elements that are comparable. But you see too that we are now back where we started: are Polish Jews recognizable (biologically of course) by Poles? Our difficulties in isolating a biological difference remain unchanged."

The Biological Figure

ONE

Let us now go one step farther: let us suppose we have made this decisive test; that
we have made it carefully and scientifically.
To my knowledge, in spite of all this up-
roar, or because of it, there is no complete
work on the subject, no methodical and
comparative description apart from the lu-
cubrations of the Nazis. Let us do even
better: let us suppose that the conclusion
is enlightening. Compared to other Poles,
Polish Jews, for example, do have special characteristics: "Undersized, emaciated,
curly-haired, enormous ears, thick lips . . .,"
as one of my Polish friends remarked ironically (I place responsibility for this sketch,
a rather poor one, on her). Thus, a certain
Jewish group would be found to have specific biological features that would distinguish it from other groups among which
it lives. Under certain circumstances, if not
all, the Jew would be biologically recognizable.

And why not? Conditions of prolonged confinement might well end by having an effect on a man's physical appearance. It is not surprising that oppression should leave its mark on the body. I have already shown that colonization marks even the body of the colonized. It deforms his soul, why would it not deform his face and his limbs? Let us suppose that centuries of confined life in the ghetto may have left profound traces, which became more marked as the result of endogamy. I am well aware there is no proof that acquired characteristics are inherited. But let us take a chance. Let us add a specific diet, the absence of certain foods, a predilection for certain others, a more extensive hygiene. I am putting everything I can in this basket. I would say that, in every way, it is really the total situation that ends by having an effect on bodies as it has on dress, speech, gestures and conduct. We are far from an original conformation, deep-rooted and obscure. Dependent upon a situation and an historico-social experience, it cannot be very profound, even though spectacular. Nor very original: on the contrary, it is neither unusual nor characteristic of the Jew. Many groups, placed in the same conditions over a prolonged period, have shown the same stigmata and the same deficiencies (for, no use hiding it, we are dealing with these and not with extraordinary beauty that would make others jealous of us). Colonial biology, if there is such a biology, was above all physiological misery, undernourishment and disease. It was not mere coincidence that we Jews of North Africa shared those troubles with the Moslems. We were the same sickly, undersized individuals—either dark and shriveled like insects, in whom one was surprised to see life functioning in the absence of any fat or flesh—or else unhealthily corpulent and yellow, billowing with obesity, and in addition most certainly suffering from tuberculosis, trachoma and syphilis. From the biological point of view, the type of the "little Jew" is only a stereotyped picture of physiological misery, of a prolonged historico-social misery. And when some of us managed to rise above the tyranny of fate, our children or our grandchildren were no longer either undersized or unhealthily fat. The last generation of young bourgeois Tunisians, both Jews and non-Jews, was already beginning to grow astonishingly taller. A richer and more sensible diet, proper medicine, the practice of sports, a new love of sunshine and fresh air, relegated to the bazaars of the past that pallor and that light umber coloring so cultivated by young girls. As for specific maladies, they do not exist or when they do they are conditional. It required an actual effort on the part of certain philanthropic organizations to ferret out cases of tuberculosis and trachoma; there is no particular predisposition to those maladies except as the result of undernourishment, faulty hygiene and perhaps, overexposure to the sun. One of my psychiatrist friends thought he had discovered the basis of his whole scientific career: certain mental illnesses, he was convinced, would not exist in Tunisia and other maladies there would take special forms. From that to concluding that our psychology, our "mentality" predisposed us to certain illnesses and made us immune to others was only a step—which he did not take. Honest man and scholar that he was, he quickly discovered that his ignorance of his patients' language led him astray. I myself have not known the life of the ghettos of Central Europe, but I would not be at all surprised if descriptions of them were equally false. What generations upon generations have built up to their detriment, one or two generations would undoubtedly be able to demolish and transform.

And what if all that were irreparable and had marked the Jews forever? (This I do not believe, since heredity of acquired characteristics is not proven and since it would suffice to mix Poles with North Africans . . . as this is done in Israel.) What would that prove save that the Jew would be a permanent victim, biologically as well, since this is a matter of deficiency traits? If every prolonged human situation ended by reacting on the body, one would not know whether that reaction was a disgrace or a glory. Those corporeal signs of the oppression of the Jew are a result of the situation in which he is placed and not of the reasons behind that situation. They are not proof of his iniquity: they are proof of the iniquity done to him. But I shall have more to say on this point, on that extraordinary reversal which makes a crime of misery, and a disgrace of what should be the object of a revolt and a demand.

Can one go still further beyond those deficiencies and their stigmata, hollowed out in the course of a corroding and tormented history; beyond those immigrants' features that are in no way specifically Jewish and that do not appear so save through an illusion of geographic perspective? Could one suppose a distant background on which all those variations have been exaggerated, a background common to all Jews who have survived the accidents of their long adventure? The hypothesis is weak to say the least; it presupposes a common biological origin, which is highly improbable. Even if we go back beyond history, as far as the neolithic tribes of Jericho, we discover not a separate entity but a nomad tribe among other nomad tribes. That hypothesis assumes, moreover, that the initial contribution has remained pure and unmixed, which is false; on the contrary, later contributions far surpass it.

"The ancient Jews were formed as the result of crossing between several groups of markedly distinct type. Later there has always been a certain amount of crossing between the Jews and the non-Jewish inhabitants of the countries where they have dwelt." (Julian Huxley, *op. cit.*).

That does not even have the merit of clarity or of

setting one's mind at rest; we would have to assume a sort of biological substratum sufficiently deep-rooted and visible to compete with all acquisitions, all cultural modifications, and at the same time sufficiently supple and residual to become part of any new combination. Moreover, do we not find again at the turn of the road, the universal biological figure, sly and masked, we had agreed to drop? We keep turning in a circle and this time in the dark. For, instead of that famous nose, or those too prominent lips, to which the caricaturist clings, all we have is a hypothetical biological skeleton.

And even if we admitted that the Jew is biologically recognizable (let us admit everything), what would that prove? What significance, what influence would that fantastic residue have on the concrete destiny of the Jew, on his life and conduct? One can, of course, suppose anything. But at this point we must turn to the scholars. What do they say? They conclude that in the present state of our knowledge, we cannot affirm the existence of any connection between mental traits and physical traits. Despite all researches, as Professor Otto Klineberg reminded us in *Race and Society*, we have not been able to discover any relation between the size or shape of the head, height and the color of hair on the one hand, and intelligence and personality on the other. Scientists will no doubt end by finding something. But at least let them not argue about eggs that are not yet laid. Such is our science that we do not know such correlations. Even when these physical characteristics are plainly visible and most apparent, and all the more so when it is a question of an historical hypothesis and, at the least, of a false lode covered with multiple sediments. I am convinced, as I have said, that certain psychological traits are common to Jews. But is not that long past of terrors and sufferings, of instability and anxiety, of oppressions and repeated traumatisms sufficient to explain them instead of turning to some obscure, and almost mythical biological community? To explain that concordance, that common denominator in Jewish life—the history of the Jew is rich enough in suffering—we do not need to interpret the shape of his head or the color of his hair especially since that hair and that head vary according to whether he is a Moroccan Jew or a Polish Jew, a German Jew or an Iraqian Jew.

TWO

I do not maintain, I repeat, that any biological description of the Jew is impossible, or that any recognition of it is fallacious. On the contrary, I am inclined to believe that every group is recognizable in some way: people from the South of France, for example, and the Alsatians, even people from the Auvergne. But recognition is a more complex and more general phenomenon of which the biological index is only one factor and not the most striking. Compared to the Jew's other traits, cultural and religious, social and political, to his memories, his obsessions and his plans, a biological distinction of the Jew is absurd. When it is not minimal, it is neither clear nor significant and is generally based on a *misunderstanding* within one same nation or more especially between one nation and another. It practically never reveals original or specific traits, but a simple biological phase, suddenly imposed by the hazards of history. Every immigration, every movement of populations, draws men closer together and contrasts them, emphasizing and contrasting their differences. The destiny of the Jew was simply richer in those disturbances and obliged him more frequently to measure up to that yardstick of history. The Jew was, in short, a perpetually displaced person. And when his hosts discovered that he was a Jew, they attributed to the fact of his being a Jew everything that surprised them. But those features they thought were characteristic of him had nothing to do with this. They can almost always be found in men who are not Jews; at least in the country to which storm and stress have driven them. One can also find them, of course, among Jews who have never left their native land. It is therefore always possible to make the Jew disappear biologically; all one has to do is to make him change his residence. Inversely, it is always possible to make him appear; "typical," "obvious," people think, whereas he is simply a foreigner. All biologists agree today that the famous "Jewish nose," is Armenian. In short, if I believe that *the Jewish condition admits of a biological aspect* it would be useless to ignore, I also think that there is no coincidence, either total or partial no stable correspondence between the Jew and the greater part of his biological description. Biologically we should not speak of the Jew but of Jews. We must add that his multiple scattered figures are, moreover, relative and changing, now like everyone else, now strange, unfamiliar, like masks that are now transparent, now opaque.

Then why all this anxiety and furor in the face of that famous correspondence between the Jew and his biology? Why, in describing the Jew, do others firmly fasten on him such a biological concept as if it were clear, distinct and sound, whereas it is confused, vague and fluid? Why do they insist upon this picture of myself when I am certainly not that biological figure they say I am? I am not satisfied to track down and denounce a few optical errors of the non-Jew. I must go on to explain those errors, which are too persistent and too impassioned to be accidental or even perhaps innocent. That very disparity forces me to pose a supplementary question; if those differences are slight, vague and variable, why are they considered so significant? Why is that supposed biological difference, always supposed *a priori*, implied, suggested, inflated out of all proportions? Why that disparity and what is the meaning of it? To that question, in truth, I see only one possible answer: if the extraordinary importance attributed to biological difference does not reside in itself it must have a *borrowed significance*. A non-Jew may be glad that he has a beautiful mouth or regret his ugly teeth, but he does not torture himself to discover what human type he resembles. For the non-Jew, in fact (save when he is another oppressed person), a biological trait has, essentially, an esthetic value. The Jew, however, reacts as though each trait had another dimension, another significance, more engrossing and more burdensome.

It is as though that significance, added to the Jew's physique, explained that physique in a particular way; gave it shadows, depths and bold reliefs. The result is that to understand and exhaust this very deceptive problem of biological difference, it seems to me necessary to reverse the usual point of view. It is not the biology of the Jew that makes the Jew, it is not his actual physique that describes, particularizes and reveals him; it is the idea people have of the Jew that suggests and imposes a certain idea of Jewish biology. The same technique probably works in most of the contexts of oppression even in the case of more remarkable biological facts, like the color of the skin among Negroes or several feminine traits.

THREE

And now I come to that formidable, and, for me, obviously difficult example—circumcision. Here, it seems, we are dealing with an undeniably biological fact. Now circumcision, which appears to be so characteristic of the Jew that it creates many illusions, jokes and aggressive attacks, is shown enveloped in an amazing conceptual fog and at the same time burdened with casual meanings. Do people realize, for example, that it has absolutely nothing to do with an ethnic identity but with a practice? And, even better, a cultural practice which stems from a social decision and not from a biological necessity before leaving its mark on the body. What does the cause matter, you will say, if ultimately, the operation is performed? It often matters so much that it is not performed. A great many Jews are not circumcised, but they do not cease on that account to be Jews or to be treated as Jews. If, in addition, one could consider the fact in itself, in its purely clinical form, what more would one find than a biological incident, a scar hardly more serious than an appendicitis? It is true that nothing in man can be divested of all significance; nor would it even be desirable. But at the same time, one sees that far from having any significance in itself, the circumcision of the Jew finds its significance in his Jewishness. Far from unveiling some mysterious aspect of the Jewish being, it lends him its halo of mystery and blame. To give an example of a counter-proof: that unveiling of the end of the penis is found in so many other men. Is it sufficiently recognized that circumcised Jews are merely a handful compared to the number of circumcised non-Jews: Moslems, Anglo-Saxons, men who have been operated for phymatosis? It is amusing to note in passing that all this business is strictly concerned with only a portion of humanity: the males. Legal society being made by men and for men, it is easy to forget that this keynote of biological recognition disappears when the Jew is a woman (however, for women they will invent something else). Does anyone think of attributing to circumcised non-Jews some special trait that will bring them closer to the Jews? That would not be impossible. Psychoanalysis may one day discover a traumatism common to all the circumcised. But so far man's restless curiosity has not been oriented toward clarity and scientific neutrality.

On the contrary, it is the secret character of circumcision, which does not reveal the Jew at first glance, that apparently makes it more irritating and more suggestive. Paradoxically one may say that this vague mystery augments the burden of significance. Undoubtedly too, the nebulous importance, the ambiguity of circumcision is common to everything that touches on sexuality. There is a vague notion that circumcision affects the Jews' sexual habits, procuring extraordinary pleasures for them and giving them power to arouse equal pleasure in their partners. But it is also true that the anti-Semite is not jealous, nor is he curious about other men who are circumcised, but only about circumcised Jews; and the circumcision of the Jew seems to him more amazing, more disturbing and more shocking than the circumcision of the non-Jew. The mystery of the Jew's sexuality is merely the mystery of the Jew himself. It is not circumcision that disturbs one in the Jew, it is the Jew who disturbs through and in his circumcision. Moreover, this time the Jewish woman is not forgotten. Everyone has heard of the exotic, exciting and scandalous picture of the Jewess. All the somber stories current about the sexuality of the Negro are only the expression of the mystery of the Negro. In each case the same fact is cloaked in an implicit and different meaning which it derives from a whole culture, a whole universe, to which it refers and which gives it special significance and a variable degree of importance. In fact the circumcision of the Jew does not have the same importance as the circumcision of the Moslem or of the Anglo-Saxon. We are finally compelled to turn to Jewishness to understand the envy or the disapproval, the secret astonishment or the aggression which the circumcision of the Jew arouses.

Must I now add that the circumcision of the Jew is related to special significances in the Jew himself? How can one fail to be surprised at our extraordinary faithfulness to the rite? Especially after the Hitler period; when the famous little scar served as decisive proof to send millions of Jews to the crematory furnaces.

"'Friedman, Friedman,' exclaims the officer. 'Why that's Jewish . . . Are you a Jew?'

"'I am not a Jew, Colonel,' I reply, 'I am an Alsatian.' I was repeating the lesson my father had taught me.

"'You're no Alsatian, you're a dirty Jew,' shouted the Colonel.

"'I can prove it to you, Colonel,' I told him. Never having been circumcised (an almost intuitive neglect), I felt that I could convince him on that score.

"I took off my first long trousers.

"The Germans leaned forward, touched me, examined me.

"'Seems to be all there,' said one of them.

"'He has the outer skin,' said the other.

"'To be all there' saved me from being shot.

"They commuted my sentence to deportation to the mines of Silesia."

(J. LANZMANN, *op. cit.*).

Why does the Jew persist in transmitting to his son that dangerous mark of the common misfortune? It is not a simple matter of religion; many atheists continue that practice. Nor of hygiene, certainly: that would be an absurd motive for it: circumcision is a mark of belonging, both a negative and a positive mark, but the most decisive; a true symbol of Jewishness. An Israeli, a revolutionary however, offered this formula: "It is at present still the best Jewish identification card." In short, in the Jew, as in the non-Jew, in the believing Jew as in the militant atheist, circumcision signifies and continues to symbolize all the ambiguity of the Jewish fate.

Generally speaking, I admit that I see my body in a certain way: I watch over it, I ask it certain questions,

I apprehend certain replies from it. But we must turn to the other view: it is not because my body is what it is, but because I have a certain picture of my body, estranged, burdened with a culture; because I know that stubborn, persistent image of my body that people suggest to me, that they claim to find in me, is running around everywhere. There is a model of the Jewish body which is part of a more complete picture of the Jew. I was told the other day that one could immediately recognize the Jewish character in the film *Grand Illusion*. But what do people recognize? The real Jew or the stereotyped picture of the Jew which the director, Jean Renoir, has reproduced and which everyone thinks he recognizes precisely because it is in everyone's mind— Jews included, of course. I shall come back again to the complexity of the Jew's connection (like all oppressed persons) with the image non-Jews suggest of him. One thing is certain, he does not confine himself solely to denying it. When a Jew is sickly and undersized, he sees the image of the little Jew run towards him. Rarely does he manage to consider calmly that unfortunate resemblance to the traditional biological entity. When a Jew has a big nose, it is as if he wore a permanent mark of his being a Jew in the middle of his face; he has the Jewish nose, that is to say, not the nose of the Jew he is, but the nose of the Jew people expect him to be. That poor nose, which would have nothing Jewish about it if it were on another face, is here swollen with all the supposed Jewishness of its possessor. At once, as is the case with the Negro's color, the Jew's nose becomes the symbol of his misfortune and his exclusion. As in the case of circumcision, it is not the Jew's nose or the "little Jew" that makes Jewishness important; it is Jewishness that is indicated by the nose, by rickets or by freckles. Otherwise, why so much interest as to whether the Polish Jew has freckles or not? Or even whether the Negro is black? Seen from Sirius, it would all look ridiculous. Now we almost never attain that degree of serenity, neither Jews nor non-Jews. Thus the problem of the biological entity takes on a new physiognomy and is integrated in a larger though no less dramatic perspective. What is that Jewishness which gives the biology of the Jew significance? And to begin with, what is the meaning of that picture of the Jew? For it is an integral part of my Jewishness of which I am incessantly reminded.

Am I an Economic Figure?

ONE

"Look around you," I have often been told. "Wherever money circulates, wherever money is being made, there you will find Jews. In business, naturally, in banks, in industry, in the most lucrative liberal professions. Jews abound in positions as middle-men. They have the necessary patience and the shrewdness for those jobs, the suppleness and (see how fair we can be!) the human qualities: cordiality, initiative . . ." This other collective portrait, with its flickering and unclear features, is, however, one of the oldest, the most routine and banal, as common and stubborn as a chronic asthma. Here the anti-Semite makes use of a true historical warrant which the biological case does not have. Tacitus rebuked the Jews of his era for the same thing. In Alexandria Jewish merchants competed against Greek merchants and earned their hatred. Judas was a traitor for money—for so little really, for thirty pieces of silver! "It would have been all right if it were for millions!" the irresponsible judgment of nations seems to say. What contemptible greed! The Jew of the Middle Ages is depicted as a usurer deserving only vengeance. The literature of today picks up and makes full use of such a convenient model. Shakespeare gives him the features of the sinister Shylock who demands a pound of his victim's flesh. Victor Hugo does not hesitate to introduce a horrible character named Deutz, who betrays a princess for five hundred thousand francs. Hugo's gross naïveté, or his shrewdness as you please, gives us as usual a picture larger than life: the misfortune of a princess; in other words, nobility, weakness and purity sullied, destroyed. Nothing is safe from this appalling malady, the Jew's love of profit. Drumont, the anti-Semitic leader of the nineteenth century and of all later anti-Semites, declares that: "Anti-Semitism is an economic war." Even on the Left there exists at least an economic doubt, extremely old and still enduring, which begins with the Socialist Toussenel and comes down to the Communist Khrushchev. "For dozens of centuries," the latter declares calmly, "Jews have never been able to make up their minds to live by themselves and to find means of support and stability in themselves alone . . ."

"If you take the building trades and metallurgy, professions of the masses, you will not, to my knowledge, find a single Jew among them. They do not like collective labor, the discipline of groups." (Remarks made to Serge Grossert, as quoted in *Le Figaro*, Paris, August 3, 1955). The remark is at least ambiguous: it does not point out a plain historical fact, but merely suggests unwillingness on the part of Jews to earn a living among themselves and their scorn for the honorable trades of the masses. The anarchistic newspaper, *Le Canard Enchainé*, wrote, in its issue of January 14, 1959: "The First Lady of France . . . the Rothschild Bank." It was only a joke, perhaps, but no joke is completely harmless. Even the Left is fully aware of the stereotype that links the Jew to economics and money, which produces a certain discord I shall refer to later. Here again, I do not intend to take stock of this folklore, but simply to note that the echo comes from afar, reverberates down the ages and is continued even in our day. From the Judean tradesman of antiquity to the modern stockbroker, through Nathan the Wise, Lessing's importer of spices; from the second-hand clothes dealer who followed the Napoleonic armies, to the rug merchant of today, a solid chain, a burdensome tradition links me to this family portrait. So much so, in fact, that people maintain they find it again in my fleshly face and they connect the two processes, the economic and the biological. Can there be any doubt that such inveterate habits must originate in the "blood," in the "genius of the race?" I, as well as all Jewish children, must have come into the world with a special love of money and fully equipped to satisfy it. To borrow an exquisitely modest expression from science, I must have what are known as "tendencies." Is it not understandable and almost normal for me to turn into a money-maker, an economic figure?

And, do what I would to feign irony or to shrug my shoulders, that economic accusation made me feel as conspicuous as would a placard marked P.W. hung on my back and on the backs of my people. Had I been the most disinterested man on earth, a Spinoza, polisher of lenses, or a leather-worker like my father (which I should have been and for which I often feel a nostalgia), I know that to others I would still have to answer to a very unfortunate reputation. Whether I liked it or not, each time the mechanism was set in motion. Whenever the name of a prominent banker or of an influential businessman was mentioned in my presence, a name I suspected of being Jewish, I pricked up my ears anxiously: another one! Can't these rich men leave us in peace? Inevitably, he was carrying grist to the accuser's mill which was already running over. I was angry at that Guggenheim or that Leibovitz for becoming a banker when his name was so obviously Jewish. To be honest I must admit to a curious feeling of satisfaction mingled with that regret. The existence of, the activities of influential Jews, the Rothschilds for example, especially when mentioned in non-Jewish circles, irritated me as much as it flattered me pleasantly. I am embarrassed by that wealth, by that perhaps questionable power, but I am also vaguely reassured by it and oddly proud, as though I shared a little of that power and that success. I think all Jews must know that rather childish but euphoric burst of pride when they are reminded of the Jewish origins of certain of their famous co-religionists. Now, economic power, the Rothschilds, for example, whether I admit it or not, is among the accepted symbols of Jewish life. I can deny it and fight it. I can try to prove that it has not the slightest connection with the essence of Jewishness; nevertheless, I am forced to recognize it. In a recent film, *Me and the Colonel*, the hero, a Polish Jew, found that to flee he needed a car. Quite naturally he goes to the Rothschilds to try to procure one, as if their garages were part of the common Jewish patrimony. The joke strikes home and makes everyone laugh because all, Jews and non-Jews alike, are in connivance. The Rothschilds as a symbol of wealth have become a part of the language common to all men, Jewish and non-Jewish.

Ridiculous, you will say. Do the Rothschilds give the car to Jacobowsky, our little Polish-Jew hero? No, he has to bribe one of their chauffeurs: what else would he have done with the chauffeur of another financier? To be sure, the accusation is, in part, a matter of language and verbal illusion. But in part only. I shall have to repeat this frequently: rarely does language express nothing at all. Inversely, the terrible efficacy of language, which has long been ranked among miracles, makes the word a genuine act which is registered in the flesh more often than one thinks. Words, whatever I may say, influence my life and the lives of my people. Jacobowsky was a fool to believe that Rothschild would give him a car; but he makes an effort to obtain it, he actually goes to Rothschild's house to ask for it. In the end he makes a deal with the chauffeur who is not even a Jew, and the owner, probably fleeing too, knows nothing about it. But would he have dared to call on a non-Jewish financier? Would it even have occurred to him to do so? The very thought of the connection, whether false or true, between the Jew and money, to my questioner and myself, influences my conduct. I know that the majority of my economic moves—for example, if I protect my interest—will be termed typically Jewish. And knowing that, I am perturbed by it, I become more discreet or more cynical. For that reason alone, if for no other, I could not be indifferent to the economic significance which, rightly or wrongly, is attributed to Jewish existence.

But there are things that go beyond the plane of language: though disinterested, even poor, to a certain extent I am responsible for those Jews who appear to confirm the accusation, even if they are odious to me. Each time Jews, whether bankers or not, are insulted or threatened because they are Jews, I hear the warning signal for all Jews. When the shops of Jewish merchants begin to be ransacked I know that all Jews are in danger of death, because killing a Jew is a frivolous and readily contagious act. As young Zionists we were so furiously angry at the rich German Jews that we received the announcement of their early tragedies rather coldly and, I must confess, almost with satisfaction: those powerful communities had always refused to receive our comrades, whether as propagandists or fund-raisers.

Favored by fate, they refused to acknowledge their responsibility towards the misery and fear suffered by other Jews in the world and even tried to conceal a resemblance that weighed heavily on them. Now the wheel had turned and that paltry sum of money we had collected, penny by penny, among the less fortunate, had to be used to save them, the men who had refused to aid us. How could we help looking upon their catastrophe as a striking confirmation of our efforts? I remember that afterwards we used "the German argument," with that unconscious and triumphant cruelty of adolescents. Our triumph, however, was short-lived: soon the Nazi wave reached us. Then we were all in the wrong, each in our turn. Since then history has amply proven that Jewish destiny is an interdependent destiny. That was the best lesson of those war years. Whether I am flattered or humiliated by it, my fate is linked with the fate of all other Jews, propertied classes included, whom geography, history or chance brings together or separates. For that is the way the others want it, and I can only suffer the repercussions of that negative solidarity.

Be it true or fictitious, in short, I am saddled with this economic role of the Jew and I must live up to it whether I myself am one of the privileged, the beneficiaries of the economic system, or one of the exploited in revolt against a social order that is crushing me. Rich or poor, I am accused of diverting to my profit, and to the detriment of others, all the wealth in the world. It is useless to hide it from me: Judas, the traitor, and Shylock, the usurer, are the caricatures of myself that circulate in the market places of the world. This concerns me personally and, in addition to consenting to it tacitly, I am required by these caricatures to take a stand about money. I must ask myself one day who this Judas and this Shylock were—whether they really were as they are depicted and whether it is true that I resemble them.

I breathed a little easier when I ventured to loosen the iron collar of history and to reject the everlasting and much too convenient accusation in the name of the past. To begin with, I was told to admit that in the past other Jews have occupied an economic place apart that is both inordinately lofty and degrading. The argument is, at least, fully reducible. One day I would like to lay siege systematically to the past and give that prestige with which it is adorned a tremendous jolt. I would happily show that its weight and its tyranny derive in great part from our weakness; from the respect we accord it and which it does not deserve. If I feel tremendously bound to all Jews now living, I confess that I do not feel responsible for either Judas or Shylock or Süss, always supposing they are what they are pictured to be. Nor, I hasten to add, for the great Maccabees or the glorious Bar Kochba! For, after all, how can I be held responsible for what is so totally beyond my volition? I consider it futile and absurd to boast of one's ancestors, for good or for bad. It is true that, in general, we assume only their glories, forgetting absentmindedly their infamies. It is also true that Jews are never given the choice and that they are thought of only as rascals and traitors. But the one cannot do without the other, and both are absurd. How dare the Italians of today boast of the military prowess of the Romans? To be consistent they would then have to be punished for the crimes of those conquerors. Should we blame the Spaniards for the atrocities of the Inquisition? And the whole Church? And insult with that memory all the priests we meet on the street? By what right do we weight down the present generation and each individual with the massive burden of a history as remote and as dubious as are all histories?

Am I even sure that there was such a man as Judas, and such figures as Shylock or Süss? Everyone knows

Fontenelle's anecdote of the gold tooth which was the talk of scientific circles and aroused the curiosity of salons, until they discovered that it was a clever fraud. Before we judge them, are we certain that Judas and Shylock actually had that unmistakable physiognomy that is attributed to them? In ancient times, it is said, Jews were tradespeople. Were they more so than the many Mediterranean peoples, the Phoenicians or the Greeks for instance? The most recent historians deny that they were, insisting that they were perhaps even less so. It would seem now that they were more often agriculturists than tradesmen, more often laborers and craftsmen than many other peoples were. P. Jaccard, a scholar specializing in the history of labor, wrote:

"Israelites are indeed the only people of antiquity who are still untouched by the influence of Oriental mysticism, which condemns work and activity as the source of all evil. The Hebrews have always honored the professions . . . On this point, Biblical authors are in complete accord." (P. Jaccard, *Histoire sociale du travail de l'antiquité à nos jours.*)

Later on, scorn and resentment were aimed at rabbis for sanctioning usury. Now looking at this matter closely, we find infinitely more texts steadily recommending manual labor; even the study of law does not exclude the most arduous physical labors. Still later, Jews became bankers. It would be interesting to have some statistics on the proportion of bankers in relation to the whole of Jewry. And were those bankers different from and more corrupt than English bankers or Portuguese bankers? If we were to set the Jewish Shylock down in the midst of the non-Jewish Shylocks we might find that he is not such a Shylock after all The past, in short, is only history, and history is often fallacious. And I would be foolish not to rid myself (if possible) of all those many historical sorrows.

But let us stop here and leave for another occasion

that tremendous and indispensable task of exorcising the past. I know so well what the answer will be: though the past enrages me, it strongly influences my life and therefore my relations with other men. To that I can only agree. We must, however, define the meaning of that influence. What can one say, after all, but that the past is, in a way, transformed into the present? What matters ultimately is not so much the memory of this process, nor even that it is still going on. The discussion therefore boils down to that question which I admit: is that tradition, or that so-called economic tradition, always handed down through Jews? Can we, the Jews of today, can I myself, a living Jew, be economically definable?

THREE

Now here, in contrast to the biological problem, I can judge by documents, and the documents exist. In contrast to biology, which is so much a part of me that I do not know what to make of it, here I know very well who I am! I have never been a money-maker and money has never tempted me. Neither do I find in myself any of the famous tendencies. When I think of it, I have always lacked money! As far as that is concerned, I have never thoroughly understood and at heart have scorned those men who wasted a precious life fighting for money. This is neither a question of merit nor of inefficiency. I know the origins in myself of such sentiments. The son of artisans, having lived all my life among small-time harness-makers and tailors, I have retained their scrupulous strictness and the idea, perhaps foolish, that money should be earned by one's own efforts. I preferred to reserve my labor for other ambitions. Later on, I was amused to notice, though I did not regret it, that my rebellions against my father were always made in the name of his own values. When, conscious of his oppression and of his reverses and even doubting the meaning of his own existence, he finally advised me to choose an occupation whose chief asset would be that I could earn my living easily and well, I refused violently and scornfully. At the time I did not see that, by electing to follow the professions of teaching and writing, as among the most craftsmanlike I knew, I was merely raising again my father's own standard—and this time against him.

Besides, where would I have met the living model of those foul pictures of the Jew? We lived at the gates of one of the poorest ghettos in the world, where we had our work, our synagogues, our relatives, our friends. For a long time I knew about gold, jewels and riches through my mother's fabulous tales, then later through the movies. If I had tried to adapt them to my people, I would have produced one of those strange and humorous effects, so dear to surrealists. When the Nazis launched the slogan of the international Jewish plutocracy, it seemed to me a bitter madness of history. I felt the same rage they did against money and the propertied classes—assuming that their rage was not feigned. We detested with all our adolescent hearts those philanthropic organizations with which we were expected to deal, although they did very much to relieve the atrocious misery of the ghetto. We agreed not to wait for the revolution in order to allow them to fight tuberculosis which was so prevalent, or death which snatched one child in five from its mother's arms. But that only increased our exasperation and humiliated us as though we were conniving at their order. True, aside from the middle classes, which fluctuated between a permanent destitution and a sporadic ease, the city counted a few wealthy families of wholesale merchants or landowners. But these were only local notables, rather ridiculous, against whom my anger wavered, since they were neither numerous, nor, above all, powerful. All the power in the colony was concentrated elsewhere. The mass of the ghetto, in short, overshadowed all, crushed all: for me Jewry was first of all the tortuous alleys which I have been long unable to revisit without a feeling of tenderness, pity, anger and a sharp and mysterious sensual pleasure. And when I faced the economic question, I found it difficult at first to understand. Fundamentally, as on other points, two perspectives occupied my mind: on the one hand, the Jew in me and in my family, and on the other, the slanders, the ugly and preposterous gossip of non-Jews. Those two spheres, the one very real, the other fictitious, lay one over the other like two liquids of different densities. I had no doubt that the real Jew was the poor Jew, for I myself was the real Jew. Perhaps, as luck would have it, the ghetto may have saved me from a little of that torturing Judeophobia so common among Jews themselves.

I expect, of course, to be criticized for that view of poverty which is so close to my heart and which, someone will tell me, is so pronounced only among us: "Once again you are bringing the general case down to your personal matters! You and your ghetto are not the only ones!" The reproach is not without value, but neither are my personal experiences. There again, I insist that the delusion is not on our side, but in Europe, in an extremely occidental Europe. Throughout all the Orient, poverty, not wealth, prevails. But it was the same in those many communities of Central Europe that today are almost decimated. The importance of Russian Jewry was essentially a Jewry of the underprivileged. The Zionist leaders, who sprang from it, were very often sons of poor men. On this point, read the autobiography of Chaim Weizmann, and you will see that the Oriental is not the only poverty-stricken Jew.

"Motol was a typical example of a district of country houses. I lived there from my birth in 1874 till I was eleven years old . . . It is difficult to give modern man of the West an idea of the life most of the Jewish families in Motol led, their special occupations, their incredible poverty, their means of existence and their privations." (Chaim Weizmann, *Trial and Error*).

And, in reporting my personal experience, I do not wish merely to note that there was a ghetto in my life and that this reference, concealed in my heart, makes it impossible for me to consider the economic accusation seriously. Yet, when I think of Jewish economy, the pictures that come before my eyes are of the Hara in Tunis, the Mallah in Morocco, the rue des Écouffes in Paris, and this explodes the theory of the Jew as an economic figure just as the theory of the Jew as a biological figure was exploded. It means that the Jew is not a universal economic figure any more than he is a universal biological figure.

The Economic Figure

ONE

Can one say then that most Jews, if not
Jews as a group, are economically definable?
I agree that the question, so conveniently
limited, is admissible. But I find it difficult
to seize on a half-truth that characterizes the
Jew as an economic figure.

First, I tried to straighten out that
vicious and incoherent description that is
so often heard. I learned that it was useless to look for accuracy and logic in the
anti-Semite's statements. On the contrary,
the contradiction in them today seems to
me more frequent and more significant. In
Tunisia, for example, we were criticized
indiscriminately for avarice and for prodigality, for exhibitionism and for sordidness. We were accused both of throwing our
money out of the window in a spirit of
boastfulness and of holding on to it tightly.
Jewish women were criticized for not pa-
tronizing the best dressmakers. One wanted
to say to the anti-Semite: "Make up your

mind." I do not say, however, that those ironic and spiteful remarks were all unfounded, but at least they could not all be true at the same time, for the same persons and the same classes. Perhaps the ghetto could have been accused of sordidness and the good quarters of opulence. But those were frequently only characteristics of different civilizations and easily clarified if one took the trouble to put them in their proper contexts. Or characteristics that were not in the least Jewish, such as that fondness for bright colors which was particularly Arab, and which was found only in the poorer sections. So also for those dazzling or would-be dazzling Mediterranean festivals, fleeting and indispensable luxuries in a drab and monotonous life, which plunged Jews and Moslems into the same periodic extravagances. So, too, for the sumptuous automobiles of the rich in those countries where there are rarely any opportunities to make a display and few occasions to exercise power. The same phenomena are to be found under other skies, in similar climates and similar social structures. The same festivals, excessive and, to foreign eyes, almost scandalous; the same passionate taste for adornment; the same contrast in living conditions—a thin layer of extremely wealthy propertied classes on a broad foundation of extremely poor populations.

All this most certainly deserves discussion. And God knows I have not restrained myself from expressing my impatience and my rebellion against my native land and against my people. I must add that, like all behavior, any customs can arouse sympathy or antipathy. We are never obliged, I agree, to like customs other than our own. But one must, if not a fool or violently prejudiced, have at least some understanding of them. Today I scarcely see which would be more moral or more alluring, the petty calculations of colonial functionaries or the bourgeois city-dwellers' obvious fear of enjoying themselves; their incredible acrobatics designed to cheat the government of income tax by living as modestly as possible, their great mystic dream of retirement and the innumerable sacrifices they make to save for "buying-a-little-house-in-the-country." I agree that those qualities are considered virtues and that they are called foresight, good management and discretion. Allow us, however, in our turn, to refuse to measure our lives and our dreams, our sudden hunger for festivities, by the standard of other men's dreams and other mass manias. I could go on at length on this subject and attempt a description of comparative customs, in which I would make allowances for what is due to the Jews and what belongs to non-Jews. I would show what poor Jews have in common with the poor everywhere and what the rich have in common with the rich. Then I would justify the residual differences through history and sociology. But such is not my intention: I am not pleading indulgence for what I am. I seek neither to arouse sympathy nor to fight antipathy. What, besides, could I do to dispel that irritation my manner arouses and which I can hardly deny? Not everything in the non-Jews' description of us is true, but neither is everything false. It is true we were more extravagant and more exuberant, more wasteful and more restless, more eager to live, more interested in food and traveling.

But is that really the basis of the problem? Is that what the accusation is built on? It would most certainly be a very weak foundation and one that could be too easily refuted. Is not the implication rather that the Jew's conduct, his way of life, affects the lives of non-Jews? That economically the Jew has an important role and an influence that gravely disturbs the economy and the lives of his fellow-citizens?

". . . Mark my words, Mr. Dedalus, he said, England is in the hands of the jews. In all the highest places: her finance, her press. And they are the signs of a nation's decay. Wherever they gather they eat up the nation's vital strength. I have seen it coming these years. As sure as we are standing here the jew merchants are already at their work of destruction. Old England is dying."

(JAMES JOYCE: *Ulysses*)

That is why I am not surprised when a more stubborn anti-Semitism goes beyond this psychological impressionism. To be more efficacious the indictment is made explicit and is focused. So true is it that there exist enemies very close to us and their hatred makes it more ingenious. That desire for money, the anti-Semite then adds, has led to the Jews gradually getting control of the economic system, with the result that today Jews are responsible for the economic systems of the countries in which they live and even of the entire modern world.

To be of a greater persuasive value, the accusation is only outwardly clear. What are those controls the Jew is said to have? And what responsibility are they talking about? Let us ignore the somber conspiracies of financiers and rabbis, almost sorcerers, united to complete a plan to conquer the world. The famous Protocols of the Wise Men of Zion stem, as we know, from a frenzied hatred that requires outlets other than arguments. The last war showed us, among other things, the futility of power and the absurdity of the so-called international Jewish collusion. Very unfortunately for us, I have to say! How happy we would have been, at that time, if there had been a combined Jewish power! We would not have had to beg the American official in vain to accept that bargain offered by the hard-pressed Nazis: a million Jewish lives for trucks. The Warsaw rebels would not have waited till they were exterminated for Russian troops to intervene.

The argument sometimes takes on a more subtle, more scientific form. The Jews are supposed to have conquered the world economically, not as the result of any occult guidance, but by a sort of spiritual contamination: there is a deep affinity between the spirit of capitalism and the spirit of Judaism. One understands immediately why the Jews are so well adapted to modern economy, which is abstract, dynamic and concerned with banking: they invented it in their own image. It is literally their creation. That is why an economist like Sombart, a talented and often perspicacious man, who supports that curious theory, finds himself forced to take careful stock of the well-known but nebulous economic qualifications of the Jew. I have perhaps too good an opinion of scholars, a hangover from my university days, I suppose; but I simply cannot understand how they can seriously defend a concept of social phenomena so linear and so nebulous at the same time. How could the Jewry of those days, relatively few men after all, downtrodden and poorly integrated, but sustained by their own efforts, by their personal needs, overthrow the social and economic structures first, of all Europe, and then, of the whole world? But perhaps the best and most objective minds are disturbed when they think of the Jew; and in spite of themselves, preserve some remnant of belief in an occult and inordinate *"virtus judaica."* For is it not easier, more refreshing to one's intelligence simply to suppose that, on the contrary, it is the profound and complex transformation of Western society which has given rise to the bourgeoisie and capitalism and which became embodied in it, or better, which is capitalism itself? The Jew benefited, to be sure, by the disintegration of society in the Middle Ages, a society in which he could have only a limited place, a lowly existence and where he was always in danger. The new society, less hierarchic, more anonymous, more dynamic and therefore more liberal, suited him much better. As society no longer pointed him out to other men, he was less exposed to their blows; as it offered him a broader field for his industry, it increased his chances of living and prospering.

But where are the evil and the mystery in that? The liberation of the Jew was only an infinitesimal part of the liberation of so many others, who were in the majority and who were the real driving power behind the revolution. There are so many parallels between the Jewish soul and that of capitalism, that they could have changed souls without too greatly upsetting the thesis! People have thought they could detect the same parallels with the Protestant soul. The origin of capitalism, it has been stated with equal gravity, lies in the spirit of asceticism, which was developed by the Reformation, i.e., the mentality of the Puritans, for whom every duty, even the most worldly, was a mission imposed by God, and to which they were bound to devote themselves seriously and in self-abnegation. Then, spurred by the same impetus, the same trick was tried with the Catholic soul. The origin of capitalism? Just look at the organization of the Catholic Church, the extraordinary order of the Jesuits in particular, you will discover etc., etc. In truth, one can go far with this little game of resemblances, relationships or so-called spiritual genetics. All one has to do is to reduce Judaism or Protestantism or Islamism to a few simple terms; then give capitalism the same treatment (or Marxism for that matter!) and the trick is turned. The reduction will be all the easier as it will be effected solely on the plane of ideas or of psychology. How many things about the natives in the colonies have been explained as fatalism or a love of dreaming! But neither institutions and techniques, nor tremendous human forces and the complex relation of those forces that make up a society, which is endlessly disrupted, eroded and renewed, can shake that amazing license of the thinker-magician idealist. So amazing that it strongly resembles fantasy. . . .

We must definitely leave the past to historians until they come to an agreement (and perhaps even afterwards), relegate inherited tendencies to psychologists (if they want them), and leave economic spirit to the dark and mystic clouds of anti-Semitic imagination. The only way to speak accurately here would have been to talk facts and figures and to work with statistical data. In the absence of a trustworthy science, we can at least refrain from speaking with assurance and from condemning. And one can only admire such casualness, such rapidity of affirmation; such strong consequences that they dare to draw from such uncertain premises. It is amazing that, in a field in which, after all, it is possible to be precise, we are so sorely lacking.

I was an adolescent during the last war and I was furious that I could not answer with conviction the allegations of the Nazis and their false testimonies. If only for my own peace of mind, I wanted to be able to say to myself: They lie! Such and such a figure is false, such and such an accusation is invented. But, with my comrades of the study group, I searched in vain through the extremely rich library of the Souk el Atlarine; I could only deplore the scarcity of technical books, compared with the extraordinary burgeoning of another literature —speeches, pamphlets, rabid denunciations and insinuations or pleas and protestations. We will have to re-examine that lack which is certainly not without significance. The difficulty involved in the research is not a good excuse when one thinks of the wealth of patience and ingenuity expended in so many less serious fields. I am forced to think that this modest but precise study and its possible results are less desired (by everyone, perhaps) than all that nonsense in which the Jew's exact place in the economy of today is lost.

Who, disregarding those many vetoes, will give us one day the great definitive study entitled simply: "The Role of Jews in the French Economy?" Or in the American, or in the English Economy? I can imagine my Jewish and philo-Jewish readers' surprise: Look out! That would be calling attention to the Jews! That would be discriminating against them, considering them *a priori* as strangers to the economy of the country! I have said enough about what I think of those false ostrich-like precautions. In my opinion, no knowledge is harmful in itself. On the contrary, I see no other way of cutting short the debate, if we want to settle it. Does not their refusal prove, once again, that in these matters the Jew and his friends prefer not to engage in the debate, for fear of having to plead guilty? Whereas we should go straight to the crux of the matter and immediately disclaim any guilt whatsoever. The only serious and honest way to envisage this problem is *first of all* to desire a solution; in other words, setting aside all preconceptions, to reduce the problem to one simple question, the answer to which is verifiable: Do Jews form a separate socio-economic class in each society?

To many people the answer to that question, even so precisely stated, would, I am well aware, seem easy: "Do the Jews form a separate class? Why, that's as plain as can be!" They can just as readily tell you which class: in any case, not the class of the small wage earner. And if the Jews are not in that class, they naturally have to be in the other. It's very simple, you see. The average anti-Semitic imagination is not noted for excessive richness; and one always finds their few basic themes cloaked in different words to fit the circumstance. Jews are said to be essentially the propertied class, financiers, businessmen and middlemen; in short the great specialists of economy, its rulers and its profiteers. This is, at bottom, merely a poorly disguised variant of the traditional picture of the fat Jew (fat, this time), smirking on his mountain of gold, while the masses groan, crushed beneath the yoke of international Jewish plutocracy. . . . That scarcely rationalized proposition finally reveals its true nature: an abusive and grotesque generalization. It amuses the real specialists, the actual rulers of economy. They know well enough in whose hands economic power lies.

"As for the widespread image of Jews as international bankers and Wall Street brokers, this amuses even the Wall Street folks. The truth is that there are relatively few Jews in either category."

(VANCE PACKARD: *The Status Seekers*)

Of course, there are Jewish bankers, and banks run by Jews just as there are banks run by Protestants or Catholics. But that does not justify so much anxious avoidance of the subject on the part of the Jews, nor so many derogatory aspersions on the part of anti-Semites. Why would there not be a Jewish bank? Let us even suppose that the participation of Jewish finance in the economy of any one country is relatively higher than that of non-Jewish finance? There again, of course, we must first be given exact statistics and not mere assumptions. But let us admit that it is so: At the very moment when I am editing these pages I am assured that Jewish bankers do outnumber non-Jewish bankers, but by a very slight margin which has dropped since the war. But why extend the accusation and the odium, if odium there be, to all Jews? If I am a socialist, I will fight against wealthy Jews too, but I shall not hold them either more or less culpable than non-Jews. And if those men of wealth are more numerous and more powerful among my people— which remains to be proved—my struggle will be more difficult and more complex. But even if there is a preponderance of Jewish bankers, that by no means justifies a special and world-wide curse against all Jews.

As far as I know, only the Marxists have made a serious effort to define the economic activities of *the majority* of the Jewish population: for, let us not forget, that is what the definition of the Jew comes down to. The problem reinforces their anxieties, it is true, and is apparently responsible for their methods. Among the young men in Tunisia who shared in our impassioned adolescent discussions, there were a few Communists. In general they were part of our youth movements, then after breaking with us, they returned to the charge, inflamed with a fresh but proselytizing zeal. When we urged them ironically not to confine themselves to the affairs of the Chinese or the Mexicans but to give a little thought to our destiny and to their own, they fell back on that key-concept that has served them well, the concept of the social classes. The Jews, they assured us, were a class; and anti-Semitism, an economic conflict which, among many others, the revolution would take upon itself to resolve—statements that at least had the advantage of clarity. The difficult and irritating "Jewish problem" would, it seemed, be settled in time. We would begin with class struggle and end with the Jewish misfortune. But not all locks can be opened by the same key—even a passkey—everywhere, and reality is not so easily reduced.

In *Portrait of a Colonized Native* I have described the similar persistence of the Communists in connecting colonial conflicts with class struggle, the outcome of which depended upon the triumph of European workers. Now the colonizers—natives were not assimilable in the propertied classes—are being dispossessed. The revenge of the native is not limited to an economic revenge. Wherever native uprisings occur, they have all the earmarks of national struggles, headed by the bourgeoisie with extremely vague and often nonexistent social programs. Not that I would minimize the enormous importance of the Marxist discovery. I am convinced that there is an economic aspect to the majority of oppressions—including the oppression of women. I myself have shown that one of the fundamental mechanisms of the colonial situation was the mechanism of privilege. But I also discovered that colonial privilege was not confined to one *class:* all colonizers, of any class whatsoever, even if they were the most underprivileged in their home lands, benefited by it to some extent. That privilege, moreover, was not solely economic. Cultural persecution and scorn for the native, the curtailment of the native's social and historical life, racism and segregation, all worked to the advantage of the colonizer; and all that gave colonial despotism its unique character. Nor do I think that the Jewish problem is a simple matter of class; nor anti-Semitism a simple economic conflict, even in disguise. In his preface to the Russian edition of *The Diary of Anne Frank,* Ilya Ehrenbourg, a very orthodox Communist writer, notes:

"The Nazis killed six million Jews, rich and poor, famous and unknown, belonging to twenty different countries."

And what class was it a question of? It was not enough to say that the Jews constituted a class, it had to be stated clearly which class. The Marxists have attempted to do so several times, but their embarrassment was obvious. The fact is that one need only look around to discover the discouraging variety of the Jews' economic activities. In spite of the existence, more frequent than one would believe, of Jewish workers' blocs, the Marxists saw plainly that Jews as a whole did not belong to the working class. Naturally, they refused to conclude from this, like the vulgar anti-Semite, that the majority of Jews were in the moneyed class. My Jewish Marxist comrades, at least, concurred in classifying Jews among the oppressed peoples, the downtrodden of history, who must be saved by the same social upheaval. Then what did they have left? That sort of catch-all, that magma, known as the middle classes. And this, in a word, is what they did when we badgered them. Under that very convenient name, they brought together, pell-mell, vast numbers of Jewish artisans, employees of all categories, the liberal professions, technicians, intellectuals, middlemen of every stature . . . provided that stature was not too great. And in a certain way, as a first approximation, it was not altogether wrong. But that grouping is so disparate, so flexible that it scarcely gets us any further. We win, of course, a decisive argument against the ordinary anti-Semite; the vast majority of Jews are not wealthy and influential men. But what distinguishes the Jew within those middle classes? If there is nothing to distinguish them, why all this anti-Semitism? The problem remains unsolved. The Marxist would say that it is a matter of a hoax and a diversion on the Jewish part of the population, and of economic difficulties of the whole of society. Undoubtedly there is a mythical aspect to the Jewish situation. I come back to it often, but it is also certainly not the whole story. We would still have to explain why that hoax and that diversion are so successful. To get the answer we should have to carry the analysis beyond that first crude approximation.

There is a fundamental confusion implicit in all Marxist thought with respect to the Jew, as with respect to the colonized native and even to woman. The confusion is based on the same significant postulate: the necessary relationship of every alienation to the social class. Now, if the Jew is really an oppressed person, his economic alienation is probably not the essential part of his misfortune. In any case, the result is a paralysis of Marxist thought and conduct with respect to the Jew. Is it not strange that after the Marxists reduced the whole Jewish situation to its economic aspects, they have never undertaken an actual examination of it? As if they were afraid of discovering something that would invalidate their original premise. From this, perhaps, derives all the obvious confusion of Marxist activity in any matter connected with the Jews; I think they are clearly at a loss as to how to treat this curious person, so obviously oppressed, and yet at first sight not always belonging to the usual underprivileged class the Marxists champion.

In short, is there nothing then? Is all economic characterization of the Jew illusory and only in the province of emotion? There again, I honestly do not think so. In the absence of statistics, I am obviously unable to determine the precise importance of the economic difference. But I believe that it exists; and I refuse to evade it by denying its existence, as my accuser takes advantage of it to inflate and pervert it. Besides, I did not intend to make an exhaustive and detailed study of my life, but to offer a true comprehensive picture, omitting none of its essential features. Now, I believe that my life has a certain economic aspect.

Even in the absence of definite information, how could I ignore, for example, the large participation of Jews in certain trades? When I walked through Tunisian bazaars I could not fail to see that those little shops crowded one against the other, long tunnels no wider than their doors, were occupied only by Jews. I need look no further: the harnessmakers, which most of us were, except for two or three strays, were all Jews. The European tailors, which my two uncles were, were divided equally between Jews and non-Jewish Italians. I could roughly estimate that the shoemakers, drygoods merchants and jewelers were recruited especially from among my co-religionists. (Those jewelers were more craftsmen than speculators, and they earned no more than copper-plate engravers).

A striking characteristic of the Jew's economic activity is, what I propose to call, a *tendency to crystallization* or concentration. Within a basic global division, let us say, in the middle classes, we quickly discover a *second concentration*, a number of groups more restricted and at the same time more conspicuous. There was no doubt about that in Tunisia. We are fortunate enough to have, at last, a thesis in the Sorbonne on the Jewish population in Paris. The author has apparently discovered the same phenomenon: he notes a concentration of two-thirds of Jewish activity in a very small number of centers, and at the same time an extreme diffusion of the remaining third scattered among all levels of the economy. (Roblin, *Les Juifs de Paris*)

I have not had the opportunity to verify that statement for other countries, but I am convinced that one would find the same situation almost everywhere, even in socialist countries where the original structures have been profoundly modified. On his return from the USSR, the president of a Jewish delegation admitted that out of 1,190 lawyers in Moscow, 500 were Jews. It was as though the economic particularity of the Jews had been in part restored.

This *dual concentration* is the basis of an effect of social illusion, a distorting halo, a blurring, which in return increases the apparent importance of the concentration. The exact number of Jews in trade is not considerable; this can be verified whenever one wishes to take the trouble. The Roblin thesis confirms these facts for Paris and the Department of the Seine. "The proportion (of Jewish merchants and employees in trade) is not much higher than the proportion of non-Jewish Frenchmen in the Department of the Seine . . ." But their concentration in a few commercial centers makes them infinitely more noticeable, more annoying and more insufferable to a prejudiced eye. Thus, even if there is nothing remarkable about the general statistics, the original character of the particular detail remains.

This tendency to crystallization is again reinforced by a frequent demographic concentration of the Jewish population: Jews of the same origin have a tendency to remain over a long period in one economic group. Jewish financiers in Paris are not only Jews, they are also three-quarters Alsatians and are almost always named Bloch or Weill. That distinction and that demographico-economic correlation are easily explained. Jews who have been settled longest in the country have more or less merged with the population; they have finally found their place in the economic system. The newcomers, as a rule penniless, are ready to accept any sort of job. The last wave of North African Jewish immigrants, for instance, provided France with a sub-proletariat that was penniless and undemanding. Later on, the better elements among them, or the more active, will be regrouped. But that effect of blurring is even further intensified. Even if the number of Jewish financiers was not unusual compared to the number of non-Jewish financiers, that very concentrated solution of Blochs or of Weills will tremendously increase the impression of saturation. Even if there were not a substantial number of Jews in the liberal professions, the 500 Jewish lawyers in Moscow cannot fail to catch the public's attention and imagination. If the anti-Semite goes shopping on a certain street in Paris, he will find there a great many Jewish hosiers. He sees this as a confirmation of his phobia and his hatred and concludes that *all* trade is in the hands of the Jews, with never a thought of *all the commercial centers where there are no Jews at all* which brings the general proportion down to almost nothing.

There are many Jews in the clothing business, but there are practically no Jews in produce, chemicals, or construction. The Jews turn readily to certain liberal activities; which should be explained. But the phenomenon is greatly exaggerated; because Jews crowd into a certain liberal profession, medicine for instance, and through sheer numbers, certain Jews fill important posts, etc . . . But people forget about the many liberal professions in which there are no Jews.

There is therefore a unique aspect to the Jew's entrance into the economic life of the city, a uniqueness less shocking than it seems, but real. It is difficult to put one's finger on it, which certainly adds to the ambiguity, but it is possible to characterize it. It is absurd to see in the Jew a purely economic characteristic. On the contrary, it is his whole position in the midst of non-Jews, which results in his special form of economic penetration; as it also controls his political and his cultural penetration. It is even more stupid to accuse him of holding the keys to the economy, since he is absent from large sectors of that economy; and since gross statistics reveal nothing in his favor. And yet I believe that one can describe an economic aspect of the Jewish fate. If we add to this objective aspect the economic accusation which weighs on him continuously, we can finally admit that the Jew does have a certain economic character.

The Meaning
of the Indictment

ONE

Convinced that, as a Jew, my existence is
unique, why should I be surprised to discover economic peculiarities in myself? I
have admitted that actual differences do
separate me from my non-Jewish fellow-
citizens; therefore in discovering those peculiarities I merely add another characteristic to that existence. The anti-Semite will
rejoice and say that my admission confirms
his hatred. But he did not need my contribution, and the accusation already existed.
On the contrary, by tracing it to its exact
origins, I can answer it confidently and
precisely.

After all, have I discovered anything so
terrible in the course of all these reflections?
That Jews do differ in some measure from
non-Jews among whom they live? But why
should that rather commonplace truth ex-
cite the anti-Semite's passion? That trait is
not even typically Jewish. What human
group, endowed with a certain autonomy,

and living in the midst of other groups, is not differentiated in several ways? That is almost a truism. Every separated group tends toward differentiation, and economic differentiation is only one aspect of separation. It is the positive and negative aggregate of differences that constitutes and maintains the particular existence of a group. Anything else is assimilated; in other words it disappears. In Tunisia, far from being an exception, differentiation was the common rule; but at the same time we did not give it exaggerated importance. Our Corsican fellow-citizens acknowledged that they held a very large number of positions in public services; Corsica, they said jokingly, exports oficials and imports pensioners. The busy inhabitants of Djerba were so active in the grocery business that we actually used the word Djerbian to mean grocer. The masons were Italians, the goatherds Maltese, and the vine-growers Spanish. It is easy to find similar divisions almost everywhere in the world. In France, it is said, most of the café owners are from the Auvergne, and the Normans supply the country with lawyers . . . but no one makes a secret of it, for no one finds it scandalous. Sometimes people are a little annoyed, but never as much as they are by the Jews, to the point of hatred. At the most it gives them a chance to laugh or to display bad temper. In Tunisia we mimicked the Corsican accent of the police and taunted the Djerbians with being cuckolds because they lived so far from their homes.

There is no evidence, in any case, of a deliberate plan to seize control of any corporation. Professional concentration seems to be the result of a sort of social mechanism. We do not need to call on the spirit of Colomba to explain the public service work of Corsicans: The poverty of their island; their tradition of emigration, the fact that they all have relatives in office in other lands, are explanation enough. And I found the same thing among my own people. Numbers of new corporations headed by Jews spring up in Tunisia, as they do elsewhere, as the result of opportunity and pressure and not from any evil premeditation. Everything urges them on— their parents, their friends, their relations—and as they are surrounded by their own people, the business struggle seems less bitter and success more probable. To this general principle, one must undoubtedly add particular motives in individual cases. Why are there so many Jewish doctors? Medicine is an ancient Jewish profession that corresponds to a geographic restlessness; not to mention family traditions that derive from it and from which it benefits. A Jewish broker from Antwerp explained to me why so many Jews of that city are brokers: it is a profession that can be carried on any place and does not require much time to establish. Moreover, children generally follow in the footsteps of their parents; as a result, in Antwerp, sons of brokers often become brokers. Elsewhere the son of an intellectual will tend to follow a liberal profession, in which he sometimes has greater success than his father, who had less help. The son of the businessman goes into business by choice and finds it easy to become a businessman. The phenomenon for that matter is not limited to the more lucrative professions; look at the group of North African Jewish proletarians that is being formed in Paris at the present time. The same thing is going on in the famous Rue de Rivoli where Algerian, Tunisian and Moroccan merchants concentrate: scarcely have they spent an hour together before they are planning to meet again. They patronize the same real estate agencies, who moreover specialize in that clientele, and their families exchange visits while waiting to find an apartment.

Even the relative social rise of Jewish immigrants, which is commonly cited and which seems to me frequent, as a matter of fact, does not strike me as symptomatic of

Jews alone: the same thing occurs in most of the old minorities. Minorities, because that need for security that assails every man, every group living among strangers, will drive a man to stabilize his position by putting down as solid roots as possible, economic roots among others. Old, because it takes time, a certain seniority in the country, to achieve a new status. Hence that astonishing and neverending waltz between the different classes of successive immigrations. The Saint-Paul quarter in Paris, refuge today of Sephardic Tunisians and Moroccans, was, even before World War II, the refuge of the Ashkenazim. But there is nothing unusual about that drive; one finds it again in most of the countries to which people immigrate, in America, for example.

No, this economic difference is neither extreme nor specific. I would have almost liked to say proudly: "Yes, there is an enormous difference. And it is in our favor! For once we have a clear advantage!" But that is not true. There are, of course—and I repeat it—economic and biological differences between Jews and non-Jews, but they are generally very slight and they are by no means as significant as the anti-Semite makes them.

TWO

Here I want to follow my thought to the end at the risk of being accused of paradox: I have always resented that economic aspect of my life as a shackle, a limitation, and not a privilege. Why do I not have, *a priori*, opportunities in all professions? Why am I obliged to forego so many specially guarded fields? Why, if I am sensible, must I advise my son against taking up such and such a career? When at the end of my high school studies, I announced that I intended to become a professor, my parents and my friends urged me not to think of it: a Jew in a public position! They were sure I would have a miserable career no matter what efforts I made. I have described elsewhere my family's anxiety and the struggle I had to keep from following a traditional path. Nevertheless, my stubbornness and my eagerness, the natural optimism of my age, prevented me from believing in the experience of other people. But today I know they were not altogether wrong; I have proven, at my expense, what my parents already knew and could not perhaps explain to me clearly. Anti-Semitism, which makes so much of the economic pretext, has particularly efficient economic sanctions against the Jew. I must stress this point: economic concentration has always been as negative as it is positive, as injurious as it is useful to the Jew himself.

People refuse to see in that concentration anything but a sign of the Jew's good fortune, the proof of his scheming cleverness. That, however, is precisely the viewpoint of an accuser; one forgets that the concentration was solely the result of the Jew's initial misfortune, that it was imposed on him by fate and by others and that it will follow him all his life. The tendency of Jews to concentrate on certain trades is said to cause non-Jews great harm. But no one thinks of the harm done to the Jews themselves by this. For the reverse side of the picture is obvious: the complement of that concentration is the Jew's exclusion from so many other sectors. And yet the same mechanism comes into play and often, also, a decision stronger than the Jew's. The *numerus clausus* is not at all a Jewish invention. But this is not the first time a despot has blamed the victim for a crime he himself has committed. We have seldom been farmers, it is true; but have we been allowed to be? For a long time we did not even have the right to buy land; and when we were finally given permission, why would we have acquired it when we were constantly in danger of having that land snatched from us? Land is too open to view, it attracts the greed of other men and brings down misfortune on the head of its owner, especially when he is too weak to demand respect. It is also too static, too tied down for us, for we are so volatile and changeable that we must always be ready to move on. The Jew was seldom a soldier in the past: he did not often have a place in the epic. For a long time he did not even have the right to mount a horse. That timid and stupid animal was too noble for him! All that we Jews are can be explained, in large part, by all that we have not been allowed to be. And all we have not been is explained in large part by oppression. There was a period, under the Moslem rule, when the Christian's life was also restricted to certain activities. He, too was not allowed to bear arms or to mount a horse, to bear witness in a law court nor, of course, to practice any kind of profession. The result was a precarious existence in which he could ply only those trades the Moslems were willing to let him have. In Tunisia, before the colonizers made their first concessions, we were not allowed to occupy government positions, we were excluded from the army except as privates and we could not be settlers because life in the midst of hostile peoples was too insecure. Then what was left for us? Handicraft, trade and certain liberal professions—which is exactly what we were doing!

"You blame us for being merchants or intellectuals as if your cruelty gave you the right to blame us—but to cultivate a field you have to think of the harvest . . . In France a generation has lived in peace and quiet, I admit it; since the Dreyfus affair we have felt we were men in the eyes of all Frenchmen. But all this time, Jews were being killed in Russia and in Turkey. Then it began all over again, everywhere. And because it is not so long since that stopped, even here we are recovering that attitude of fear which is our only defense, we bend our backs, we hide, we huddle together." (Clara Malraux, *La lutte inégale*)

It is true that Jews were sometimes induced to go into

ignoble trades; for example, as money-lenders or tax collectors in the service of men of power. It is true that Jews sometimes found themselves libelously portrayed as disreputable historical persons. (One usurer in the whole country and every Jew is accused of practicing usury. In the same way, all natives in colonies are said to be thieves, all women wantons, etc.) It is easy to understand that certain populations have hated those symbols of their economic misfortune. But even in those extreme and rare cases it must be obvious that Jews filled positions nobody wanted and the reason why they were given them was precisely because they were considered degrading occupations. Jews were, in short, executioners, Jacks-of-all-trades for men of power—they did their dirty work for them. That is where the ambiguity of this miserable power of the Jew comes to grief; as an agent of power, and therefore in a measure power itself, it adds to his odium and his alienation. A role as disgraceful as executioner could only be offered to a slave or a criminal. At the same time those men of power made up for those indignities by emphasizing his disgrace. They freed him and at the same time they branded him; they consecrated him by clipping his ears. When the Jew's economic role is not wretched and sordid, it can be the instrument of his survival or even the opportunity for his revenge; it is, nevertheless, one of the signs of his hateful singularity and of his humiliation.

The first victim of economic specialization is the Jew himself. It is neither right nor healthy that he should thus be restricted to certain specific economic areas, even if he succeeds in making an honorable place for himself in them. The anti-Semite is hypnotized by the economic success of a few Jews. The Rothschilds have cost us many a slander and much anxiety! While far from denying the relative success of certain Jews in some fields, it would be infinitely more instructive to draw up a picture of the vast permanent percentage cf Jews who live in a condition bordering on endemic catastrophe; what race has such a high percentage of emigrants, for instance? If we examined the total economic aspect of Jewry we would find it astonishingly unhealthy. When, in our study groups, we reflected on the nature and situation of our scattered peoples, we discovered, among other things, that they were economically sick. The Jew's professional aspect can be compared to an inverted pyramid, standing on its point. Whereas among most nations, peasants and laborers, the backbone of all social construction, form the base of the pyramid, there are no peasants and almost no laborers among the Jews. Jewish merchants, middlemen and employees, on the other hand, are too numerous compared to the average among other peoples, and even more so in relation to the Jewish pyramid. The proportion of craftsmen among the Jews is excessive. Intellectuals are overabundant in some sectors, nonexistent in others.

If additional proof of that morbidity of the Jew's economic situation were wanted, we need only think of his extraordinary weakness. Personal vexations and hindrances are not the most serious difficulty; the Jewish community as a whole is regularly in danger. Every time a nation goes through a crisis, its Jews are the first to suffer; whether from legal action or from the peoples' intense xenophobia. After World War I, that mechanism worked throughout almost every country in Europe, wherever economic or political tensions arose. After the last war, it was more difficult to attack Jews directly; they were too exhausted, they had been too much victimized and yet history has often repeated itself under another guise. Most of the young nations, in particular, removed Jews from all governing positions. They explained to them politely, regretfully, that the present generation, the new classes, sprung from the masses this time, were claiming the positions and the responsibilities; and in this there is

some truth . . . but they implied that Jews were not genuine offspring of the people. It seems to be a law or a
general custom of history that whenever Jews are not
indispensable, whenever they can be replaced, this is in-
exorably done. Make no mistake: this is not the price of
wealth or of power. In North Africa I was able to prove
that the poor are the most vulnerable, the most quickly
affected. For example, they are the first to emigrate; not
because they have nothing to lose as the bourgeois in-
timates, but because they are the weakest. Deprived of
their jobs or their shops, they soon lost everything and
were stamped out in a few weeks. The wealthy were able
to hold out longer and if they could save part of their
possessions, the loss was only relative.

Here again we have one of the dilemmas of the Jewish
fate. Segregation forces the Jew into professional specialization, and specialization fosters segregation, emphasizes
the difference and the particular character of the Jew.
Difference and particularization contribute largely to the
weakness, the precariousness of the Jew's existence. What
conceals the phenomenon here is an ambiguity that has
worried all of us; Jews are blamed for specializing in the
professions as a means of power, money seems to express
the Jew's victory rather than his defeat. It is also true
that, to the Jew as to any other man, money can be an
admirable compensation. Crowded out, confined to a few
fields, it was inevitable that Jews should do their best to
make the most out of it, and that certain of them should
actually succeed. But how many of them are there? If all
roads had been open to them, no doubt they would be
scattered among all of them and without any particular
distinction. They have been deprived of that freedom.
In short, even the successful cases are merely the reverse
of a situation of weakness and exclusion. And I am convinced today that the oppression of the Jew is indicated
as well by his economic oppression. It would be surprising
were it not so: economic oppression is certainly most fre-

quent and most common among various oppressed groups. Many professions are still not open to the majority of women; natives in a colony could have access only to the most menial trades and the most poorly paid; the proletariat, of course, is defined precisely by its economic weakness. Though, among the Jews, economic oppression is not the most obvious, I am convinced that the liberation of the Jew must include his economic liberation.

THREE

Then why such an accusation, and why such disproportion between facts and the interpretation ordinarily put upon those facts? The Jew is neither an economic figure nor a specific social class, nor even the sole representative of an economic class. He is concerned in a certain way with the economy, it is true, and he prefers to concentrate in a few professional sectors. But he is driven to them as often as he decides upon them, he is as much resigned as consenting. He establishes himself as best he can on whatever land is left him and sometimes ends by living there in comfort, just as from long habit a man eventually becomes accustomed to old clothes or to old dwellings. But the Jew pays dearly for this adaptation. His very success is the ambivalent sign of his limitations and his isolation. He is quickly punished for it, impoverished and dismissed as soon as another man, better connected, can replace him. Thus, we find ourselves face to face with the same impasse as in the biological investigation. Starting with one question we end with another. Why are certain rather nebulous characteristics supposed to be so important when they are not considered disgraceful in the non-Jew and when they are really more harmful to the Jew himself than to other men? Why is the economic aspect of the Jewish fate given the most unfavorable interpretation for the Jew?

Again I see only the same reply: *it is not so much the*

Jew's economy that draws attention to him and makes people condemn him; it is the Jew's Jewishness that draws attention to the economic side of his existence and earns for him this added anathema. Jean-Jaurès, the French Socialist leader, was amazed at the extraordinary violence of Drumont, front-rank man of the anti-Semites of his time.

"Why," he asked Drumont, "do you attack Jewish financiers and not all financiers?"

"My God," the French racist is said to have replied, "it is not the financier in the Jew that arouses my hatred, but the Jew in the financier!"

Let no one charge me with idealism. I have shown plainly that I do not deny that there is a certain objective economic difference. But I am obliged to reverse the point of view of the explanation. Economic difference is not the real motive of the accusation. It is the Jew's whole existence, including his economic position, which is repudiated and which makes that economic difference at once striking, paradoxical and disastrous.

The fundamental reproach made of the Jew is that he will always be an economically privileged person. This accusation is so absurd when one looks at the Jew's actual existence, that it is suspect. There are, to be sure, economically privileged persons among the Jews, on whom it is convenient to focus popular anger. But the Jewish masses are as wretched as, and frequently more so, than others. There are groups of Jews on each rung of the social ladder. Jews are not often laborers, it is true—though more often than one thinks! "Between 1900 and 1914 most American Jews belonged to the working class" (P. Aubry: *Arche*, No. 45, October, 1960). But how does it happen that all those who are not workers incur such discredit? Is there such a thing as moral poverty and immoral poverty? If one has to be poor to be moral, let us rejoice! There are enough artisans, employees, little middlemen, and poverty-stricken intellectuals among the Jews to call down blessings on us. But the truth is that Jews are not permitted to fill any but the lowest rungs of the ladder.

It is amusing to note that the objection does not come from the workers or from their usual defenders. All this righteous indignation comes from people who have no desire to suppress the privileged. In a society based on profit, private property and economic freedom, and controlled by the propertied classes and the middlemen, how dare they hold it against certain Jews for sharing ever so little in those profitable mechanisms? Do they imply that Jews do not have the same rights as non-Jews? God knows I have no special goodwill towards merchants and middlemen whose psychology I dislike and whose economic role I question. I am prepared to disapprove of all trade and to confess to a desire to reform the whole field of distribution. But I reject the particular case brought against Jewish merchants. Is it not better to deny the Jew the right to be a merchant simply because he is a Jew and not because trade is a bad thing in itself?

Of course, by prodding the anti-Semite a little we discover that the Jewish merchant is an outdated model: with dishonesty, dubious practices, crooked deals, the Jewish merchant is said to be disloyal, he never plays the game. What game? Here we leave the element of quantity for the element of quality. The affair now becomes esthetically revolting. The spectacle of the Jew working secretly to amass the greatest possible sum of money is not a pretty one to contemplate. As if the Jew were not criticized for earning too much money, but for earning it by underhand and crooked methods. As this criticism is made by people who by no means look down on money, it is difficult for them to stress the amount of the earnings so they fall back on the method by which he gains them; the means of earning money is apparently more important than the amount earned. The Jew, so they contend, would corrupt good manners and fine traditions that do honor to an old established firm, etc. Of course, this is not only a matter of esthetics. The Jew would be dangerous in business. Dangerous to whom? Here we will better understand it all. To his client? No, on the contrary, he would be too assiduous in his attentions to his clientele, excessively obliging, obsequious, never letting the customer go, procuring the article requested even if he does not have it in stock. If he were unfair to the customer, the latter would leave him. Now the trouble is that the Jew succeeds too well. We are amused to learn that he is considered unfair towards other merchants; other merchants and businesses suffer from the Jew's assiduousness and ingenuity. But how do other merchants suffer from the activities of the Jews? Are they cheated? Do they receive damaged merchandise? Are not their contracts honored? No, one seldom hears such complaints. Moreover, they would be absurd. Why would the Jewish merchant be more of a crook than other merchants? I am convinced, on the contrary, that his social instability, his insecurity, make him more respectful of the law. The Jew operates within the law; he "cuts" prices (an expression that gladdens the heart of the consumer), he is satisfied with a smaller profit, he is too alert, he opens his store too early and keeps it open too late . . . At last we come to the heart of the matter: it is all a question of competition. The non-Jewish merchant is simply defending his own profits. Driven by his own greed, he accuses his Jewish competitor of the same fault. How many times have we been told that competition is the backbone of business, a statement that is not contradictory. Competition consists of defeating and, pushed to the extreme, eliminating one's competitors. Which competitors? Naturally the most poorly defended, the easiest to eliminate. Now, who is easier to eliminate, more vulnerable than the Jew? The Jewish merchant is so quickly suspected, accused and condemned merely because he is a Jew and not because he is a merchant. It is his Jewishness that suggests, encourages and permits him to be maligned, plundered and put to death. Otherwise, once again, why just the Jew? Why not all merchants? As James Joyce writes in *Ulysses:* "A merchant, Stephen said, is one who buys cheap and sells dear, jew or gentile, is he not?"

Another example? There is furious rage against "Jewish money." It is suspected of all sorts of evil influences and collusions. I have no particular liking for money or wealthy persons either. But I see clearly that wealth is not always condemned wherever it is found. In fact, it is really attacked only when it is considered harmful and unwarranted. (Some of my readers will immediately protest that they condemn all wealth, at least all extreme wealth and even all private property; but those very people are not generally anti-Semitic and they do not make a point of decrying Jewish wealth.) Except in times of revolution, when society as a whole is called to account, what is challenged and criticized is the money of the newly rich. As he has not always had it, he seems to have no right to it; and as he has no right to it, how did he get it unless by fraud and at the expense of others?

Now the fact is a Jew's money is always considered censurable. It follows him like an odor of illegitimacy and of doubt. The expression "a rich Jew," contains one part ambiguity, with a dark core which gives rise to sneers and disdain: "God only knows where and how he made his money and where he keeps it!" But did not the fortunes of other men have a beginning? How have those "old families," those "reliable old establishments," made their money? There was certainly a moment when they first became rich, and when they were newly rich. But as time passed they ceased to be illegitimate. The Jew, however, will never cease to be so: he is the bastard of the economy, and as for the rest, at best an adopted child however long he may have been in the country. It is not so much the Jew's money that is more scandalous or more dubious than other men's money, it is the scandal of the Jew's whole existence, the illegitimacy of the Jew's whole approach which makes his money a definite scandal and stamps his economic conduct with suspicion and illegitimacy.

All this discussion of the harmfulness of Jewish money, Jewish business, Jewish banking, is shown to be futile the moment we move on to other fields; to the liberal professions, for instance. There one finds the same bitter quarrel, even though money and profit are no longer dominant themes. Someone will say that a certain Jewish doctor earns a great deal of money, but this time the principal approach is on the concentration, on the monopoly of the profession. Jewish doctors are not so much accused of being more expensive or of robbing their patients or of shady practices. But the cry goes up that "all medicine is *in the hands of* the Jews, etc." It is clear that it is the Jew's participation in the economy which is questioned and declared bad. At the beginning of the last war, the Vichy regime put a *numerus clausus* on us, as is well known. Only a limited number of Jews had the right to be doctors, lawyers, teachers or even students.

Some of my comrades, and even a few moderate professors, upheld a decision they considered equitable. "I am not anti-Semitic," an old classmate assured me, "but I want my country to be healthy and I want justice. There is no reason why the proportion of Jewish doctors should be any greater than the proportion of Jews in the population."

That arithmetical argument, under the guise of impartiality, profoundly revealed the anti-Jewish rage. Was it necessary to distribute professional positions according to the various categories of the population? If so, the people from the Auvergne would see the number of cafés they owned reduced and the Normans would have to give up being judges and lawyers. As a matter of fact, my Vichy classmates meant something quite different: they implied that the case of the Jews was very different from the case of the Auvergnats, the Normans or even the Corsicans. The Corsicans could all be public officials if that is what they wanted, but not the Jews, for it was not good for so many Jews to be officials, doctors or merchants. That is the true, implicit substance of their argument. During that same period, moreover, more openly avowed anti-Semites disclosed their ulterior motives.

"We don't want to trust our wives to Jewish doctors," they dared to say, "our children to Jewish teachers, and our business affairs to Jewish lawyers."

Why not? Are Jewish lawyers less able, Jewish doctors less competent and Jewish teachers less equipped to teach? No. The anti-Semite has never said that: on the contrary, paradoxically, he will speak of a certain Jewish doctor or a certain Jewish lawyer as particularly clever. But, he implies (confusedly, it is true) that there is a certain danger, a certain harm in letting Jews practice these professions. What does that mean if not that the Jew himself is dangerous and criminal; that they are not attacking the doctor or the lawyer in the Jew, but the Jew in the doctor, the lawyer, the teacher or the merchant? The profession the Jew practices is, in short, of little importance. In any event, I am convinced that the Jew's economic activity would have aroused the accusation and provoked the sanction. Thus, if the Jew confines himself to any one professional field, it is said he is monopolizing it; if he is scattered over a wider area, the complaint is that he is everywhere. The heart of the matter resides not in the Jew's economic activities, but in what he is as a whole. It is the Jew whom men suspect, judge and condemn, because the Jew can and must be suspected, judged and condemned, and not the craftsman, the merchant or the intellectual who are neither better nor worse than their counterparts.

It is, in short, the Jewishness of the Jew that gives the economy of the Jew an infamous meaning and not the reverse. Here again, to understand the economic aspect of the Jewish fate we must place it in the full context of that fate.

The Myth

I therefore found myself before a mythical
portrait of myself; like the mythical portrait
of the colonized native which I have described and a mythical portrait of the poor
which I hope to discover. These imaginary
portraits are not, however, wholly imaginary. Rarely are such false portrayals, which
trouble so many different people including
the victim, without some foundation. The
accuser would have to be out of his mind or
an extremely clever faker; and even so, cleverness must be supported by at least some
verifiable references. But the few Jewish
characteristics I recognized in the accusation are either derisory or have a different
meaning. I immediately felt that the quarrel they were trying to pick with me was so
inconsistent with my supposed defects, the
accusation so out of proportion to its possible origins, that I was forced to look elsewhere to understand it.

I have therefore insisted upon following

the anti-Semite step by step in two directions as far as he wished to lead me: in the direction of my biological figure and in the direction of my economic figure, simply because those are the most common today. But I can have the same experience, I can go over the same ground, with reference to my metaphysical, cultural or political figures. For many Christians, the Jew is supposed to have, above all, a marked theological aspect: it would be a mystical destiny, condemnable and most certainly condemned for various grave crimes, the most shocking of which would be the murder of Jesus Christ. Do not tell me again that this is an outmoded point of view, an *affaire classée*. The Church has never explicitly abandoned it, and another time I shall tell why it can never do so. For that matter, contemporary Catholic writers still refer to it frequently in their books; and the most representative of them all, Paul Claudel, does not hesitate to ride that theme hard. How can one fail to see, in any case, that it is always the same story, told in a different manner? In this theological description of myself, I recognize the same familiar and fundamental accusation; my existence in the world of other men is a calamity, or, in theological terms, an irremediable curse for me and for others.

The same reasoning holds good for the cultural accusation. An amazingly evil person, I would contaminate and warp the minds of other men as my people have always contaminated the growing minds of men. If anyone thinks I am exaggerating let him re-read carefully the literary production of these past decades. I am not referring to Celine's curses, to Ezra Pound, or to any other fanatical anti-Semite, but simply to the most temperate authors. I have just learned from one of Mr. Lawrence Durrell's books that Moses' morals have poisoned the whole of modern civilization. The same reasoning applies to my supposed political role: the Jew is supposed to have had an extraordinarily heavy, occult and of course injurious influence on the social and historical destiny of others. Thus, the Jews would not be without responsibility for the outbreak of World War II. Every man, in short, expresses in his own language, through his own ideology, his particular concept of the Jew; theologians use theological terms, writers a cultural description, and politicians political characterizations. But it is always the same idea and the same outcry: the Jew is pictured as an absolutely formidable being, possessing an extraordinarily maleficent power.

In every case, it seems the accusation (based on some perhaps genuine observations) is magnified and finally becomes a veritable myth. In other words, it retains just enough distant connection with the initial reality to live its own life. Two characteristics are always cropping up in those different figures of myself; their *casual connection* with reality and their *convenience* for my accuser. The convenience is not always obvious, it is true, but the anti-Semite's slightest description teems with incoherence and contradictions. I might hesitate over a certain detail of some of my supposed characteristics; I have always found it impossible to take seriously any sort of whole, and of course, any entire construction. The few differences that separate me from other men, and which I have acknowledged as clearly as I could, seem to have run wild. I have been accused of other differences which either enrage me or make me laugh.

Most of them, normally incompatible, are frankly contradictory: my mind is said to be both intelligent and blind, I understand everything and I do not understand anything, at least in several important fields such as art, mysticism and emotion. How could that extremely sharp intelligence be also narrow-mindedly weak? When I press the point I am told that my mind is analytical, abstract and inexpert at "intuition." The chairman of a board of admissions astounded one of my colleagues by saying bluntly: "You see the details clearly, but you do not know how to make a synthesis of them: that is an Israelite turn of mind." One might just as well believe that my anxiety, my difficult life had developed special antennae, making me especially sensitive. This the anti-Semite would grant me, provided it was another weakness, a morbid trait, a maladjustment of sensitivity and not of "intuition," which is too noble to function in the mind of a Jew. German doctrinarians have stated at intervals that a Jewish capitalism and a Jewish Bolshevism do exist. How could those two exist side by side? Nor was that a purely Nazi statement, meant only for the consumption of the German masses of those days. The Nazis invented very little, to tell the truth; they more often took over and developed ideas already ingrained in the German tradition. Is that contradiction peculiar to Germanic anti-Semites? The beliefs that Jews control the economy of the world and that they foment revolutions co-exist with the greatest of ease in a multitude of minds. The Jew's body arouses the same contradictory judgments as do his mind and his conduct. I am supposed to be sickly and weak, a biological wreck, and at the same time swollen and fat as the Golden Calf. This is the result, I suppose, of superimposing two pictures of different origins; one comes from the wretched inhabitants of ghettos and the other from the too well-fed usurer. (That must be more complicated, for the usurer is often depicted as a miser who starves himself.) In any event, no one ever tries to make those outlines agree. The racist accusation commonly marks the Jew as a quasi-pure race; it holds his rather aloof personality against him as an aloofness that has made the Jew unassimilable for centuries. In that case the Jew would have remained a foreign body in the midst of nations. But just as often we meet the reverse characterization: the Jew is said to have borrowed something from all the people through whose midst he has passed. This would be a dubious and despicable conglomeration of traits for of course, he would have taken the worst and the result would be disastrous for him and for those who have received him. Julius Streicher said of the Jew:

"The Jew is monstrosity incarnate . . . in his veins flows the blood of Nordic Germans mingled with the blood of Mongols and of Negroes. Whence his physical appearance."

I could go on at length drawing up this catalogue of incoherences and inconsistencies in my mythical portrait. It is clear that the important point is not my real character, but the profound desire to see me in a certain way. Now, far from being embarrassed by those inconsistencies, the myth seems, on the contrary, to be reinforced by them. Objectively incoherent, the myth ideally serves a purpose: to show, at no matter what cost, by adding repeated and even incongruous statements, that the Jew is harmful; and that ultimately he is absolute evil. At the same time that fanaticism, that madness has a meaning, a goal and a visible trajectory. The myth of the Jew is not a pure lie, it contains a modicum of truth, but the truth of the myth is not the reason for the myth: what is that secret coherence and that hidden significance? They are what I have called the myth's *convenience:* my mythical portrait always turns out to the advantage of my accuser. It is easy to understand why incoherence does not trouble the anti-Semite: his interest and his rage inwardly justify everything he says about me. That is why theologian, politician, economist and writer, each portrays the Jew that suits him. In general the accusation rebounds on the accuser.

TWO

The strategy is common to most oppressions: an accusation, a calling to account of the oppressed person, which because of its magnitude and radical method makes the accuser himself suspect. We quickly discover that the mythical figure of the Jew is literally built up by the society in which he lives, as the mythical figure of the colonized native is imagined by the colonizer. At the same time, to understand the myth of the Jew, we must first examine the needs and the attitudes of the non-Jew. It would seem that the Jew's whole being, all his activities, everything he produces, must be affected by that systematic denigration. Nothing escapes ridicule, neither his body nor his mind. His fingers are like claws: but don't think for a moment that this is simply a rheumatic deformation; on the contrary those are suspicious symptoms of a fundamentally unhealthy physiology. Moreover, those fingers are very often dirty! But why dirty if not to accentuate that repugnance he cannot fail to inspire? The Jew is flat-footed: that too is not simply a physical deformation which is particularly embarrassing to him; those flat feet are the pretext for all sorts of anxious mistrust. The whole man is filthy, deformed, sick, an easy prey to certain maladies, slyly immune to others, his sexuality is obviously disturbed, *"projectissima ad libidinem gens,"* as Tacitus said. He has, in short, all blemishes, all ugly traits, both acquired and innate. You think I am exaggerating? No, indeed, we have only to collect and put end to end all the articles and books lying about in the homes of the well-known writers of our day.

"Skada was an Israelite, about fifty years old, from Asia Minor. He had a hooked nose, an olive complexion and as he was very near-sighted, he wore glasses as thick as the lens of a telescope. He was an ugly man, with short crinkly hair pasted down on an ovoid skull, enormous ears . . ." (Roger Martin du Gard: *Les Thibault-l'été* 1914).

I may add that Martin du Gard was not being especially malevolent towards his Jewish characters; he was merely translating a convention: the Jew is ugly. In his

Portrait of Dorian Gray, Oscar Wilde is not so restrained: his Jewish character is both deceitful and homely.

But can one hold a grudge against an invalid or a cripple? We do not quite forgive an invalid, it is true, unless we are fond of him, unless he is one of ours. The others get on our nerves or disgust us: and the Jew has some of the characteristics of that sickening aversion: he is obviously considered a strange invalid, aggressive and dangerous. Does he not carry malignancy to the point of spreading ailments he himself does not catch? That is the epitome of biological evil! But after all, one can say that such things are beyond his control; no one is altogether responsible for his body; the outstanding ears and the big nose are not necessarily dishonoring. That is why physical illness, in a strict sense excusable or without great significance, is almost always followed by moral illness for which there is no excuse.

"A mixture like that," Julius Streicher also said, "has formed his soul, ill-assorted, inharmonious, vile. As the blood is, so is the soul. The Jew's soul is the sum of all turpitudes."

The Jew's ugliness, infirmities and illnesses do indeed reveal a hideous soul. His clawlike fingers show his avidity and his malice and their filth adds moral taint to physical disgrace. Biology leads to a particular psychology, the one explaining the other. This is why contemporary anti-Semites encourage all themes upholding a linear relation between the two fields. Scientifically we are far from it; and it is probable that environment, education, culture and history play at least as large a part in the psychology of individuals as do their bodies and their heredity. But such proofs would be so convenient for the anti-Semite that he applauds them in advance. Biological negativism has need of spiritual negativism which supplements it and completes it.

Everything about the Jew, in short, is said to be bad,

even what at first sight may seem to be a virtue. Is it said that the Jew is intelligent? Can we consider that a virtue? No indeed, he is *too* intelligent, his sagacity is destructive, corrosive. Is he said to have a hunger for knowledge? That means he is afflicted with "intellectual bulimia," with a voracious appetite, as though everything about him that is not already negative is made so through his maleficence. I have shown that, although the colonizer unwillingly admitted the qualities of the colonized native, he nevertheless interpreted them as defects: generosity as prodigality, gaiety as vulgarity. The differences that separate the Jew from other men are not condemned solely because they are differences, as we have seen, but on the pretext that they are harmful. The Jew is not only economically different, he is said to be economically dangerous. The entire characterization of the Jew is implicitly or explicitly governed by the same method: a systematic, progressive negativity which is carried by its own momentum to the limit.

At the worst the Jew is depicted as absolute evil, the devil of the Middle Ages, which means, to be specific, that his accuser demands the death penalty for him. Carried to the extreme, negativity can end only in nothingness, in the removal of the Jew from the anti-Semite's horizon. It is always the same coherent absurdity. The anti-Semite appears insatiable, the Jew's gesture of refusal seems to lead him on and on. The drama lies, in great part, within the anti-Semite himself rather than in his victim's actual existence. It is not enough for the Jew to be slightly guilty and slightly condemned for certain perhaps displeasing actions. He must be more and more condemnable, therefore more and more guilty. The culminating point is obviously complete negation: the Jew posed as absolute evil and the accusation to be erased only by his death. From this point of view the traditional theological image—the Jew is cursed for eternity—is the most expressive, the most revelatory of the anti-Semite's profound desire. It is also in this light, I think, that we must understand the astounding and terrible accusations of ritual murder. Why is the Jew accused of murder? I shall answer bluntly: to give his accusers an excuse to kill him. The Jew killed Christ, he profanes the host, that is to say he continues to kill Christ throughout the ages. The accusation is not confined to symbols, the Jew kills concretely: every year at Easter a Christian child disappears. This theme of the Jew as a murderer goes back far beyond Christianity. The historian, Jules Isaac, found it among the ancients: a Greek was periodically carried off, fattened and sacrificed. Moreover that theme is still present in a new guise. The Nazi accusations are only a secularization of this theological method of radical condemnation. Modern racism is merely employing a language more adapted to the present day. "The Jews plot to conquer the world and suppress all peoples," explains an Arab tract distributed in Bonn in 1959 by delegates of the Arab League. The same arguments are broadcast daily to the four corners of the world by numerous sources of intrigue, Belgian and Canadian among others: the Jews are the cause of most of the wars, social cataclysms and mass murders. This is complete madness: how could the Jews conquer the entire world? And even if they did conquer the world, why would they kill all the people? That madness, however, is significant and deliberate: the Jew commits the most atrocious crimes, therefore one need have no scruples about killing him. To understand the argument we must look at the reverse side of the picture: it is a means of preparing for the death of the Jew. It is simply the rejection of the Jew by others, carried to its symbolic and concrete limit.

That mechanism of liquidation, fortunately, does not always run its full course, otherwise the Jew would have vanished. Not that the definitive suppression of the Jew is so shocking to the nations' consciences; from time to time someone envisages it and a beginning is made. I persist in thinking that the Jew is permanently in danger of death. However, the mechanism contains its own brake. The effective massacre of the colonized native would have put an end to colonization, therefore a sort of equilibrium was established between a spontaneous movement towards annihilation of the native and a relative acceptance of him in order to perpetuate the profits and privileges of the colonizer. The same dialectic is found again in the relations between employers and their employees: the employer's natural temptation is to get the maximum from his wage-earners, but the employee has to live and to live well enough not to rise in revolt. Fortunately the Jew is, in a certain way, necessary to the non-Jew! Not only for the non-Jew's psychological well-being (it is undeniably a convenience to have someone inferior to oneself, a scapegoat, etc . . .) but because the Jew fills several specific roles among non-Jews—those roles for which he is so bitterly criticized. If the Jew had not instinctively discovered that he has to make himself indispensable, if he did not occupy a series of social posts that make him, at least temporarily, irreplaceable, he would no doubt be immediately replaced, ignominiously driven out, or in danger of death.

THREE

The function of the mythical portrait of the Jew is obviously to justify oppression; and therefore, to a certain extent, to help maintain it. It is not always, of course, a consciously and deliberately mounted attack, but more often a sort of regularizing function. Faced with the oppression of the Jew, the non-Jew, I have noticed, acts as though he were confronted with a fact; whether he approves of it or is indignant about it, he always shares a little in it, either directly or indirectly. The exclusion of the Jew benefits all non-Jews. The oppression of the Jew results from the functioning of society as a whole; anti-Semitic language belongs, in varying degrees, to the whole world. In a recent film, *The Defiant Ones,* a white man who had insulted a black man by calling him a nigger, excuses himself by saying that he did not invent the term. The black man replies: "You did not invent the words and the customs that crush me, but you make use of them." Confronted with the situation in which the Jew is placed, the non-Jew discovers a problem which is also put to him and to which he must reply as best he can: the myth is the non-Jew's most common, most current and most convenient reply to the Jewish situation.

Certainly the non-Jew would also oppose the oppression of the Jew. But that opposition is not easy for him, I am willing to admit. Aside from renouncing appreciable privileges, the non-Jew would have to transform the whole of society, overthrow existing human relations and their system of values, and seriously attack the social order that permits oppression. But when has the world ever seen such devotion, such efforts solely to save someone else, and moreover someone held in contempt? Must the non-Jew turn revolutionist and rise up against his own society because the Jew is unhappy in it? Especially when he is not even convinced that the Jew's misery is not deserved?

But, someone will say, the non-Jew is sometimes a revolutionist for reasons other than rushing to the aid of the Jew. It is lucky for the Jew, after all, that there are many men who long for more justice. Moreover, those men too are oppressed by that same society and their cause coincides in part with the Jew's cause. But here the parallel stops. The Jew is the oppressed of *all* that society, including its other oppressed members, any one of whom, even the most underprivileged, feels in a position to despise and insult the Jew. That is probably the explanation for anti-Semitism among the working class, an anti-Semitism which is not altogether aberrant; for *all* members of society, without exception, it is advantageous to have a few Jews. Just as every man, no matter how low he may be, holds women in contempt and judges masculinity to be an inestimable good—and in this he is not altogether wrong since he manages to benefit by it concretely—just as every colonizer, without exception, feels superior to every native no matter who he is, because every colonizer finds certain advantages in perpetuating the colonial situation. But the transformation of society and the adjustment of the Jew's lot obviously lie in the more or less distant future. For the present, the Jew is the oppressed person of a society in which the non-Jew is the beneficiary; every non-Jew must put up with the relation that unites him with the Jew. He can approve of it, as the colonizer approves of colonization, or reject it as the good colonizer criticizes the policy of his own country, though he cannot avoid carrying it out, at least to some extent.

He will therefore have to account for it. At the very best he will argue, and he will admit his share of responsibility, throwing the rest back on the Jew. And this I understand. It is hard for him to admit full guilt in such an involved set of circumstances. Then too he is more or less carried away by the myth. It is a vicious circle: oppression creates the myth and the myth keeps oppression alive. But more often the entire fault is placed on the Jew: the non-Jew's guilt is transformed into the guilt of the Jew; in other words, into anti-Semitism, into myth. Once again it is clear that I am not making a special effort to overwhelm my accusers. To be sure, there are degrees in rejection, but it seems to me hard for the non-Jew not to blame the Jew. If the non-Jew is not guilty, then the Jew must be. If the vagrant and the prostitute are not guilty, then we are; therefore the vagrant and the prostitute are responsible for their own misfortune and for the disorder they introduce into society. Guilt must be changed into its opposite, the guilt of the oppressor must become the guilt of the oppressed: the mythical Jew is, in short, a defensive argument of the non-Jew.

With the situation thus reversed, everything becomes clear and everything becomes possible, a genuine mechanism of debasement is released. Worse still: that defense argument and that mechanism have, from now on, their own laws, their own destiny; the more the non-Jew oppresses the Jew, the more he accuses him; the more he accuses him, the guiltier he feels towards him; the guiltier he feels, the more he must say the Jew is evil, the more he must get the better of him . . . it is an endless circle. It is what I have proposed calling "the Nero complex." And the myth keeps on growing bigger and bigger, the accusation being carried to incredible extremes: the Jew becomes almost a monster. He carries misfortune with him and sows it around him. As *Fortune,* the magazine of the French national lottery, which is circulated gratis throughout France, writes amusingly (?):

"The Wandering Jew, whose name is perhaps Carthaphilus, perhaps Ahasuerus, perhaps Isaac Laquedem, is obliged to walk till the end of time. And if he chances to stop, the city where he pauses is destined to be destroyed . . . Hamburg in 1542, Strasbourg in 1582, Beauvais in 1605. And that is what happened in Saxony; one may verify the fact that there is no trace left of the city on the Matterburg where he was so imprudent as to wish to rest. Has he paused at Herbauges? We may be allowed to suppose so . . ." (*Fortune,* No. 5, 1961).

On this course which runs from negativism to annihilation we find the essential and necessary stage of racism. One could almost say that racism is independent of real biological differences. The racist accusation is an additional and too convenient rationalization of the rejection of the Jew. I have said again and again that the oppressed person has no special biological characteristics: it happens that the biological index may be striking, as it is for woman or for the Negro. But considered apart from the accusation and the myth, no biological characteristic is bad in itself, no difference is condemnable. Moreover, when biological difference is absent, the anti-Semite invents it. Racism is an abusive and pejorative generalization of a real or an imaginary difference. It is not the race that calls forth and justifies oppression, it is oppression that calls forth the racist ideology. From now on what matters is this effort of radicalization, of substantification of the Jew. Through racism he can be attacked for everything in his life: his whole being is affected, as are all the individuals in the same group and the degradation is definitive and irremediable. Now at last the Jew becomes incomprehensible, obscure and mysterious. He communicates a feeling of malaise and of strangeness: "He is a ghost," wandering about in the midst of nations, an unpleasant apparition that must be driven away. Somewhat more nobly, people will speak of the "mystery of Israel." But do not be fooled! That mystery is poisonous, it contains the death of Christ, the Jews' refusal to acknowledge the triumph of Christianity, the eternal punishment that follows the "Wandering Jew." By a simple antithesis, the Jew is at the same time accused of not understanding others, their art, their culture, or their sensitivity; and of not being comprehensible *to* others. The Jew, in short, is not of their world: degradation ends in de-humanization. The myth is complete: it has reached its goal.

How can one fail to reject and condemn such a creature? Physically hideous and corrupt, morally despicable, economically harmful, politically dangerous, spiritually evil, theologically damned, why would one even pity him?

"Jews must be cut off as a whole and not even a little one should be kept," the French writer, Robert Brasillach, declared during the last war. Stripped of all human qualities, the Jew becomes, indeed, an animal. We can understand why, periodically during anti-Semitic crises, to crush the Jews seems to the anti-Semite almost a duty. It is a kind of hunt to track down a dangerous animal— from whom the anti-Semite must protect himself.

So far I have not mentioned a secondary aspect of the myth, but one that often supplements it. The Jew is so guilty that he ends by admitting his own guilt. What a triumph then for the anti-Semite when the Jew confesses his confusion as he stands before that false mirror! Now all of us have our moments of doubt: the accusation is so general, the insults so varied, so repeated, that sometimes we hesitate. What better verification could there be for the accusation? The accused has confessed: we can calmly mete out punishment, the oppression can and must be continued. If the Jew himself is resigned to the situation created for him; if he accepts the limits imposed upon him, if he ends by behaving as expected, then the oppression is firmly established. To sum up: the mythical portrait of the Jew paves the way for and adds the finishing touches to his actual oppression. It is the symbol of his oppression; its preliminaries and its crowning point: the myth justifies the oppression in advance and makes the consequences lawful. If it first appears as a bitter and fanatical argument of anti-Semitic imagination, it is also an efficient excuse for and an absolution of the anti-Semite's conduct and institutions. The myth is, really, already oppression, since it announces the concrete manifestations of oppression and contributes to its perpetuity: it contributes to the actual crushing of the Jew. This explains better than all "mysteries" the stubborn survival of that absurd myth-making: the Jew continues to be oppressed today. The myth is not only a collection of prejudices and arguments that we must combat and refute, it is the verbal barb of the anti-Semite's constant behavior. That accusing and oppressive myth is indeed the best introduction to understanding the actual life Jews are forced to lead.

"There is no sense," Einstein noted sadly, "trying to convince non-Jews by all sorts of inferences that we are equal, for their behavior does not have its roots in the mind." (Albert Einstein, *The World as I See It.*)

part three

THE SHADOWY
FIGURE

"What do all those faces, of which one can only say they are not Christian, have in common? Is it the stigma of suffering?"

ISRAEL ZANGWILL

"The isolated man is never likely to use the full measure of his powers, unless one of those collective representations which is called an ideal should come to his aid . . . The archetype has been called the mystic participation of primitive man with the soil on which he lives and which alone contains the spirits of his ancestors. The stranger is misery."

CARL J. JUNG

The Jew and
the Religion of Others

ONE

Now that we have tracked down, unveiled
and reduced the myth to its proper size, the
question remains: Who am I? What is a real
Jew, in his life, in his suffering, in his joys?
The best approach to understanding my
actual life would have been to describe its
positive aspects: traditions and institutions,
collective habits and values, economy, religion, art. I will return to this later. But I
quickly realized that the life of the Jew is as
remarkable for its limitations and its lacunae as for its positive characteristics. At
every step, the difficulties of maturing, if
not of living, hindered, distorted and transformed the direction of my life. The misfortune of the Jew is not so much what he
is, but what he is not; he frequently becomes attached to his misfortunes, and to
such an extent that he is vaguely afraid he
may cease to exist when the misfortune
ends. I remember having written, a long
time ago, a story in which the hero lost and

found again and again a marvelous necklace, an amazing jewel of black and white pearls; but the black pearls were so luminously black that one could see nothing else, and the brilliance of the white pearls was so dimmed that they almost seemed to be invisible. One day, tired of this, the hero thought it a good idea to get rid of the black pearls. It was no use: the necklace disappeared again, and this time for good. When I wrote that story I did not know how closely it concerned me. There are as many dark beads as light beads in the necklace of the Jew's life (and they are as thick, as heavy to the touch as the most brilliant stones). Today I would not write that tale in the same way. I believe in the possibility of a Jewish life which is independent of age-old black misfortune. But I honestly do not know if it will be the same life, and if we will still be able to talk of Jews and Judaism. For the moment, in any case, it is not possible to understand the positive aspects of Jewishness without referring constantly and, above all, to its negative aspects: to everything the Jew is not, everything from which he is excluded. When, several years ago, I left Tunisia to come to France, I knew that I was leaving a Moslem country, but I did not understand that I was going to a Catholic country. A few weeks were enough to impress that fact on me—it stares you in the face. Seen from a distance or from too close at hand, things are equalized and are sorted out the way literature and history textbooks would have it: on the one hand Bossuet and Fenelon, on the other, Voltaire and Diderot; on the one hand a Catholic section, on the other a non-sectarian one; here a clerical district, there an anti-clerical and atheist district. So that a man would have only to choose his reading, his friends and his city to live his life peacefully and without undue conflicts. But I quickly discovered that French reality is an inextricable mixture of liberalism and Catholicism, clericalism and anti-clericalism at the same time. A little more Catholicism in one place, a little more liberalism in another, but the common Christian background is everywhere—sometimes more or less buried, other times more or less obvious.

This truth is, to be sure, sought after; by the conservative, who wishes to live in the past and forces himself to believe that nothing has changed; by self-styled progressives, who, because of their impatience to live in the future, end by not seeing the present. But the real fact is that, in spite of considerable changes, France remains a profoundly Catholic country just as America is a Protestant country. How this situation will evolve and how long it will last, no one knows. I am told that the struggle is bitter, and this is true, as I discovered recently a propos of the free school; working men have a tendency to turn from Christianity and this is perhaps true, though one must take into account the ebb and flow. But at the present time, two out of three young Frenchmen are practicing Catholics: "Out of all young Frenchmen between eighteen and thirty years of age, more than eight out of ten practised Catholicism in their childhood and made their holy Communion; more than seven of them still profess it . . ." (Survey made by the Institute of Public Opinion). More than half of the secondary school education in France is in the hands of Catholic parochial schools. When I travel in the interior of this country, what do they show me with righteous pride? What do I myself ask spontaneously to see because I know that they are worth seeing, if not churches, chapels, baptisteries, statues of Virgins, objects of worship and very few other things? I have verified the accuracy of those descriptions by orthodox writers: the villages are crowded around their churches, around bell-towers that can be seen from afar and that really do seem to protect them.

Is this so only in France? By no means. I was stunned, outraged, and then wryly amused, when I read in the

Italian newspapers the solemn declaration of Togliatti, leader of the Italian Communists, encouraging and blessing "the Communist communicants." I am well aware that it was only a matter of *strategy:* but if there must be strategy, there is a reality to evade. Now the reality of the Italian people is profoundly Catholic, like Polish reality, like Spanish reality, etc. . . . And in Moslem countries, from which I come, Ramadan or Achoura mark the rhythm of social life as Christmas and Easter mark the rhythm of life in Catholic countries. The importance of religion in Anglo-Saxon countries is well known; it is inextricably bound up with their institutions.

I have tried hard to fool myself: Why do I pay so much attention to the religion of other men, I asked myself, when I myself am neither a believer, nor scarcely ever a practicing Jew? Do I stop work on Saturday? Do I seriously celebrate Passover and Yom Kippur? Do I speak often of the synagogue, as some people do, to praise it or attack it? No, I scarcely ever think of it. On the other hand, many Christians do not go to church any more frequently than I go to synagogue; are not most of my non-Jewish friends as indifferent as I am to religious matters? But all these were only imaginary arguments in a polemic against myself, to reassure myself. It is not a question of religion, nor only of the religion of other men, as I know very well, but of a more complex rapport. I am not excluded and considered different solely because of the dogmatism of my own religion; I am excluded and considered different because of the dogmatism of the non-Jew's religion which is thus transformed for me into a sly negation, a situation that is always more or less oppressive, more or less destructive. My religious situation is the result not so much of the degree of my profound religion, but of the fact that *I do not belong* to the religion of the men among whom I live, that I am a Jew among non-Jews. And this also means that my children, my relatives, my friends frequently find themselves in the same situation. I am always in a certain way outside of the religious world, the culture and the society to which I otherwise belong.

It is not solely a question of private or of customary practices, but of legal and official practices that rule our societies. The law of Christian countries is a law of thinly disguised and often proclaimed Christian inspiration; the law of Moslem countries is a Moslem law, taken for granted and openly acknowledged. It is not merely a question of organized public demonstrations but also of dreams, impressions, and the most confused and most obvious ideology. The religion of non-Jews is, in fact, everywhere—on the street as in institutions, in shop-windows and newspapers, in monuments, in conversations, in the very air itself: art, morals and philosophy are as Christian as law and geography. The philosophic tradition taught in the schools, the great motifs of painting and sculpture, are as impregnated with Christianity as are the laws of marriage and divorce. When I was on the Riviera last year I amused myself noting the villages that bear the names of saints: Saint Tropez, Sainte Maxime, Saint Raphael, Saint Aygulf . . . Their number is astonishing. It is the same, for that matter, in the stations of the Paris metro. My first irritation against Paris, a city I love so dearly in other respects, had a religious basis, if I remember correctly. Working for part of the day on a miserable job, I used to stay up late at night to get ahead in my studies. Every morning I was awakened—and to my exasperation several times in succession—by bells ringing at full peal, continuing at great length, pausing, and then returning to the charge just as I was dozing off again! True, I was living in a small hotel a few steps away from a church but in this city you are always two steps away from a church. Slight though the experience was, it is significant because I still remember it. It seemed to me doubly symbolic, I suppose: those bells summoned men to duties they shared with other men and were a symbol of their union; at the same time, for me they sounded the signal of my exclusion from that community. I was in a Catholic country; everyone must find those matin bells normal and perhaps pleasant—except me and those like me who were embarrassed and annoyed. A hopeless rebellion, however: the non-Jews, who were not annoyed, nor perhaps even awakened, represented numbers and power. Whatever concerns them, whatever they approve of, is lawful. Those bells are merely the familiar echo of their common soul.

Do I exaggerate? Is this a morbid reaction? Let others call it what they will: I have never said that the reactions of the Jew, in this respect, were indisputably healthy. Is it a completely personal reaction? I do not think so. I do not think I have forced an interpretation of those incidents, which so perfectly symbolize the religious situation of the Jew. I was not surprised to find the same irritation in Freud's biography and I sensed in him the same malaise. I have even noticed in my Protestant friends that same disagreeable feeling that troubled me during those interminable and obligatory visits to churches in all the cities through which we passed. Do Christians realize what the name of Jesus, their God, can mean to a Jew? For a Christian, even an atheist, it evokes, or at least has evoked at some time, an immense virtue, a being infinitely good, who offers himself as The Good, who desires at least to carry on the torch of all bygone philosophies and all morals. For the Christian who is still a believer, Jesus epitomizes and fulfills the better part of himself. The Christian who has ceased to believe no longer takes that ideal seriously; he may even resent it, accuse the priests of incompetency or even of deception; but though he denounces an illusion he generally leaves no doubt as to the grandeur and beauty of that illusion.

To the Jew who still believes and professes his own religion, Christianity is the greatest theological and metaphysical usurpation in his history; it is a spiritual scandal, a subversion and blasphemy. To all Jews, even if they are atheists, the name of Jesus is the symbol of a threat, of that great threat that has hung over their heads for centuries and which may, any moment, burst forth in catastrophes of which they know neither the cause nor the prevention. That name is part of the accusation, absurd and frenzied, but so efficiently cruel, that makes social life barely livable. That name has, in fact, come to be one of the signs, one of the names of the immense apparatus that surrounds the Jew, condemns him and excludes him. I hope my Christian friends will forgive me. That they may better understand, let me say that to the Jews, their God is, in a way, the Devil, if, as they say, the Devil is the symbol and essence of all evil on earth, iniquitous and all-powerful, incomprehensible and bent on crushing helpless human beings.

One day in Tunis, an idiot Jew (we always had a certain number of them who haunted cemeteries and community gatherings) seeing a Christian funeral pass, was suddenly seized with an uncontrollable rage. Knife in hand, he flung himself on the funeral procession which scattered terror-stricken in all directions. But the idiot, paying no attention to the crowd screaming in terror, rushed straight to the acolyte . . . grabbed the cross out of his hands, flung it on the ground and trampled it furiously.

I did not understand his action until later. Anxiety expresses itself as best it can; the idiot reacted in his own way to our common malaise before that world of crosses, priests and churches, those concentrated symbols of the hostility, the strangeness of the world that surrounds us and assails us the moment we leave the narrow confines of the ghetto.

It is, in short, impossible not to notice that breach which the religion of non-Jews introduces into the life of the Jew, that separation of the Jew's daily life from that of his non-Jewish fellow-citizens, no matter how independent *their* thought of or *their* loyalty to traditional dogmas. But at the same time there is a Christian aspect of the Jewish fate which is inseparable from the life of the Jew, which the Jew cannot forget, except in a moment of abstraction or bewilderment. On the collective plane, the matter is perhaps even clearer. I am now convinced that the history of peoples, their collective experience, is a religious history; that it is not only marked by religion, but lived and expressed through religion. It was one of our greatest and most disastrous naïvetés to have believed, like our Leftists, in the end of religions. It was a great mistake, in our efforts to understand the past of nations, to try to minimize the part religion played. There was no need either to rejoice in or to deplore it, only to note its extraordinary importance and to take it into account. It is clear to me that today every phase of the collective life of Christians is still attuned to Christianity; both in their past history and in the history that is still being made. Look at that long series of consecrations that mark the life and history of France: the consecration of Charlemagne and the consecration of Clovis, the consecration of Jeanne d'Arc and the consecration of Napoleon. The place of the church and the part it plays in morals and politics is well known; entire regions are completely subordinate to the dictates of their parish priests.

All that is so well known that one scarcely ever gives a thought to its significance. The strength of the pious is most evident on their feast days when their devotion reaches a new height, when the collectivity becomes aware of itself as a unique being. That, ironically, is the moment when the Jew feels most excluded. The other evening I was at the theatre. The play was amusing, the actors excellent and we all laughed heartily. All of a sudden the tone changed to one of seriousness. The actress, deeply moved (perhaps really so), in a gesture of fervent exaltation, invoked the Holy Virgin and Jesus, and implored Christ to protect the audience, herself and the entire city. At those words the audience, overcome by emotion, was silent; and exactly at that moment it was all over for me—even my aesthetic pleasure was ruined. I was embarrassed. To me the protection of that Holy Virgin and that God I did not recognize was like an hypocrisy; I could not accept that profound or temporary accord of the audience; I could not be one of them. After all, was I really part of that audience and that whole city, since I withdrew from them in those very moments when I felt I had become one with them! As usual I was again suspicious of that need to win all. It is at the moment when society is most united in a renewed communion, in its memories of tragedies and victories shared, that the Jew best measures his distance from the community. Then everything reminds him of his loneliness, more insistently than ever: newspapers, radio, the streets, the public speeches of the nation's leaders. During Christmas week, scientific and political speeches on the radio and on television, all begin with the invocation: "In these days when the hearts of all men are as a little child's . . ." All men? Not mine certainly; I do not belong in that communion. One of General de Gaulle's first gestures on assuming power was an address to the Pope in which he asked him to bless France and the French. Is the Jew a part of that France? If so, how would he like to have his country blessed by the Pope, and to have himself included in it? In reality, the heads of state act as if the Jew did not exist. And it is true that he scarcely counts, that he dare not even count himself: otherwise why would he permit the chief of state, his representative, to appeal to the Church in his name? The Papal nuncio is doyen of the diplomatic corps: by what right if not by an admitted preeminence of the Catholic religion, which is not his? It is always at the moment of the greatest effusion, during ceremonies and rites open to all, at the burial of heroes, or the celebration of victories that the Jew confirms his loneliness and his lack of importance, that his heart sinks on discovering that effusion, that general reconciliation, when his fellow-citizens gather together and discover anew their common origins and projects—and leave him outside. It is then that the distance is most strongly re-established.

I realize, even as I am saying this, how unconvincing, how ridiculous my rebellion may seem and how exorbitant my demand. Would I pretend to impose my law on the majority? Is it not normal for a nation to live according to the desires, customs and myths of the greatest number of its citizens? Perfectly normal, I admit immediately. I scarcely see how it could live otherwise. I must even confess that, today, I have a different understanding of the religious phenomenon. I still believe that a clerical ascendancy is harmful to the life of a nation; I still believe that it is necessary to fight any political use of religion. But I also believe that the religious phenomenon is not an invention of priests or of a single ruling class; it is an expression (one of the most important and most significant) of the life of the whole group. And if a nation expresses itself thus, in the moment of its history, and manifests its unity and its existence either by sacrificing chickens or by organizing processions, the priest can do nothing but bless the chickens and the processions. When, last year, the Pope blessed scooters and suggested a Madonna of scooterists, he did not invent the importance of Vespas in Italy; he merely acknowledged it. The priest fosters and feeds collective illusions and mysteries, it is true, but to a very great extent he merely translates them and endorses them in his own way. Of course, on that point a reactionary ideology, a utilization, a perversion of those primary emotions may be grafted, but those sentiments exist, they correspond to vague needs, and their manifestation is to a large extent natural and normal. What is not normal in all this is my life, different for that reason, in the bosom of the nation. The Jew is the one who does not belong to the religion of the others. I merely wished to draw attention to the difference and those consequences I have experienced, and which are not part of that normality. It is clear that I must live a religion that is not mine, a religion that regulates and sets the rhythm for all collective life. I must take a holiday at Easter and not at Passover. Do not tell me that many non-Jewish citizens also condemn this contamination. Theirs is merely a theoretical condemnation: their daily life is ordered by the common religion, which is at least their own religion and which does not tear them to pieces. "The trouble with you," said one of my non-Jewish friends, half seriously, "is that you have never been a Christian!" The Jew, believer or non-believer, accepting or rebelling, must live more or less the religion of others, which displaces him and repudiates him. Often he will even end by willingly celebrating Christmas and New Year's Day; he will dance, exchange presents, have a tree at home and attend midnight Mass. But he will celebrate in anxiety or in irony, in ambiguity and in bad faith. He will explain that the tree "is for the children, so as not to deprive them," that the midnight Mass has a great esthetic value. The truth is simpler and at the same time more compelling. How could he help participating in the general celebration? And besides, why should he refuse to do so? He has neither strength enough nor conviction enough to refuse everything; the effort of refusal is greater than the anxiety of participation. How could he help seeing the splendor of the city's shop windows, the Christmas illuminations in the department stores, the unusual wealth of the food markets? Why would he not, like everyone else, breathe in the euphoria, the gaiety in the air? If he should ignore the fact that it was the Christmas season and not leave his house, his friends would come after him. He and his children are invited to the Christmas tree lighting at the bank, or to the veteran's celebration, or to several tree lightings at the same time. Should he also refuse to accept the dolls they give his little girl and the little autos they give his son? Is he such a sectarian? He feels slightly strange in accepting, but he would feel even more ridiculous if he refused. And, besides, he would be excluding himself of his own accord, he who complains so bitterly of being excluded.

The Jew,
the Nation and History

ONE

I have written elsewhere that as adolescents
and later as young men we refused to take
seriously the persistence of nations. We
lived in enthusiastic expectation of a new
age, such as the world had never known before, signs of which we thought we could
already detect—the death (which had certainly begun) of religions, families and nations. We had nothing but anger, scorn and
irony for the die-hards of history who clung
to those residues. Today I see more clearly
why we expended so much energy on cul-
tivating those hopes. Certainly the impatient and generous nature of adolescents
which drives them to free themselves, and
the whole world, of all shackles, is particularly suited to revolutionary ideologies. But,
in addition, we were Jews: I am convinced
that this had much to do with the vigor of
our choice. Beyond our desire to be accepted by the families, religions and nations
of non-Jews who rejected and isolated us

because we were Jews, we longed to be one with all men and so, at last, become men like the others.

Unfortunately, whether we were deluding ourselves, whether we may have relapsed since then into a period of regression, or whether it is simply that I have grown older, I have to admit that those residues were as stubborn as weeds and persisted in remaining fundamental structures in the lives of nations, essential aspects of their collective being. War was waged in the name of nations and peace stabilized the oldest nations and brought new nations into being. The postwar period saw an indisputable religious revival which swept the orthodox parties to power thoughout Europe. Because they understood that situation, the Communists, who keep their fingers on the pulse of nations, extoled the "Catholic communicants," offered their "outstretched hand" to Christians and called themselves patriots and nationalists. The Socialists did not even need to resort to trickery; their chauvinism was very real; colonial wars soon gave them an opportunity to expand. To all appearances we were doomed to religions and nations and for a long time. Once again I am not passing judgment, I am simply stating facts.

What was going to become of us, of our adolescent hopes? What we felt confusedly, what we were trying to suppress by rejecting the society of those days, I neither can, nor do I wish to make a secret of any longer. The religious state of nations being what it is, and nations being what they are, the Jew finds himself, in a certain measure, *outside* of the national community. And here again, of course, people are going to protest, and I am ready to concede, out of weariness, and to avoid a discussion in which reason alone does not speak, that this is particularly a question of, let us say, a personal situation. Because, even today, people live their collective lives as nationals, I feel more or less set apart from that life of communal nationality; I cannot live spontaneously the nationality modern law grants me (when it does grant it).

So then, is the accusation confirmed? As a Jew, you admit to being stateless and cosmopolitan? Of your own accord, you reject the nation! I do not reject anything! What is confirmed? Do I really suffer from my own refusal or from what other men refuse me? As if, on this point, I had enough strength and pride, serenity and independence to be able to refuse! I have often wished, but so far in vain, that like a former lover who has become indifferent, I could refuse dispassionately, that I could be calmly ironical about those residues, about what I liked to think were relics. But one does not really scorn till after one has been surfeited, and my non-Jewish friends manage this infinitely better than I do. The truth, on the contrary, is that I have longed with all my might for that integration, I have longed to become a citizen like other men. Yes, on this point I confess my humiliated disappointment. How heart-warming it would have been to the stranger to feel that he was an integral, definitive part of the institutions of the country, instead of finding himself constantly called to account! The Jew's enemy shouts for joy at the slightest confession of that non-co-existence, that rootlessness of the Jew. How can he call us to account for the very object of our nostalgia, for that misfortune imposed on us by fate, not to say by the enemy himself? How can he make capital of our exclusion? I have not rejected anything; unfortunately it is the nation that has rejected me, that leaves me outside. Whether I like it or not, the history of the country in which I live is, to me, a borrowed history. How could I feel that Joan of Arc is a symbol for me? Would I hear with her the patriotic and Christian voices? Yes, always religion! But show me a way to separate national tradition from religious tradition. I cannot forget that the national heroine carried a sword shaped like a cross: like most of the heroes of history, the dying Bayard, for instance, asking to kiss his sword, a double symbol. How could I have identified myself with Clovis, that good, naïve and glamorous ancestor of primary school textbooks, but who, it seems, would willingly have exterminated the wicked Jews? Or with Napoleon, so ambiguous, so annoyed by the Jews of his era? Or, with even greater reason, with the Czars and their pogroms or with Oriental sovereigns? It is impossible for me to identify myself seriously with the past of any nation.

For a great part of the citizens of the country, it is true, that history and that past are not exactly theirs, either. But they are not aware of it. Happily for them, the great collective oblivion has been going on for a long, long time. Their foreign ancestors intermingled in the vast cemetery of the past, that common grave in which all disappear together. Today the descendants reap the benefit of anonymity: where could they come from if not from here? He who succeeds in inscribing his name on the genealogical tree, salvages enormous roots, and ends by believing that he has sprung from time immemorial, makes himself legitimate and legitimatizes his descendants. There is always something mystical in all collective memory. The Jew himself, because he is a Jew, preserves his relationships integrally. Even though he be more ancient than all those successive grafts on the body of the nation, no matter how long ago he first appeared, by definition people agree that he is an outsider, because he has not always been there. Thus in Tunis, we sometimes used to boast of being authentic Berbers, or Phoenicians, settled there before anyone else, since the days of Queen Dido. That alleged nobility isolated us even more.

There is, in short, neither anything to reject nor anything to rejoice over. I live out my social and political destiny not as something marvelous and exceptional, but

as something separated cruelly from the lives of my fellow-citizens. From this come my embarrassment and my
apprehension the moment they speak in my presence of
anything that touches on that historic past. No Gauls,
please. Enough of Celts, ancient Germans, Slavs, conquering Romans and conquering Arabs! For then, I find myself naked and alone: my own ancestors were neither
Gauls, Celts, Slavs, ancient Germans, Arabs, or Turks.
How can I be sure of that? Who is sure of his ancestors?
But this is a question especially of the heart's confidence
and of the approval of opinion. And, above all, not of a
positive, but of a negative feature of Jewish existence.
Difference in this case is negatively fundamental: my
fellow-citizens may not have been Gauls or Arabs, but
that has no importance. As for me I may not have been
an Arab or a Roman; but that is considered a certainty. I
have never been able to say "We" in referring to those
historical pedigrees on which my fellow-citizens pride
themselves. I have never heard another Jew say "We"
without wincing, without vaguely suspecting him of an
inadvertent blunder, of complacency or of a slip of the
tongue.

I must add that I seldom express myself this way. I
detest historical grandiloquence, past or even future. I
scorn the slogans "immortal France," "imperishable
Tunisia," or "eternal Judaism." I believe that, sooner
or later, death shows its face entirely and that all those
eternities and immortalities so auspiciously asserted, are
merely the pathetic guarantees we try to give ourselves
against death. "It is just that you are a Jew," someone will
retort. "You scoff at countries because you haven't any!"
That is only partially true. I have said too that several of
my non-Jewish friends were much more violent than I,
more calmly scornful of their collective myths. Unfortunately I do not have their confidence and their serenity;
my mind also argues and decides, but my heart suffers

and protests. I would so much rather have shared in those illusions, if they are illusions, even though with ironical dignity I rejected them afterwards. I would much rather have been part of them the better to free myself of them. A man may succeed in being casual about the collective past of his own nation, history and traditions, but it is almost unbearable to have them denied to him by other men. André Gide noted in his diary that it was almost impossible for him to think like Maurice Barrès, whom he admired, because he, Gide, was Protestant and not Catholic, and because his father and mother came from two different regions of France; in a certain measure he felt that he was too scattered, heterogeneous, as it were, and he suffered because of it. And yet no one thought of calling him to account; no one doubted him and he had not the slightest doubt himself that his destiny and the destiny of France were one. With what country, what corner of the earth, am I sure of identifying myself? With what culture, what collective experience? It is true that I can pretend to find a certain strength in that dissipation, a greater freedom: "See, I do not belong to anything, I am therefore free of hindrances!" There may be some pride in that solitude and distance I am obliged to keep. And I do not scorn those days of courage and health. But I believe that the price for them is too high. Illegitimacy sharpens the mind, to be sure, but it is a very uncomfortable condition, and one that it is better to be spared. One of my friends, a somewhat scatterbrained psychologist, told me: "I come from Lyons, my father comes from Lyons, my grandfather too . . . But with most of my Jewish friends, their father comes from one place, their grandfather from another, and their uncle lives in still a third place." And she added consolingly: "Compared to my Jewish friends, I feel a little cramped, a little poor."

Those, however, were a rich woman's words, the romantic regret of someone who has the wherewithal to live and enjoy life, and sighs after poetry. If she only knew how her Jewish friends would have preferred her solid poverty to their too rich dispersion, her geographical and historical uniqueness to their volatile instability.

TWO

I can do nothing to prevent that constant rupture and gnawing negativity from weighing significantly on my destiny. They are among the major signs and components of my oppression. It really seems that one of its most serious attacks is directed against the historical dimension of the oppressed person; levelling it out, flattening it, in the hope perhaps of clarifying it, of making it less awkward. The oppressed person is not credited with any historic past, and if the oppression lasts, history being stolen from him progressively, he has less and less of it and ends by forgetting it altogether. For several generations colonial troops have paid for the plans of European nations with their suffering, their blood and their death. But are theirs the profit and the glory, if there is any glory and since it is permitted to speak of glory? The battle for Cassino is therefore "inscribed forever to the immortal courage of the French Army." Do they specify that that army was composed of a large percentage of North Africans and Jews? In the very heart of the nation, women, as women, have almost no position: the history of all nations is a purely masculine history. In that masculine world, also, there are rich and poor. Historical memory seems to be dispensed according to power; only the leaders and men of importance have a right to a specified past. Who would ever think of drawing up the genealogical tree of a poor family? It is all right that they participated collectively in the genesis of the world, that they have served as the raw material that they have been regimented masses or tremendous forces with desires that had to be deceived. The Jew does not even have the right to that vague collective participation. Historically he seems never to have fought, or conquered, or suffered; never to have invented anything, to have left nothing behind him, no monuments, no traces, no memories. If it were not for a few accidental references in the archives of the non-Jews to such and such a collective slaughter or such and such an extraordinary tax imposed on him, one might doubt that the Jew had ever lived in the land. How could it have been otherwise? History being national, and the Jew not actually part of the nation, how would he have had a historical past? Did he even have a past at all? Did he even exist? That may seem paradoxical when one looks at that splendid testimony of a splendid past, as they say to be kind to us. But that past is too splendid, too remote as a matter of fact, too far past, with no continuity with what we are today: it is a *mythical* past, the past of the Bible, of the Passage through the Red Sea and of the manna in the desert. Since then, nothing—or almost nothing. To be sure, the history of nations is also in great part mythical, but it is not lived only as a myth, it is renewed, brought up to date and revived daily. The Jew has to balance between his legendary history of which he is often ignorant and a contemporary history in which he is not recognized, in which he has no place. Carried to extremes, the truly oppressed person no longer has a past at all.

How could my removal from the universe fail to have serious and very concrete consequences? I do not suffer from my non-integration in the body and continuity of the nation because of any fetishism for nation, history or the past. I would not have made myself clear if I had not succeeded in suggesting that the negative conditions of the Jewish existence were as heavy with consequences as the more positive. Far beyond any sentimental claim, any purely emotional frustration, I am not on a truly equal footing with my fellow-citizens in the life we share, in our common history which is being made every day. Most often I am prohibited from looking forward to the same expectations even when I no longer fear them. Since the past is far from reassuring, I dare not believe completely in my national future. Many Jews, I know, act as if they did believe in it, as if they were fooled by it. But it takes very little to discover their hesitation and doubt. To make future plans in common, one has to be sure of staying together. Now, my marriage with the nation is always in danger of being questioned. How, under these conditions, can I settle down forever without a worrisome, secret fear of having to argue or even to move on? I live, I cohabit, in the hope that it may last, that I shall be left in peace. Perhaps (supreme hope) in the end they will have become so used to me that my children will finally be adopted. But any day, at any moment, an incident may remind me that the tacit contract is weak, that I do not have the right to the same considerations, the same security as my fellow-citizens. A few years ago, the French were thrown out of Egypt. Then, when relations between that country and France improved, they were again authorized to return . . . all except the French Jews. That, strictly speaking, could be the point of view of Egypt, at war with Israel, which has frankly adopted an anti-Semitic attitude, but not the point of view of France which, nevertheless, forsook her nationals of the Jewish religion. "The French government," writes one of them, "in aiming to renew relations with Egypt at all costs, has accepted the principle of sacrificing the French citizen of Israelite faith . . . We therefore consider that the mother country . . . has sacrificed a group of her children . . . by ignoring the sacred principle of racial non-discrimination guaranteed by the constitution." (*Le Monde*, August 25, 1958.)

Would the nation as a whole have consented so easily to abandoning the inhabitants of Brittany or of the Midi? Let us not forget the protests against the treaty of 1870 which ceded Alsace-Lorraine to Germany, albeit under pressure of force. The Alsatians are still bitter about it today.

That questionable integration of the Jew with the collective body denotes after all an actual insecurity, a latent historical weakness. The Jew cannot look behind him, but he cannot even look ahead except with due precaution. The past is denied him, the future challenged, and this is even more serious. Behind him, emptiness; before him uncertainty to say the least, if not threat. Do we need to look farther to find the sources of his unrest and his permanent dissatisfaction?

THREE

As a matter of fact the Jew's whole relation to history and time is thus perverted, constantly agitated, constantly prone to upheavals. Again and again it has been said that the Jew is interested only in the present! By that is meant, undoubtedly, that he is a sensualist and a swine; that he is lacking in respect for traditions, for the most sacred foundations of national life, that he has no "sense of the past." Presented in that light, the statement is stupid and as false as usual; how can one reconcile the Jew's preoccupation with the present with his anxiety, acknowledged in other respects by a stubborn adherence to a secular tradition? Besides, it would be hard to find a pig who is as dissatisfied and disturbed as the Jew.

And yet that accusation is not entirely false. I admit that I am essentially interested in the present: it causes me enough worries! Cut off from the past, rejected by history, with no assurance for the future, I have nothing left but the present: it is not a preference, it is an obligation. The only choice permitted me is, in short, between eternity and the immediate present. To be on the safe side, I always keep eternity in the innermost depths of my being, as a last resort for my thought, an ultimate recourse in times of catastrophe. If violent death were to strike one day, perhaps my lips would instinctively move in the ancient prayer for the dying. What can one do when the present fails, when men become too cruel, history unbearable? "Our eternal God . . . Abraham . . . Avinu," our time-honored fathers, that is to say, beyond the ages . . . Meanwhile my present as a Jew has neither the same coloring nor the same burden of anguish and hope as has the present of my fellow-citizens. I remember discussing the meaning of the last war with my non-Jewish friends. I read in the war memoirs of the German novelist Junger, all the names of the French writers who received him in the midst of war, and who had excellent relations with him. I do not even reproach them for it. We did not run the same risks, our stake was not the same, our evaluation could not be identical, I willingly admit that. A great French novelist whom I like and admire, wrote at the beginning of the war in Spain: *"Anything, rather than war! Anything, anything!* (the italics are his). Even Fascism in Spain! And do not press me, for I would also say: yes . . . and even 'Fascism in France'! . . . Nothing, *no test, no* servitude, can be compared to war, and all it engenders . . . Does the partisan stifle the human being in you? *Anything,* Hitler rather than war!" (Roger Martin du Gard in a letter dated September 9, 1936, published in *N. N. R. F.,* December, 1958).

Are those the sentiments of a class? No, not entirely. After all, every human deed is justified by a balance sheet, profits and losses. The French could think they would lose more by going to war than by accepting the German conditions. They thought so for a while; why would they not have hesitated? What was Roger Martin du Gard risking? He could believe that the misfortune of war outweighed all else. For us, Nazism managed to surpass even war in horror: children separated from their parents, little girls turned over to the brothel, the gas chambers, the dehumanization of the camps, and torture. In truth, we were not at all equal to the present that was moving towards us. The King of the Belgians had permitted the Germans to pass through Belgium; was he wrong to do so? Was he right? I have heard many discussions on this subject in Belgium and it is perhaps questionable; by yielding he saved his country from destruction, he could swiftly rebuild his few ruins and re-establish the nation's economy.

"When we saw the destruction in other parts of the world, the number of your dead," Belgian friends told me honestly, "we were not so harsh towards the King." Many people, I believe, would have adapted themselves to Hitlerism, to any Fascism whatsoever, at least in the beginning. Many thought, and perhaps with reason, that they personally would come out of it. In the long run, perhaps they would have discovered that they had made a bad historical calculation. For the Jew, there was no discussion, no delay, no adjustment possible. It was an immediate fact, a matter of life or death, and of utter degradation before death. One month after the Germans arrived in Tunis, we understood that everything was at stake and almost everything was already lost: our dignity as men, our children and our wives and soon even our lives. The few spasmodic efforts of the terrified community would have only served to delay and spread out the payments.

One need not even wait for such crises to verify that insufficient integration and all the weakness that flows from it. The Jew, as a Jew, can almost never have an effect on the national destiny; he is however, part of it; but he is not consulted, and the greater part of the time, he does not even ask to be consulted: he is only too pleased to be forgotten and to have others act as if he did not exist. But were he to make demands he would immediately discover his own helplessness and the hesitant attitude of others towards him. When the Jews came back from concentration camps, from prisons or from exile, they found their apartments occupied or their possessions stolen—sometimes by their immediate neighbors. Shouldn't the thieves have been forced to make restitution? The embarrassment of governments, the horrified astonishment of the public, quickly turned to annoyance and bitterness. After so much misfortune, was it good taste to make demands for so little? Should we not be glad that we were still alive? We were so accustomed to misfortune that it was not worth the trouble to defend ourselves for such small losses.

There has been much discussion, and there still is, about the fate of Europeans in colonies that are gaining their freedom. I hasten to say that it is legitimate to discuss this: whatever political mistakes a population conquered by a new fate may make, that population becomes, as a result, worthy of attention. But, are there in those colonies only ex-colonizers on the one hand and ex-colonized peoples on the other? In North Africa the Jews far outnumber the French. Who has heard anything about them? What future has been foreseen for them? It will be said that their fate is the same as the fate of the Tunisians or the Moroccans and, tomorrow, of the Algerians. But everyone in North Africa knows perfectly well that this is a pious lie, that their difficulties and their aspirations are different: most of them have chosen French culture, the French language and French schooling. I do not say they are right or wrong; I say that this is a fact, for a number of reasons connected with recent history. And everyone knows this, but no one says or does anything about it. Can it be said, on the contrary, that their fate is identical with the fate of the French people? That is equally false: in Tunisia and in Morocco it was even legally untrue. The French who left those countries were helped financially; they are still making claims, but they have received subsidies for housing and help in finding new employment. What has been done for the Jews? As far as Algeria is concerned, we shall soon see; but does anyone honestly believe that the French Army would have revolted for the sake of the Jew? In short, each side pretended to believe that the Jews belonged to the other side, so that they would not have to bother about them.

In fact, history is made without us and we are used to it, as are the majority of oppressed persons. And like the majority of oppressed persons, we reap all the bitterness of it, we are the most afflicted of victims. The moment a nation is struck by a catastrophe, we are the first to be abandoned. Vichy promptly gave up its Jews and in Tunisia we were the first to be handed over. Don't tell me they also gave up the Communists and Freemasons! A man is a Communist of his own choice: it is a free action, which he can abandon if, for example, he considers the danger too great. Dignity demands perhaps that he continue in it in the hour of danger, but it is always a question of a choice, of a free and continuing action. To be a Jew is, first of all, not a choice. We shall see that men often add a confirmation that gives it the appearance of a decision, but it is, first of all, a fate: to refuse that fate does not change much either, for it depends more on other men than on oneself. Now the others hand over their Jews, apparently with no great difficulty, almost spontaneously as one tosses overboard the thing one values least, the thing least worth protecting. When a nation is in trouble, when the world is in trouble, I know now, from the experience of my short life, there is danger for the Jew: even if the malady has no connection with Jews. Hitler did not invent German anti-Semitism: he utilized it and brewed a poison already widely secreted by the German nation.

"From 1926 on, it was almost impossible for a young Jew to be employed in one of the great banks or one of the great industries . . . Germany was crushed under the burden of unemployment, but the percentage of unemployed Jews was much higher than their percentage in the population and certainly much higher than their percentage among salaried men." (S. Adler-Rudel, in *Jewish Balance Sheet*).

We are, in short, the forsaken as far as history is concerned. We would like to go our way unnoticed: but history in doing without us, also frequently acts against us. Everything happens as though the Jew offered himself as an expiatory victim, specially marked out for the meager imagination of executioners, dictators and politicians. This is not an accident: the Jew is, sociologically and historically, the weak point in the nation, the weakest link in the chain, the one who should, therefore, be the first to give way.

The Jew and the City

Under the Vichy regime a professor of the law school wrote: "The reason it is impossible for Jews to attain public office is the same one that prevents naturalized citizens from attaining these offices: patronage, protection of the offices . . . The Jews," he added, "are considered to be even more dangerous politically than naturalized citizens." (M. Duverger).

So, public offices have to be protected from the Jews! What is this madness that overtakes Jews? Why would they destroy the social structure in which they have found refuge and which protects them? Here the negative myth raises its head again: the Jew's venomous nature, like the venom of the scorpion, causes him to act against his own interests. Did not the German, Niemand, accuse us of building the crematoriums in which we were forced to throw ourselves like so many sheep on the verge of insanity? The less violent French anti-Semite merely accuses us of corrupting French social life of which we were a part. But enough of those ravings. That whole period was insane, someone will say, and it was a question of a government, imposed and inspired by the Germans.

And yet today I am convinced that the French laws of that period merely crystallized, and codified, a sentiment that was widespread among a majority of the French people; the Jew is not truly part of the French population. One could suggest to the man in the street, in a modified form, that after all the Jew cannot have the public interest fully at heart; and I do not believe he would be shocked. But why would the Jew be less civic-minded than other people? Because he is less a citizen! One could add, hypocritically, that this is regrettable, unjust, etc. . . . Indeed, in that form the statement is almost acceptable. And, I must admit, I myself hesitate, I am confused: am I less a citizen? Yes, perhaps a little less. Or more precisely, I know that is the way non-Jews look upon me and treat me, and so I feel that I am actually slightly less a citizen than my fellow-citizens.

Naturally my accuser draws unjust conclusions which I reject indignantly. Far from wishing to harm the city, to weaken my ties with my fellow-citizens, I long to consolidate them; I hope to become day by day more a citizen like other men. That is why, far from shirking duties, from doing less than other men, I generally do more than the average; except of course in times when oppression becomes too unbearable, when injustice and misery weigh so heavily that the Jew looks on with indifference as the enemies of the city take over. In normal times, the Jew redoubles his public demonstrations of loyalty, his proofs of a zealous citizenship. The other day at the entrance to a public building, I read the list on one of those marble plaques on which museums, hospitals and universities engrave the names of their benefactors; names of Jews filled almost half the list. I have also said that Jewish delinquency is relatively rare. But here again, there is some truth behind that popular, rather vague, but firmly established impression, an impression that is shared by Jews themselves. I myself am not greatly surprised at the anti-Semitic accusation: I know that my integration with the city is not a matter of course. Each new blow of fate does not seem so shocking to me; I am becoming accustomed to suspicion and special treatment. Just as my relation to history and to the nation is distorted and perverted, so is my relation to the city. A Belgian Jew, born, raised and living permanently in Belgium, showed me around Brussels and spoke of the Belgians as objectively as if he were looking at them with the eyes of a stranger.

"They wash their own sidewalks themselves," he told me. "They are very clean."

"You speak of the Belgians as if you were not one of them," I remarked.

He hesitated, then said simply: "Yes and no . . . I love this city and this country dearly. I know them like a book. Twice mobilized, I would fight for them again. Nevertheless, I feel that they are not quite mine."

He refused modestly to explain ("It's too long, too complicated . . .") why he does not feel completely at home in that city to which he is so devoted and which he cannot do without (he returned to it after an unfortunate attempt to live elsewhere). But I know so well that pang of disillusioned love: to love and not to be loved in return, to long desperately to be liked and to be permanently accepted, and at the same time to be almost certain you never will be: that, in a nutshell, is the civic tragedy. Those countries the Jews care so much about probably do not care for them—a familiar doubt that haunts the Jew all his life. Everything reminds him of it, everything emphasizes it, everything adds to it.

Even when Jews do their utmost to pretend they belong to the collective whole, the phenomenon both escapes them and is thrust on them. No matter what the Blums, the Blochs, the Weills may do, the Duponts and the Smiths never consider them as one of them. After all, when a man is named Bloch or Weill, or especially Rabinowitz or Benillouche, how can he feel as much at ease as a Dupont does among Duponts? But, you will object, the Jew is not always named Blum, Rabinowitz or Benillouche. He often takes a "very French" (or "very English") local name in keeping with the language and the country. True, but there are always his brothers, cousins, friends, associates, men of the same religion, newcomers, refugees, immigrants, who stupidly continue to call themselves Rabinowitz, Benillouche and Cohen . . . Should he erect a wall of fire between them and himself, should he cease to know them, should he forget them? Sometimes he does. But that, after all, is rare; a man cannot break off all ties and live alone. Generally he sees more of those relatives than he does of other men; or better still, his daughter or his son may choose to marry among them—and there they are back where they started, Rabinowitz or Benillouche again. Fine progress for a man who has succeeded in calling himself Mr. *Almost*-Dupont, if his daughter's name is again Mme. Grunbaum! The mechanism is self-perpetuating; it automatically perpetuates the non-integration of the Jew with the city—his marginality, as they say today.

And then why not admit it? That illegitimacy is no longer either purely sentimental nor purely superficial. I have before my eyes comparative statistics of French Jews, naturalized Jews and foreign Jews (drawn up thanks to the good offices of the anti-Semitic Minister Xavier Vallet.)

"According to the Prefecture of Paris there were, in 1942, 46,542 French Jews as against 46,322 foreign Jews. The two elements therefore seemed to be equal. Those same statistics show us again that the 13,231 naturalized Jews are almost as numerous as the 17,068 Jews of French origin. Thus, according to Roblin, 75 per cent of the Parisian Jews appear to be naturalized or foreigners, the remaining 25 per cent include those of Algerian origin as well!"

Paris, I said to myself, is a melting pot; let us see what the country as a whole is like. But it seems that the phenomenon is valid for the whole of France. The same author mentions the department of the Vaucluse: 550 French Jews to 663 naturalized citizens; The Tarn: 362 French to 336 foreigners and 704 naturalized." A crushing majority, he concludes (p.79), of foreigners and naturalized citizens.

In Tunisia, we were merely colonized citizens, that is, second-class citizens and Jews to boot; in other words, perpetually fluctuating between Europeans (with whom we would have liked to identify ourselves by becoming French, Italian or English) and Tunisians whom we actually resembled. We did not know what we wanted most, and would not even have known how to define ourselves. The Suez affair in 1956 showed me by chance that most of the Jews in Egypt were of French nationality! How often in various countries have I heard Jews announce triumphantly: "I think I've made it! I'm going to get my naturalization papers!" I was not even sure they were going to gain much by that change of civil status, but they believed it would mean being settled at last! Normalcy! For centuries Jewish populations, subjected to constant migrations, have been continually torn from the nationality they had acquired at such pains. Too often the Jew is the humble candidate for a new citizenship. Yes, too often the Jew is objectively and legally a man with a precarious nationality or about to be deprived of his nationality, a foreigner or a naturalized citizen, which is not much better.

I am well aware of the seriousness of that statement
and the danger that it may be used against the Jews; I
anticipate and understand my people's anger at this
harmful publicizing of a fact that may cause many men
anxiety. But I can only say to them: is it not true? Is it
not better at all events to have the truth on record? To
non-Jews I ask: for whom then is this situation most
catastrophic? The reply is obvious. In any case does that
mean objecting to something? Does that mean distrust-
ing society? I no longer know. Let the non-Jews judge.
I helped my fellow-Tunisians to the best of my ability,
in my own way. But never—why not say so?—have I felt
that they really and completely adopted me as one of
them; and perhaps because of that feeling I did not act
as if I really belonged among them. It is a vicious circle.
Our Tunisian-Moslem fellow-citizens did not include us
when they asserted their authority as a nation, and we
were not referring to them when we said "We." I remember my conversation with the poet, Aragon, after the
signing of the Franco-Tunisian peace. Whether out of
courtesy or because he meant it sincerely the great writer
complimented me extravagantly on the exemplary conduct of "your marvelous little country," of "your heroic
people." I was as embarrassed as if I had claimed for myself that heroism and that exemplary conduct. And yet
I had done neither more nor less than most other Tunisians.

The vicious circle had to be broken, we were told, we
had to make a special effort, meet non-Jews halfway . . .
Perhaps we would then have had the strength and the
right to rejoice in their victories, in our common victories. For a long time I myself tried to convince my co-
religionists of this; and perhaps it was possible. But after
all, there was a circle we had to break; we always had to
make an additional effort, greater than the efforts of
other men. How could we fail to tire of all those efforts,

all those advances and all of them so one-sided? How could we keep our faith in the city, in our fellow-citizens? What amazes me, on the contrary, what has long humiliated me, I admit, is the persistence of my people in seeking to be admitted into the confraternity of their fellowmen, something they have sought so humbly for centuries.

TWO

Every time I brought up those questions, one of my friends, a democrat and a trade-unionist, would say:

"Give it up! Always the nation with a capital N, the city with a capital C! Do you have anything to do with all the inhabitants of the country or even of the city every day? Actually our social relations are conducted in terms of classes. Choose your class and stick to it; fight for it and for yourself, and you will no longer feel that you are without a country, without nationality and without citizenship."

I pointed out that, nevertheless, the city and the nation did exist; if I refused to take them into account, I would only emphasize my marginal status, my exclusion and my difference from my fellow-citizens. I was not at all sure that a man could get on without the nation and the city and live solely in his class. Morever, I added, what revolted me was to be forced to this choice because I was a Jew.

"Other men have to do the same," my friend insisted. "Workers don't get along so well with the Nation. Do you remember Marx's famous words? 'The proletariat has no fatherland! Workers of the world, unite!' Do you remember that French general who said: 'I feel more affinity with a German tramp than with a French Socialist!' Financiers and industrialists have connections with international business circles; 'the international plutocracy' is not just a phrase."

My friend's remonstrances were not altogether unfounded. After all, I said to myself, why not try? Since
integration with the Nation and with the City have
proved to be so difficult, if not hopeless, why not rally to
my social class? But at once, I was embarrassed: what
class did we mean? The strangest thing in that argument
was the advice itself, the choice suggested. As though it
could be a question of a deliberate choice! Having passed
that exuberant period when everything seemed to be
within grasp of my youthful powers and all my goodwill,
I had to admit that important commonplace, that one
does not choose one's class or even one's group; instead
one is chosen; one is born in it, lives in it, dies in it, at
least as a rule. Individuals may now and then cross the
line and change their station in life; changes can and do
take place within one group. But over a given period the
character of the whole remains practically the same. This
type of advice, especially when given generally, is foolish
and Utopian. "Then fight for your class!" But first you
have to be part of one. Now I quickly discovered that the
Jew's relations with social classes were also seriously
disturbed. My friend's advice therefore merely retarded
and transposed the difficulty. Not only do Jews not form
a definite class, but they find themselves spread over an
extremely wide socio-economic area; and even their social relations, their integration with different classes, are
fraught with difficulties.

There is an excellent reagent to this situation: the
Jew's adherence to political groups. How can we fail to
note the difficulty of identification with any political
groups at all? I am well aware that this identification is
not always easy for men in other categories. Intellectuals
especially are not very successful at it. Naturally, I have
wondered whether my position as an intellectual and the
relatively high number of Jewish intellectuals did not
tend to make me exaggerate that discordance. Sooner or
later however, in cases where they do not abstain from

joining political groups, most Jews are overcome with anxiety and hesitations which they more or less admit. There again what is deceptive, what makes them conspicuous, is their relative concentration in a few groups. Nevertheless, the distance between a country's political life and its Jews is greater than anywhere else. Are the Jews wrong? Perhaps. I realize, however, that when a group of men turns away from a movement or adheres to it, the fact of their being right or wrong is unimportant: the important thing is to find out why.

The difficulty, not to say the impossibility, of militating on the Right, is obvious: wholeheartedly, I mean, and for the majority of Jews. Of course, you do find Jewish names on the Right, but they are always the same names —just a few families who carry on a tradition or who benefit from certain political patronage. A "good" marriage often leads a man to adopt the political interests of his in-laws. Sometimes, and more stupidly, it is a matter of a kind of snobbery: I knew boys who joined the Fascist Youth Corps because they wanted to impress their girls. In the end, however, adherence to the Right generally arouses astonishment, irony and mistrust. The average Jewish opinion is fairly skeptical of the right-wing Jew's sincerity; it suspects him of being odd at least. How can a man be a Rightist when he is a Jew? That instinctive condemnation is not unfounded. The alliance of Jewry with right-wing movements can never be anything but temporary. Sooner or later it reveals a fundamental contradiction. To preserve the existing order, the Right has to stiffen and emphasize differences while at the same time having no respect for what is different. To preserve itself as a privileged group, it must repulse, restrict and oppress other groups. Now it may be that a Jew would desire the survival of a given social order in which, by chance, he is not too unhappy. But in addition, he wants the differences between himself and the non-Jews in that class to be forgotten or at least minimized. The Right, either openly or covertly, drives the Jew back to his Jewishness and can only condemn him and burden his Jewishness. Not to speak of times of crisis when the Rightist doctrine, whipped to a frenzy, is driven to violent solutions, to the use of sentiments and methods that debase the lives of the Jews. I wrote all this in one of my earlier books and drew down upon my head the indignation of a number of my readers. The Right is not essentially anti-Semitic, I have often been told. That statement is open to question: it is possible that there may not be any logical or metaphysical compulsion there. And yet it looks as though the plans and actions of Rightist groups are a constant threat to Jewry.

I am also aware that certain Jewish politicians and university law professors claim to be completely apart from all Jewry. They envy French or English bourgeoisie who belong to a nation and a class which they defend and which defends them. How, they ask, does Jewry enter into that? They rarely mention it and in their speeches and their actions, they refer to it parenthetically. But is this what they really want? Economically and culturally bound up with his class, can the bourgeois Jew be politically bourgeois unless he has an ulterior motive or is ignorant? Can he prevent the course of the world, the affairs of the nation, from reacting in one way on his destiny and in another way on the destinies of other bourgeois citizens? If Fascism were to prevail, what would he do to avoid the catastrophe that would befall him as a Jew? He hopes vaguely, I suppose, to escape it thanks to his connections, his friendships, and, in the end, the power of his status as a bourgeois. But the obligatory Jewish solidarity would then come into conflict with class solidarity. And he is not sure that the advantages of class would outweigh the misfortunes reserved for the group. Rich Jews are said to have suffered less from Nazism than poor Jews. That is true on the whole, but only in the early days: they could appeal to their connections, they could leave the country more easily and re-establish themselves in other countries. But the passing of time also worked against them. As their financial means dwindled and their social position became weakened, their Jewishness came to the fore and became more apparent. Soon they ceased completely to be the natural allies and protégées of the government and became its victims. The bourgeois Jew knows this well and does not require such extreme circumstances to confirm it. He knows it so well that he is practically paralyzed by it, and this explains the relative scarcity of Rightist Jews. But nobody can live in that ambiguous position, that abstraction. For that matter, it is possible that those difficulties and the resulting separation may cast a favorable light, even in my opinion, on the portrait of the bourgeois Jew. Perhaps I am presuming too much, but it seems to me that one often finds in the bourgeois Jew less stubbornness in favor of his class and more misgivings and therefore, relatively more perspicacity. That undoubtedly is why we find more liberals among bourgeois Jews than anywhere else, a fact I consider a virtue, but one that makes their position more ambiguous and separates them from their class.

As to the Jew's relations with the Left there is much to be said. The Right has never been worried about liberating peoples and putting an end to oppressions. On the contrary, they are always afraid that the established order, the guarantee of their privileges, may be upset. In spite of some disturbances, the Left consider themselves bearers of a solution, of the only solution, to the Jewish fate. It is, of course, impossible to examine the different issues connected with the Jewish problem without examining their propositions. I will refer to that later and at greater length. Meanwhile, how can we fail to note those huge disturbances? How can we fail to realize that, far from having brought balm and healing to Jewish wounds Socialist revolutions have enflamed them almost everywhere? Far from being regulated under a Socialist regime, the Jews' difficulties seem to increase or at least to remain unchanged. Admitting that those might be merely growing pains, what is the reason for even those relative reverses? It is not enough to talk of failure and the perversion of all revolutions. The degradation of the Jews would still have to be explained: why that inability to solve the Jewish problem the solution of which was part of their good intentions?

It seems obvious to me today that Jewish reality has escaped the classic Socialist analysis: the Jew does not really belong to any particular class. Revolutionary action being essentially class action, the Jewish fate was doomed to escape it. Even worse: in the great upheaval which swept the nation, the case of the Jews burst suddenly like a strange phenomenon; the Jew appeared to be an astonishingly irreducible element, not bound to any group. But how could the Jew feel solidarity when his oppression is not identified with the oppression of any other group, when the liberation of other peoples will not free him from his status as a Jew?

Here I expect the usual impatient question from my readers: is it so necessary for the Jew to be liberated as a Jew? Can't you simply make common cause with other oppressed peoples? To tell the truth, I cannot see any other line of conduct as long as the Jew continues to live among non-Jews. And that is what Jews do in general. Their participation in the parties of the Left in every country in the world is relatively very important. My first impulse, an immediate sympathy, urges me toward the underprivileged, the downtrodden of history and of the city. I am sure that my Jewishness is largely the reason for this: my heart understands them and my mind agrees with them. But today I have been forced to admit that this instinctive solidarity with the downtrodden, which I do not deny and which I shall continue to proclaim, will not save me . . . even if those downtrodden of yesterday were finally to take their revenge; for their cause is not exactly mine. Besides, it was foreseeable that this common struggle would be concerned only with what is common to all and not with what concerns me particularly, not in the peculiarly Jewish aspects of my oppression. Usually as soon as I refer to this "peculiarity" my friends become annoyed. This annoyance would prove that I have not made myself understood. Do I really want to cling so to my peculiarity? I must say clearly, in any case, that for me it is neither a claim nor a specific ideal: it is simply there. I see it in myself, in the eyes of other men and in their gestures: it is a dimension of my life, the sum total of differences, positive and negative, that separate me from other men. Having said this, why should I not be entitled to note this: why should I, among all men, forget who I am? For any man, one must admit, the struggle loses its interest if that is the price he has to pay. But suppose I agree to it. I have agreed to it for a long time, as it is; I have fought a long time, with all sorts of groups anxious for the freedom of all men. By a tacit agreement we almost never referred to the existence of Jews, to my Jewishness. And in a certain way I admit, that reassured and calmed me. But the activities of my political friends, which I shared as much as possible, have seldom solved my own difficulties. I could not be saved by chance, and indirectly. During difficult, trying days, that modestly silenced peculiarity would burst forth again. I therefore gave up trying to link my destiny with the destinies of other men. I finally discovered that the suppression of my Jewishness does not depend solely on me and on my friends. It was not enough for Leftists and all the Jews of the Left to avoid using the word "Jew" for the problem to disappear, or the Jews' difficulties in life to end.

The truth is I am assured of nothing in the heart of the city, as also before the courts of history. The natural, and frequent, temptation of the bourgeoisie is to harden into Fascism or into a reactionary regime: reaction excludes me. The temptation, the natural vocation, of Socialists is revolution, overthrow of the social order; but Socialism and revolution reject me. They explain that if I did not insist upon remaining a Jew, they could neither exclude nor reject me. I answer that it is all those negations and exclusions that in great part make me a Jew. My abstention neither makes me remain a Jew, nor would it save me. Other men than I have carried self-effacement as far as possible and have not escaped the misfortune; after all, why should I not keep to myself, since that is the only thing I am sure of? But at least let it be understood that I hesitate, that my adherences are most often apprehensive and faltering.

The Jew and Politics

16

ONE

A paradox affects my political life. As a
Jew I am deeply concerned with politics
and, at the same time, politically paralyzed.
My fate is too uncertain for me not to take
an interest in the passions and fevers of the
city. My life is too vulnerable for me not to
make an effort to foresee the fluctuations
of power, for me not to dream of a way of
acting upon it. Jean-Paul Sartre has noted
the Jew's dependence on society, his concern for the opinion of his fellow-citizens.
In the ghetto we argued passionately about
international and local events; we were familiar with the men prominent in government affairs; in the synagogue a prayer of
blessing was regularly offered for the new
chiefs of state. But though to the Jew, politics is an ever present concern, a constant
temptation, that temptation is doomed
never to be completely satisfied. Of course,
one meets Jews in political circles, but there
is practically no Jewish influence in the po-

litical life of the country. Many Jews attempt to be politically active and even succeed, but never as Jews.

There is nothing obscure about the mechanism of this paradox. Though the Jew is deeply concerned with politics, he cannot be politically active except by putting aside his Jewishness, by forgetting it himself and above all by making others forget it. But though the Jewish situation has greatly improved since the French Revolution, it has still not gone that far. Today it is possible for me to participate in civic struggles and action, but on condition that I pass unnoticed. In the most liberal periods I can even make a success of it, but only to the extent that I conceal my real identity and disappear as a Jew. I am given proof of this daily: the best weapon to prevent me from action, to check my impulse promptly, to take the edge off my effectiveness, is to broadcast the fact that I am a Jew. Show me the Jewish politician who has not been considerably embarrassed by that public reminder!

Am I about to yield once more to that persecution complex, to that sensitivity and lack of trust that disturbs and colors my judgment as I readily admit? I do not think so. During these last decades, France has had only two prominent Jewish politicians: Léon Blum and Mendès-France. Léon Blum was literally driven by a curious ambition for a Socialist leader: all his life he longed passionately to be acclaimed by the entire French nation. He succeeded to the detriment of his own party and thus lost on two counts: for that adoption by the entire nation was never anything but a nostalgic mirage. Precisely because he was a Socialist and a Jew.

Mendès-France's experience is told frankly by a Catholic writer (this detail is important: The Catholic party, M. R. P., has been the most bitter enemy of the Jewish politician). ". . . . Now this young Minister who claimed he would give France a 'pure and hard Republic' . . . was a Jew . . . a role especially difficult to maintain for a man who, every time he made a speech or acted, felt that he was surrounded by antipathy and suspicion because of his origin. This resulted in a natural but unfortunate reaction, that mixture of firmness and timidity that surely embarrassed P. Mendès-France in the decisive moments of his career." (P. H. Simon). Mendès-France's political friends also criticized his timidity and his unfortunate reactions. In the opinion of all, he made the mistake of reacting like a Jew, of allowing himself to be affected by anti-Semitic accusations. But how could a politician who wishes to represent and defend his fellow-citizens, to act in their name, not consider their moods, and especially their reservations as far as he was concerned? It is then, on the contrary, that he would have lacked clear-sightedness. The suspicion with which he was surrounded was not limited to verbal comments. It was translated into action and effectively prevented him from remaining in the government. That, however, is not the most serious point. After all, those men have never wished to act or speak in the name of the Jews; nevertheless they have been brought to the attention of their fellow-citizens; and have been accused of that, of all sorts of duplicity and Machiavellianism. They tried to forget their Jewishness so that they might better devote themselves to their constituents; and yet those same constituents worked to bring about their downfall. All is fair in love and politics, I know. Nevertheless the weak point of Jewish politicians is their Jewishness, even though they deny it and try to camouflage it. And in that one recognizes the fundamental irony of the Jewish fate, imposed on them and denied, heavy and yet transparent. Blum and Mendès-France did not act as Jews, but they could not prevent their actions from being hindered and thwarted in the name of their Jewishness.

But here is where the paradox appears even more

striking: let us suppose that, in spite of my handicap, I succeed in working my way into the political life of the city. Let us say that I have succeeded in disappearing as a Jew in the eyes of my political clientele; for example, by changing my name, by carefully limiting my Jewishness to my private life, or by stifling it altogether. We must now add that I must be careful never to further my political position or the political position of other Jews. I can never act overtly in my own behalf with the result that my political destiny continues to escape me. "Is that so important?" someone will ask. "Why are you so anxious to be politically active as a Jew?" To tell the truth, we are going in circles: we always come back to the same question and the same answer. Why should I sometimes act as a Jew? Because the Jew exists! Because the Jew exists as a Jew, to himself and to others. He exists and at the same time he is never recognized politically except to be made use of, defeated and killed. Why should he be condemned never to defend himself as a Jew? When it is necessary, of course, when differences play a part. To break this paradox (which we understood instinctively) we young Jews took a passionate interest in politics. To escape the same paradox many Jews seek shelter among powerful groups, solicit unexpected protection, for example, the protection of the Pope or the protection of a rival church. But that is skating on thin ice and counting on luck more than on oneself. The city and history ask the Jew direct questions, impose specific tests on him, which demand specific replies. The Jew can almost never answer, for politically he is *almost* speechless.

TWO

The Jew is politically speechless because he does not exist politically, because he lives politically in the abstract. After the events of May 13, 1958, when the French Army of Algeria rebelled against its own government and almost installed a Fascist regime in France, a reporter interviewed one of the leaders of the Jewish community in Paris: Guy de Rothschild. This is what that man, responsible for his own people, said:

"My first answer, and the most fundamental, if I may say so, is that in my opinion, the political changes that have taken place since May 13th do not interest and do not concern the Jews in any way. The Jews as Jews, naturally—and not as Frenchmen (we are all French). The Jews as Jews had nothing to do with it and are neither touched, interested, nor concerned in any fashion, neither closely nor remotely by what has happened. These are political phenomena in the organization of public life and of the national government, but the Jews are neither objects of nor subject to changes."

Now, living in the abstract has never prevented a man from coming up against reality or from being harshly punished for it. If Fascism had triumphed, how would it have helped us to have declared derisively through the mouths of our leaders that we had been "neither interested, nor concerned in any fashion, neither closely nor remotely . . ."? Perhaps that great financier did not see the Fascist danger. Perhaps, so blinded by class sympathies, he did not want to see the connection between Fascism and the Jewish fate. But no: he added honestly:

"It is quite obvious that at certain times, elements that can be . . . said to be Fascist, have almost dominated the French political scene. As for Jews in general, Fascist elements are not our friends."

That might appear devious, unless one remembers the paradox which throws important light on the political conduct of the Jews. Last year the walls of Paris were plastered once again with anti-Jewish slogans and symbols. A publishing house chose the same moment to bring out a dictionary containing numerous definitions insulting to the Jews. M. Weil-Curiel, a city councillor who happened to be a Jew, thought it his duty to protest at a meeting of the Conseil de la Ville. That was a dignified act but what did the honorable councillor have to say?

"I have no complex about this question," he said. "I am a Jew, but I do not come before you here as a Jew, but as a Frenchman and as a Frenchman through and through. As a Frenchman I am shocked that a subtle poison like anti-Semitism should be instilled into a work destined for children . . ."

In short, the councillor considered it inopportune to protest simply as a Jew. He could protest in the name of France, in the name of the Republic, of childhood, of humanity . . . but not in the name of the Jew which, nevertheless, he is, or of Jews who were being attacked.

One could imagine a scene in a comedy in which honorable Jewish politicians, unworthily accused, attacked, beaten to death as Jews, reply worthily as Frenchmen, or as Englishmen.

"Dirty Jew!"

"That has nothing to do with me, sir . . . but as a Frenchman, it revolts me!"

"If you are not hurt by it as a Jew, why would you be revolted as a Frenchman?"

"Because the Frenchman I am does not approve of insulting orphans, widows, the oppressed . . . and Jews."

"That is to your credit and to the credit of the French too . . . but nevertheless you are a Jew: why do you give the Frenchman, who is not insulted, the task of defending the Jew, who is insulted? Why the devil does not the Jew which you are defend himself? Is he deaf and dumb? Or have you yourself reduced him to silence? Or do you claim he is not hurt merely to keep him from protesting?"

The profound contradictions of the Jew's civic life

give him a strange political modesty which is, perhaps, merely an expression of his helplessness. He sees the danger, he is aware of the outward demonstration, but he practically never dares to act on his own behalf.

"I have retained a bad memory of the thirties," declares a Jewish professor, "a memory of inaction when I knew from reliable sources that Hitler was preparing for war. But, in those days, I was paralyzed, too, by my university work. I had no rostrum and I considered it useless to interfere in matters of that sort." (Raymond Aron).

The Jew knows, however, that he will be the first victim; the most sorely afflicted. Why would it be so shocking for him to shout a warning, to prepare to protect himself and others at the same time? Would he not be more useful to everyone by being useful to himself? Did the Jews raise their voices sufficiently to warn the world against Nazism? The Jew refrains from doing anything precisely because he is more in danger than other men. The result is paradoxical, misleading. He who best foresees catastrophes because he is the most vulnerable, who would have the most interest in warning other men and in averting the disaster, does not make a move . . . Were he to defend himself, he fears he would be suspected of thinking of his own interests. The danger, however, is frequently general! True, but it is more serious for him. At such times, as the professor says, he is most often paralyzed. Like the fowl that lies on its back, eyes opened, staring at the knife that is being waved above it, but perfectly inert and yielding, he has found it "useless to interfere in such matters." Out of discretion he shrinks from meddling in those matters that concern his life and his death and that ended in the crematorium. Or if in the end he does make a move, he will never act directly in his own favor. He will always submerge his motives and his interests, his fears and his hopes, assuming he admits them to himself, in some larger movement that would benefit him indirectly, in some party or syndicate which would of course protect him but in some negative way. Never would he dare to ask openly for aid, for an adequate and positive security. There are, in short, no public Jewish policies, properly stated. Even among the great Jewish concentrations in cities like Paris or New York, it is above all a matter of a diffused fear instilled in the future candidate by such a solid mass and not of a clearly expressed will. It is periodically suggested that the Jewish population of such and such a city voted for a certain candidate (for De Gaulle, for Kennedy etc.) and often it may be so. But the Jews take care not to proclaim it; they do not openly assert their will as a power, and therefore as the stake of a transaction, which is necessary in politics. Contrary to the claims of the anti-Semite there is no Jewish policy either good or bad, but rather a political absence of the Jew in the city.

That, also, is why the Jew who wants to have a political career promptly puts himself at the service of non-Jews and never at the service of his own people. One scarcely ever sees a Jewish deputy introduce a bill on behalf of Jews, as non-Jews do normally and legitimately on behalf of their own people. Of course, there is the Cremieux law in favor of the Algerian Jews, but this astounding exception shines like a solitary light in the political history of French Jews. The Jewish politician is self-assured only when he is not speaking as a Jew. The Jewish politician Trotsky was no less bold than his adversary Stalin: the Jewish politician Léon Blum was as good as his successor Guy Mollet: but the fact that they were Jews never interfered with their political conduct. They had made up their minds to ignore it once and for all. Trotsky denied flatly that he was a Jew: Léon Blum felt obliged to pull off a logical sleight of hand. "He silenced the Jew in himself the better to attain the Judaic ideal of the Just," writes his intelligent biographer, C. Audry. The universal values of Socialist moral philosophy embraced the best of the Jewish traditions: why then did he need Judaism? The matter can be discussed from another point of view, but we can already see how the wind blows.

And I cannot even altogether blame them, acting, the one as a Russian, a Communist and a philosopher, the other as a Frenchman, a Socialist and a man of action, they assume and earn Russian legitimacy or French legitimacy, philosophical clarity and the resoluteness of men of action. If these same men had been responsible Jews their courage would have weakened, I am sure, their vision dimmed. What would they have represented then? Far from being the expression, the agent of tremendous forces, they would have been the emanation of a fusion of weaknesses, of a community eager to pass unnoticed, of an ideology that has been defeated for centuries. Far from leading aggressive and redoubtable troops in combat, they would have had to protect their constituents, prevent them from becoming victims. "Our policy," a leader of the community, declared seriously "is essentially a policy of survival." The moment a Jewish politician feels responsible for Jews, his policy becomes weak, visibly hesitant, his political voice wavers. He tries to please everyone, he avoids taking a stand except in favor of the established power, which is actually not choosing but yielding. And if that power wavers he immediately begins to look around for openings, which causes people to suspect him of duplicity and despise him. And it is only too true that such, too often, are the leaders of our Jewish communities, for leaders there are. I can understand that it would be more tempting for an ambitious, proud, young Jew, to identify himself with non-Jews rather than with his own peo-

ple! The game is so much more exciting, apparently so
much freer! For a long time I declared that I would
never accept any position in any line whatsoever if the
limits were fixed in advance, if the entire route were not
potentially open. Merit alone is law. I was obliged to
change my tune; I had to accept my handicap or give
up. There are very few careers in which a distinctly
Jewish name is not a hindrance, more or less fixed, more
or less visible. And I am not speaking of those social
roles in which the public identifies itself with men it
admires. Seldom does an actor, of stage or the movies,
dare to keep his name if it is Cohen or Levy. Moreover,
is that so shocking? The last American elections have
taught us how important it was in spite of Kennedy's
success for a candidate for the presidency to be of the
same religion as the majority of his electors. I can well
understand that, in the state of culture we are still in, a
nation may want to see itself in its representatives. This
is one of the difficulties all minorities have to face. In
this respect, France is still a fortunate land in which the
Jew can have a successful political career more often than
anywhere else. It is noteworthy, however, that there has
never been a Jewish President of the Republic. A Jew
may be allowed to occupy an important post in the
government, he may even be prime minister, but he may
not become the symbol of the nation: the prime minister
is, in fact, the best possible present-day servant of the
nation and the most able. If he is not successful, they
change him; if he antagonizes, they can criticize him and
insult him. Of course, a Jewish prime minister, even
though he carefully denied his Jewishness, would be
criticized for his origin. But by denying his background,
he can come to represent non-Jews solely. The President
of the Republic is no longer simply an agent of the
nation, he is the symbol of the nation and the substitute
for it; it hands itself over to him and identifies itself

with him. That is why there has never been a Jewish President of the Republic: so far no nation has ever consented to be identified with a Jew.

THREE

A deep gap, a systematic distance separates me from any political activity. Though I try to fill in the gap and frequently pretend to ignore it, I know and see confirmed daily, that my civic efforts are more or less short-circuited as is also my integration with the nation and with history, with my class and with the city. I belong to the nation and yet I do not quite belong to it, for it claims me unwillingly. I am of my own class and yet I am not, since it mistrusts me and I confess that I avoid it in part. I mingle in the life of the city, and my activity always has the embarrassed look of an artificial addition. Though I am particularly exposed and vulnerable, I am politically suspect no matter what I do. I do all I can never to act as a Jew and, too often, I am suspected of behaving like one. And when, on hearing one of my decisions, people say: "He is a Jew," that also means: "What is he after? What aims beyond those of his class? Beyond those of the nation?" I am always tempted to take part in community affairs in which I am deeply concerned and I learn, at my expense, that it would have been better had I abstained. In every way, the price I pay is higher than that paid by other men. Whatever my intentions and my political purpose, fundamentally I am penalized as a Jew.

I confess that my life, my conduct, does not seem to me free of ambiguity, should I show that I am a good citizen and a good patriot, a super-patriot *sans peur et sans reproche,* a conforming citizen, stubbornly loyal and unflaggingly ardent? I admit that people might be astonished: why should I be so zealous when I have so little encouragement? Either I am said to be tricky, shrewd, calculating, obsequious and false; or else people are genuinely delighted, and pay me such exaggerated compliments, that I am instantly on my guard and irritated: I see that they are not equally flattering to others. They mean more and they mean less; being what I am, I deserve more credit than the others, they did not expect so much from me! Should I decide, on the contrary, to rebel, to deny a society I consider unjust and chaotic? "All Jews are rebels; they destroy," they will say. Or benevolently: "What do you expect? That is the only solution left you." And that is not altogether false! It often enrages me to have to admit it. Why would I not be tempted, more than non-Jews, to criticize and stir up that society which rejects me, doubts me and tramples on me? We know that many young Jews took an active part in resisting the Nazis in infinitely greater proportions than most other groups. How many times have we not been told that they did not deserve much credit for that! what else could they do? Or else that courage, unusual among Jews, long unaccustomed to fighting, is greeted with astonishment. In short, I never benefit from my decisions, except in the worst way, I can never pursue spontaneously, naturally, my civic and national interests. I am never permitted to be a patriot, a citizen, a rebel or a member of the Maquis without arousing suspicion and astonishment and without being subjected to restrictions. Undoubtedly, to answer a romantic objection, there are not only disadvantages in this distance and estrangement. Making the best of a bad thing, I have even congratulated myself at times. That difficulty in being politically active, I said to myself, makes me wiser, keeps me from being impatient, which is my nature, from putting myself too much at the mercy of events that elude me. Prevented from having a normal social and political life, the Jew limits himself to spiritual adventures, wisdom, art or philosophy—fields in which he thus excels. This choice is, however, imposed on me; I am limited from the start, and bullied, and I could have been finally smothered by it, as many were, who were meant to have public lives.

The French philosopher, Jean Mahl, to whom I read these pages, reminded me that all men in history, in the City and outside of the City, were like this, and not only Jews. True, all men are oppressed to some degree and on some levels. Many efforts must still be made before we can reveal, denounce and put an end to the many oppressions men suffer. Each oppression, however, is specific, and each must be described *in its way* in order to understand it better and fight it. It is, moreover, a matter of degree. Now the Jews are particularly oppressed, more seriously, more generally than other men. The Jewish fate, I insist, is only an abridged form, more condensed and gloomier, of the general fate of mankind.

From Uneasiness
to Persecution

ONE

Whether it is my particular lot or merely
the bad luck common to all men, only
more intensified in my case, I am practically helpless before my political fate. My
civic and historic life is a destiny imposed
on me; it drags me along in its train. And
at first sight, I can find no solution to a
truly ambiguous situation in which I am
neither free to act nor to refrain from acting.

I had been told in Belgium that many
Jews had backed and financed the Flemish
movement whose leader, Leon Degrelle,
had ended by allying himself with the
Nazis.

"Why?" I asked. "Out of fear or careful
calculation? To safeguard their future, I
suppose . . ."

"No," I was told, "because the Jews
understood and sincerely approved of the
nationalist claims, especially the appeal to
national unity . . . Later the movement be-

came anti-Semitic and then, of course, they had to give it up."

That was really being too frank. But ideological considerations apart, I must confess that I was not greatly surprised. I know well that longing for action in common with all other men! Unfortunately, the communion is always lacking, collective action has always passed me by. I can even understand that national movements might be the most tempting to Jews. They are, in fact, most deceptive but particularly in the beginning they revive national myths and insist on the complete unity of the nation. Fascinated, grateful, deeply moved, many Jews fling themselves, regularly and childishly, on the vast bosom of the collective mother they have at last found, a mother who no less regularly proves to be a harsh stepmother. When society becomes strong, in short, sure of itself, it hardens and soon becomes distrustful of everything that is not itself. The great hope of identifying with other men vanishes once more; and the Jew finds himself outside and only too pleased if he is not persecuted. Thus, and not merely as a stupid calculation, must we explain the successive adherences of Italian Jews to Fascism, of German Jews to Nazism, of Belgian Jews to Flemish nationalism and even, all niceties aside, of many French Jews to De Gaullism. The political loneliness and the impossibility of having any truly Jewish policy explain that desperate effort to identify with the politics of non-Jews. Now this effort is regularly frustrated. It always happens at the moment when the wave recedes and leaves the Jew stranded on the beach, unwanted, deserted by others and often by himself.

Must I then abstain? Prudence and experience, if not pride, obviously seem to advise me to do so, since I cannot count on the supporters of the established order and the mystic past of the nation, nor on the supporters of a new order and the future. Even a brief experience has taught me that I always end by regretting having believed in the early promises of candidates for power. In any case, I am never sure that the new era will not hold many steps forward and backward that will crush me out of a benevolent necessity. Since no political action can benefit me and since I am not wanted, why not withdraw of my own accord from that dangerous ferment? In that respect Jewish masses have acquired a kind of resigned wisdom. Their first reaction when a Jew is appointed to a high position, is not one of pure joy, as one might think, but a touch of pride mingled with a great deal of mistrust. The two or three times when Jews became premiers in France, the only time when a Jew was minister in Tunisia, a delegation was sent to ask them urgently to tender their resignations: it was better not to arouse the envy and anger of non-Jews. They also received a vast number of letters imploring or demanding that resignation: after all, the punishment would be borne by all Jews.

And yet I know, too, that I cannot safely abstain either. In a hostile world, abstention would be the worst of policies for it hands me over without a fight. When a Jewish professor of literature was asked if she was going to take part in a strike, she gave me the best summary of the Jewish abstentionist attitude. "The game is fixed," she told me, "and always against us." She told us how she had seen Jews being arrested by Germans in the very heart of Paris.

"We had been told," she said, "if such a thing should happen, the French would never stand for it! You would see them rush out on the street. They would even fight with sadirons! I have seen many things. I saw my neighbor throw her children out of the window to prevent them from being taken away by the Germans. No one in the building, no one on the street, moved. None of those people who protest today, who shout so loudly because they are being deprived of their comforts, would lift a finger if Jews were carried off to concentration camps again. These little matters of strikes, of wage disputes and of various protests leave me cold because I know, when it comes to essential matters, I can never expect any help from anyone."

How can I say she was altogether wrong? The game is, in fact, fixed, since I am always in danger of paying infinitely more than my partners. How can I have any real solidarity with them if they play only for small change and desert me when it comes to serious things? The professor of literature was right . . . and yet she was wrong, too. The game is fixed, my chances are ridiculous, the stake is greatly to my disadvantage and yet I am all the more eager to play. Unions do not fight for me and perhaps one day would drop me at the most critical moment in my life: However, they postpone that moment and perhaps prevent it from arriving. Keeping democracy alive will probably not suppress all anti-Semitic demonstrations; but the death of democracy could bring with it my own death. I have to fight, even with selfish or unworthy companions. We will always find under various forms the same paradox and the same contradiction. Action does not save me, but abstaining from action condemns me. The Jew cannot do much for himself politically, and yet politics is so much a part of him that he cannot dissociate himself from it.

Any gratuitousness is moreover forbidden me. I try to tell myself sometimes, to the despair of my many non-Jewish friends, "What does it matter if so and so is a Fascist, if, on the other hand, he is a good artist, a talented writer or simply an honest man?" But I know that it makes a great deal of difference to me. It can mean that he desires my death or will consent to it one day. This would be my chance to cite such and such an artist, art critic, or scholar, all of them Jews, who decided once and for all to turn their backs on public events and devote themselves exclusively to art and science and who were quietly successful to the day of their death. But what does that prove? Did they really succeed in guarding themselves against the Fascist threat? Or simply in shutting their eyes and stopping their ears and in having had the luck to escape?

If a man is not a Jew, he is free to consider only the writer in a Fascist author; if you do not stir him up about his political leanings, he will probably let you alone. But all that is impossible for a Jew. "Cut out your tongue and you will live in peace," my good mother once advised me; but she was only half right. Even if I had had a better disposition and enough humility to keep silent in the face of insult, provocation and insinuation I would not necessarily have found peace, for the anti-Semite is never satisfied with my cautious neutrality. He forces me to a war in which I must defend myself or be destroyed. I would have preferred to ignore his vile newspapers and for them to ignore me, but they expose me to the attacks of my fellow-citizens. In spite of all that, I can try painfully to conjure up a wisdom superior to political events. Perhaps I could even bring myself to scorn the stupid cruelty of the world and so steel myself against it. But the only result would be a greater lucidity and an ironical resignation, and not that fine indifference and that gracious casualness so many of my colleagues, artists and scholars, display. For neither their lack of interest nor their ignorance of political affairs have saved Jewish scholars from being driven out of Germany and Jewish writers from going into exile or from committing suicide. I am permitted neither moral nor esthetic relativism, neither pure art nor pure science; and it is perhaps best for me to realize that anxiety is my real fate.

In no role, under no circumstances, in short, can I profit from any historical comfort whatever. True, I am not the only one towards whom history has almost always been unjust and deceitful; it has always robbed the poor, lied to women, crushed the vanquished. But how does that change my position? To live in that anxiety I would have had to stop being a Jew. But in the world as it is, I could not do that, even if I wanted to. Nor would it have helped if I were "colorless, odorless, tasteless," the three "lesses," as one of my old professors of chemistry used to say. From time to time some demonstration, some act of aggression, pulls me up short out of this cautious and almost transparent existence.

At a congress of Catholics on the war in Algeria, which I attended, demonstrators crowded around the door. What did they shout to remind the Catholics of what they thought was their duty? "Throw the Jews out!" "Don't play the Jew's game!" "What have the Jews to do with this argument?" One demonstrator explained to me that they meant Jews in Algeria who would be interested in seeing the French leave. That was completely ridiculous. No one can be more worried, more shaken and more divided than the unfortunate Algerian Jews. But there were Jews in Algeria: they could therefore be blamed for the misfortune that has befallen that country. I should perhaps exist without existing, I should be there without being there. The cautious men, the conformists who can do this, have the right idea: the Jew's position, his every act, his life in the city can never be free of ambiguity. I must try to live without living, to act without acting. In every way, in short, I am the displaced person of society and of history, I am doomed to that historical and social discomfort.

I have not always seen this so clearly, I admit. I was,

first of all, a Zionist for semi-moral reasons and from pride. Thus, for a long time I misunderstood that extraordinary waltz of European Jewish populations. Not till I came to know thoroughly the historians Graetz and Dubnow was I convinced that constant immigration was the normal lot of the Jew and not a stray accident in his life. Those blond, blue-eyed German and Polish Jews who came from so far away to settle in Tunis seemed to me almost unreal. Whether those Yiddish writers who talked incessantly of departure, packs on their backs, of uprootings and successive resettlement in almost every generation, were suffering from a sick imagination or from their own lives, I was not too certain, especially where Jewish artists from distant lands were concerned. I must admit that I was rather impressed by the non-Jew's scorn for so much agitation, for the instability of all those strange people, who could not stay put like other men in their corner of land or in their ghettos. By comparison I felt infinitely saner. Poorly integrated, ill at ease, in somewhat straitened circumstances perhaps, but nevertheless permanently settled, my life was spent between the docks of the port of Tunis and the hills of the Belvedere. To my youthful mind, my inner and my outer worlds seemed to me nearly definitive, with no connection, in any case, with the lives of other Jews in the world.

Since then, I have revised that impression! How quick we were to join the general exodus! In the beginning, some fools, the most restless among us, those whose antennae were the most sensitive, the most alert, left us, to all appearances gratuitously, to go elsewhere. After that, the ghetto was beset by a sort of mass unrest: people went off to Israel, to Paris, to Marseilles, sometimes even to America. The well-to-do said condescendingly: "The poor are always the ones who leave; they have nothing to lose, why wouldn't adventure tempt them?" But soon the bourgeoisie themselves were at it, arguing passionately, ridiculing each other, with finally the ridiculer catching up with the ridiculed. What was going on? It would be hard to explain. There had been the war and the postwar period, of course; but we had not suffered more than other men, less if anything. I must emphasize that point: in Tunisia and in Morocco we had not suffered any great catastrophes because we were Jews, not even pogroms for a very long time. I pay homage in passing to our Tunisian compatriots and even to the Europeans of those countries; the inevitable anti-Semitism of certain people among them did not degenerate into bloody massacres, so frequent elsewhere. Then why this emigration? Simply, I believe, that our life had begun in its turn to verify, to confirm the common destiny. Today one of my sisters is settled in an Israelian *moshav*, after having experienced of her own free will the adventure of a ship-exodus with internment on Cyprus, etc. One of my brothers, a hero, as they say, went through the Sinai campaign, another sister married a young Frenchman, slightly ultra-Gaullist, who persists in staying in Bizerte and declares he will leave it only by force; other members of my family are living in Paris; as for me, for a long time I no longer knew . . .

How easy it would be to accuse us of being nomads, wanderers! Or to recall the myth of the Wandering Jew or the various curses that are said to pursue us as the result of our famous sins. But our example is precisely the contrary to those wanderings. The little artisans of the Tunisian ghetto have not budged for centuries from that little corner of earth. Crowded between the mosques of Sidi-Mohrez and the Cathedral, steering a course for a century between Arabs and Frenchmen, carefully locking their doors at night, but punctually celebrating their Sabbath and their various ritual festivals, they were poor, without recognized rights, but, in spite of several alarms, almost at home in that geographical area and psychological restraint. My grandfather liked to boast that he had never gone farther than twenty kilometers from his house, eighteen, to be exact and that only because he had to take the children to the la Goulette beach. My mother would undoubtedly have had the same fate if . . . And I myself, am I a nomad? No, I am sure I am not! I have a horror of trips, I detest all those material confusions that people add uselessly to their inner confusion, which they take with them in any case. If I could, if I had been able to, I would have settled down permanently in the same apartment in the same town, and there I would have pursued my daily routine, so that I could think, dream and write really at ease.

But one day, as had happened to so many other Jews, a series of fresh historical events shattered our unsteady equilibrium. We were stunned by it, as helpless as an insect on its back. The ground we had thought to be so solid, was swept from under our feet. The world looked upside down and far away and we realized how weak we were and how rootless. Obviously, history and the city functioned very well without us; of this we had daily proof. As colonized Jews, we were neither socially well integrated nor provided with all our dimensions, but we lived in a sort of stupor common to the majority of the people around us. Suddenly we were jolted out of our lethargy, questioned about strange problems that required urgent replies. Thus brought face to face with ourselves, we made the cruel discovery that we neither knew how to reply nor were we able to, that socially and historically we were nothing.

Do not tell me again that this is my personal problem, that North Africa is too special a case. On the contrary, there are too many examples of that sudden imbalance, that questioning the life of a Jewish community which shows the community suddenly how precarious, how fragile and how dependent that life is. On the contrary, I repeat, we were the last to believe that one day we would prove the general scheme: and we were almost the last that History caught up with after all of Central Europe, after the Jews of *la douce France* and the Jews of *la bella Italia,* after all the countries of the North and all the countries of the Mediterranean. I realize that all this deserves discussion: however, I am still too stunned by it, too close to the event to be sure that I see it clearly. And I admit that it is not easy to understand from the outside. We have been too much criticized for not having participated more boldly, more completely in the struggle for the independence of Tunisia and Morocco and the reconstruction of those countries. I am not speaking, of course, of individuals who often contributed generously, each in his own way, to the different movements that faced each other in the struggle; I am speaking of the Jewish group as a whole. How do I explain that situation? The independence of Tunisia and of Morocco, the Tunisian experience, was not directed against the Jews, but neither was it made with the Jews; it was made without them. It is in the very way in which new nations were born that differences became clear, were confirmed, showed us plainly that we were not part of it. It is in the way that Tunisia became a nation like other nations that we became, as we were everywhere else, a civic and national negativity.

But why did you not become a positive factor and thereby share the destinies of the new nation? That in substance is the retort of a number of friends who were surprised, disappointed and vaguely suspicious of our reserve.

I am sorry to have to tell them that is idle talk and in the abstract. As if belonging to a nation depended on mere will-power. We did not recognize ourselves in that nation which was being born and taking its place among other nations, in its institutions, in its decisions. One of the Tunisian government's first decisions was to write the Islamic religion into its constitution as the state religion. What became of us denominationally? Nothing. Like every national rebirth, the Tunisian rebirth legally restored its own language; now Arabic had ceased for a long time to be our official language and we did not want to go back to it again. Result: we no longer knew what language to use. We saw with anxiety the time for the schools to open drawing near; where should we send the children? How could we decide so quickly, so radically not only their linguistic future but their very future itself?

Our fellow countrymen were as reticent as we were. For we could do nothing about it and neither could they; the situation engulfed us and surpassed both of us. A professor of literature, who was not a Tunisian, but who had taught a long time in Tunisia, told me, laughing, that if the Tunisians had really treated the Jews as their own, the Tunisian government, which was greatly in need of administrators, would have been 75 percent Jewish. But let me add at once that this was politically impossible; for them as well as for us. We were not actually their people. As regards language, school, institutions, even religion, I believe that anyone would probably have acted as they did. I do not say they may not have made mistakes, they were fumbling for what best suited their people. What else could they do? But what suited them did not always suit our reticent, hesitant people, on the outside as we were. Moreover, finding ourselves constantly outside the system that was being built up, how could we give ourselves to it body and soul, cheerfully?

Another blow, our mutual friends would say. Why not share in it, if not gladly, at least willingly? Why elsewhere and not here? A reasonable objection. The Jews could have stayed, too—and for that matter a great many did. But do you not see what we are coming to? To a new weak, unstable equilibrium that a feather could push to one side or the other. Therefore, the Jews may as well stay as leave: as regards integration and a new citizenship, the victory is slight, we must admit. We would only have exchanged a bed of bricks for a bed of stones, an old discomfort for a new one, one malaise for another.

The Shadowy Figure

Every new social upheaval, in short, worries us, arouses our suspicions; the future might be worse than the mediocre but unsurprising present. What part would we play in that upheaval? What blows would be especially reserved for us? When De Gaulle assumed power in France, one of the remarks I heard most frequently among the Jews in Paris was: "What is it going to mean for us?" I heard the same query again some time later when the generals in Algiers nearly succeeded in bringing off their *putsch*.

Contrary to what is frequently claimed, I have never found that Jews are particularly revolutionary or in a hurry to see the social order changed. It is true that life in the ghettos was often so miserable that it would seem we had nothing to lose by that change, that we were natural subjects for all revolutions. Even rich Jews had worries enough to keep them from being calm and carefree conservatives. The fact is that the inhabitants of the ghetto as a group were far from being revolutionaries. In Tunis, and also in Paris I believe, Communist recruits were drawn, paradoxically enough, from among the bourgeoisie. Even Zionism was a relatively late and extremely slow development; our relatives were violently opposed to the first departures of our comrades for the Palestine of those days. And yet the Promised Land was part of their collective being, of their daily prayers, their popular tales, their dreams; the Israeli adventure was a continuation of their own story. They were not Tunisian, Moroccan or Algerian nationalists any longer. At bottom, they had almost become accustomed to French colonization; in exchange for a little contempt, they had a relative security. They did not have full rights, but they could not remember ever having had them. And even the poorest and most downtrodden among them hoped to get on without those rights, and by hard work and stubborn tenacity, gain a partial success that would offset the contempt with which they were surrounded.

Impatient adolescents, propagandists of one cause after another, each of which seemed better than the last, we tried to draw the ghetto into new political adventures. By turns irritated or persuasive, we explained that all governments were bad: that the French Front Populaire would surely bring Bread, Peace and Liberty to all, Jews included. Later on we added that one could not expect anything from the "French Imperialists;" that government by the Colonized would surely be more just than the government of the Colonizers . . . The ghetto listened patiently and always raised the same objection: "Perhaps. But who can guarantee us that our own position will not be worse?"

They believed that there was always a chance that their existence would become more difficult and more dangerous. Why exchange a known evil for another condition, another domination, which might result in new and therefore less bearable problems? Dissatisfied though they were with the present, they preferred to hold onto it rather than call for a change, the consequences of which they could not foresee. The obvious result was that they lived in a kind of discrete isolation, both civic and historic, to which they themselves contributed, but which was in other respects imposed on them.

How can we altogether blame them for that cautious anxiety, that resigned timidity? For ages their disillusionments have far surpassed their happy surprises. A Yugoslav Jewess, a former member of Tito's Maquis, who is now living in Paris, told me she understood why most of the popular democracies had failed to liquidate anti-Semitism and solve the Jewish problem. She tried to explain it to me at length. She blamed Stalin's influence, the presence of the Russians, Catholicism, etc. But as for Yugoslavia, her own country for which she had fought so wholeheartedly, she still could not understand. How could Tito permit anti-Semitism to survive? The evil was difficult to wipe out, of course, but the regime had worked other and even more striking miracles. Why should the Jews be the only ones to continue to pay? I had the impression that this former fighter had left her country more in anger and disillusionment than because of actual suffering. In North Africa the first gestures of the young Arab nations fed and confirmed, but fortunately without too serious effects, the anxieties and the hesitancies of the ghetto. One of the first acts of the new governments was to tighten the bonds of solidarity with other Arab nations, an understandable and legitimate move. Now one of the foundations of that solidarity today happens to be a pronounced anti-Judaism. In vain we pointed out to our co-religionists that anti-Judaism was still fairly half-hearted among Moroccans and especially Tunisians. So far Bourguiba has refused to make it a government weapon. The Jews acknowledge it gladly. "God save Bourguiba for us!" But later on . . . Who can guarantee that . . .

No one could guarantee them anything. Not masters of their own fate, set apart from the collective will, anything can happen to them. And their anxiety is no longer unfounded. Moroccan Jews can no longer write to their relatives in Israel; all postal connections are prohibited. Any truly Jewish activity, in Tunisia as in Morocco, is always in danger of arousing a suspicion of Zionism. A young Tunisian minister, who should have known better, used these very harsh words one day:

"We do not want the Jews to have their wallets here and their hearts elsewhere!"

Let us overlook that contempt (which is constantly raising its head) and that identification (traditional, but very unfortunate in that minister of good will) of the Jew with his wallet. Why, the young minister should have asked himself, do the Jews have a bit of their heart elsewhere? Why do they so often live with part of their being outside of the country in which they are actually living? If people only knew how harassing it is not to be sure of dying in the place of one's birth! I remember a saying of some artisans, colleagues of my father, though at that time I did not understand all the concentrated bitterness of their words: "A man is never sure of anything but his birth."

Arab solidarity is a fact, as I well know; the Arab people feel it, governments utilize it. The Moslem religion is another fact; the leaders are obliged to take it into account and naturally are tempted to make use of it. The result is that Jewish citizens find themselves once more sacrificed to necessities that are always to some extent legitimate and respectable. Doesn't this suggest at least that they are not citizens like other men, that they are less valuable than others?

I could not guarantee, no one could guarantee, that my
co-religionists' situation would not grow worse: because
no one could foresee the end of the uneasiness. Long
experience has taught us on the contrary, that uneasiness
may always be whipped up into a crisis. In a way that
astonishes, revolts or causes them to be admired, most
Jews do not consider persecution a monstrous phenomenon. When young men, born in Israel, heard stories of
the sufferings of Jews throughout the world, their indignation turned against the Jews themselves. How could
they put up with that persecution without revolting?
Happy the man who is born free! How can one explain
to those young men the inner wear and tear, the resignation to their fate, of men who have been too long oppressed? Before an oppressed person can rebel he must
not only have a goal, but he must also believe that he
has a right to it. Unlike the colonized, the Jew has been
oppressed for so long that he no longer even believes
strongly in his right to live among other men. In any case,
to the inhabitants of the ghetto—and every Jew carries
within him his own ghetto—for the Jewish masses, persecution seems vaguely to be a natural calamity. It
seems to them to flow almost of necessity from their lives
among non-Jews. They admit it without a protest in
tales of misfortune, oppression and massacres. This explains the success of a book like Schwarz-Bart's, *The
Last of the Just.* And that popular belief is, I am convinced, fundamentally correct and historically justified:
persecution is the paroxysm of social and historical discomfort; now malaise is consubstantial with the Jewish
fate.

Once again I shall be accused of dramatizing. One of
my liberal and intellectual bourgeois readers told me,
with that ironic compassion we grant worn-out ideas,
that I sounded like a Russian Jew of the year 1800. I did

not find the comparison either absurd or insulting. As I read the memoirs of Chaim Weizmann, first president of Israel, and as a matter of fact a little Russian Jew, I was frequently struck by the similarity of our experiences. And this confirmed my opinion that there actually is a Jewish fate, since it is common to both Russia and Tunisia. The difference lies in the date and the pride of Western Jews at having benefited from the tremendous and decisive European progress. Not till I had left my questioner, did I remember that he, too, had known exile: since he must have had to flee Europe, his home and his profession, to take refuge in the United States for the duration of the war. Or else what does he call exile? That desperate blindness of so many intellectual Jews to anything that touches on the Jewish fate might have prevented him from admitting it. The flight to America was not exile, he would have explained to me, and the Nazi experience was only an incident, and postwar European anti-Semitism is only a temporary sequel. The fact is that Jewish history goes on, always as aberrant, as monstrous and as rich in accidents, flights, uprootings, resettlements.

Persecution is only the ever-possible outcome of discomfort. It is the hardening into permanence of an unhealthy situation, the least evil side of which is malaise and the latent hostility of other men, and the crisis of which is the pogrom and open persecution. Exile, the wrench from one's home, material flight is only the extreme point of Jewish behavior when faced with the non-Jews' exasperated rejection; when that rejection calls for his physical disappearance; in other words, his death. In other words persecution and discomfort are not two ideas that I combine fortuitously from a love of the dramatic, but two expressions, more or less intense, of one same reality: the social and historical negativity of the Jew. Discomfort, more or less sharp, is its habitual norm, but persecution is not an accident, a negative phase among other negative conditions: it is evidence and proof of it enlarged. It reveals nothing, it confirms a chronic condition. That is why the actual absence of crises and catastrophes proves nothing, never completely reassures me. Hatred is more or less diffused, more or less easily managed; but it can always crystallize and gradually increase until it grips and paralyzes the Jew's whole life. Inversely, various negative conditions are only the explanation in detail, the small change, of the basic negativity of Jewish life. "To be a Jew means that nothing is given us," Clara Malraux, first wife of the writer, said to me once.

There is a negative unity of all Jewish destiny and of all individual Jewish destinies; an actual unity, a concrete negativity, as I have sufficiently explained, that crushes and marks that destiny in a certain way. It is not just the simple accusations, mere glances, calumnies, "insults that fly with the wind," I had already written about in regard to the colonized natives. The negative conditions of Jewish existence are as much actual difficulties in living, impossibilities, iron collars and knives, wounds and amputations, in his flesh and in his measure as a man.

To be a Jew is, naturally, not to have received as an out and out gift, those traditional blessings of good fairies: a native land, nationality, a place in history, etc. . . . As a Jew, those things will be bitterly disputed us; granted, taken back again, questioned, so that rarely can we measure up naturally to the current social dimensions of most men.

Those lacunae, those amputations and that emptiness in the life of a Jew, take different forms, of course, according to geography, historical incidents, special customs and the people among whom the Jew lives. They explain obviously the various physiognomies of the Jew throughout the world. Sometimes where religion is all-important in the non-Jew's life, the religious difference is very important: the Jew is excluded and punished chiefly because he is of a different religion. So true is this that, through a conjunction easy to understand, the Jew seems to care little about his own religion when the religion of non-Jews is friendly to him; but in countries where faith is intense and ritualism strictly adhered to, the Jew serves his own religion most faithfully. Sometimes the Jew appears as a national minority; he is then primarily a foreigner, who speaks the language of the country poorly and is fairly ignorant of its customs. Sometimes, as a recent emigrant, he is even ethnically different, in biological contrast to the people who accept him. But, in every case, at the base of the Jewish misfortune, one finds the same absence; it is another name for his misfortune. Through the diversity of individual Jewish lives scattered over the globe, and his social activities, it constitutes one of the fundamental threads of Jewish existence. And, unfortunately, it does not take me long to recognize it and find it again among all those people like us; under every clime I have almost always found the same shams and the same idiosyncrasies, the same hurts, the same fears and the same flights. Through the body and diversity of negative traits, that absence of Jews in the world in which they live, gives them a negative destiny, a true face in the shadows.

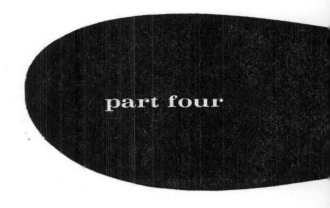

part four

THE HERITAGE

"Old Greenfeld lives in a world petrified into symbols and make-believe; but the rules of the make-believe have to be strictly adhered to. For the last two thousand years the believers left their doors open on Passover-eve for Messiah to walk in, and laid a cover for him to partake of their meal, and assured each other that "next year we shall celebrate in Jerusalem." They also sold all their plates and cutlery which had been in touch with leaven to their gentile neighbours, and bought them back when the festival of the unleavened bread was over. It was all make-believe, but this stubborn ritual alone held them together during the centuries of dispersion."

ARTHUR KOESTLER
(THIEVES IN THE NIGHT)

"They are peculiar . . . in preserving, in their dispersal, a definite, though fading, cultural unity. Among dispersed people they are probably unique in their spiritual and intellectual gifts, in the contributions they have made to civilization in general and to modern European civilization in particular."

JULIAN HUXLEY (WE EUROPEANS)

The Will to Live

ONE

I do not doubt that some of my readers are becoming impatient: is there nothing positive, no light side in Jewish existence? Is the history of the Jew and his life nothing but a long misfortune, an incessant persecution, more or less suppressed? Is the figure of the Jew nothing but that painful grimace that alone distinguishes him from other men?

It is time indeed to look at the other side of the picture; and I shall also answer clearly: whatever the importance of the Jewish misfortune, the Jew is by no means confined to his shadowy figure. In my personal history, the positive aspect was for a long time as vital as the negative. Even today my parents still periodically gather around them the whole family (surprisingly enlarged) at the tables of Passover, Purim or Rosh Hashanah; and I always rediscover with pleasure the blessed atmosphere of my childhood. Most of my brothers and sisters have made traditional marriages and Judaism is not unknown to my nephews. I have also said that I was brought up in a Jewish culture which I have certainly not forgotten. So one of my greatest surprises, on arriving in Europe, was to hear people deny any positive aspect to Jewish life.

Why have I dwelt at such length on the weaknesses and catastrophes in the life of the Jew before speaking of his hopes, his happiness and his opportunities? Why did I spontaneously begin with the passive? It is not so easy to explain and I will have to prod myself again. I have, however, an excellent alibi: in telling, above all, the story of my life, I preferred to tell it as it came to my mind. Now what came to me first, what fascinated me in this effort to recall and set the record straight, was the burden, the general nature, the persistence and the diversity of the misfortune. Nor was there anything original about my astonishment: I found almost always that my opinion was shared by Jews and non-Jews, friends and enemies. Everyone agrees that the life of the Jew is at least difficult to live, even if the difficulties are not the same for everyone, nor the responsibilities clearly established. As Heinrich Heine has so amusingly put it in *The Baths of Lucca*:

"Judaism? Don't speak to me of it, Doctor; I would not wish it on my worst enemy. . . . Abuse and disgrace, that is all it brings; it is not a religion, it is a misfortune."

I am not sure, however, that those were the best reasons. I ask myself, honestly, whether I am not even more embarrassed to speak of the positive aspects of our life. As if I were unveiling some fragile collective nakedness, I am not too eager, I well know, to undertake the chapter of positive differences: traditions, values, religion, collective habits that are strictly Jewish. Nor am I the only one to feel this. Too many Jews only speak of themselves negatively; often they even end by thinking of themselves only in the negative; to be a Jew is to be only a victim;

it is an absurd injustice. In that attitude there is nothing
but bad faith: in every way, most Jews today feel less
actively than passively Jews, a condition infinitely more
oppressing and heavier to bear than Jewish culture or
Jewish traditions. These latter, moreover, are lived and
breathed and noticed less than the restrictions. Even
when the Jew is a traditionalist, dedicated to his values
and his rites, he forces himself to treat that tradition, his
family life, the synagogue and his communal relations as
strictly private affairs, of which as little as possible must
be allowed to transpire before the eyes of his non-Jewish
fellow-citizens.

Why that more or less voluntary modesty or blindness,
that persistent discretion? It is, I believe, part of every
oppressed person's rejection of himself: in at least one
stage of his life, every oppressed person rejects himself.
The negative aspect is oppressive enough and conspicuous enough to call attention to itself. One understands
why so many Jews instinctively avoid emphasizing other
characteristics that might plunge them again into absurdity and injustice. By making a desperate effort to reject
himself and to camouflage his Jewishness, the Jew often
ends by not seeing it anymore, by no longer seeing himself
except as an embarrassment to himself, a hindrance to his
life as a man. The result of that embarrassment is that
curious agreement frequently noted between the Jew, his
friends and his enemies. I have already mentioned this in
another chapter: to everyone the Jew seems to be essentially a negative figure.

For what the enemy of the Jew believes the Jew to be
is *a priori*, a figure of evil, more or less somber, more or
less harmful. There is only a difference of degree, not of
nature, between the so-called objective and apparently
moderate remarks of certain intellectuals and the open
and, occasionally cruel, hatred exhibited by little Fascists
who regard the misfortune of the Jew as nothing but the

just punishment for his ugly nature or his vicious conduct. The Jew's friends, on the contrary, are moved either by generosity or by ignorance. Wishing to adopt the Jew, they force themselves through a natural reaction to believe that he is like them and not to see him as he is. Besides, as a rule, they honestly do not know him. How could they? Since the Jew conceals his real nature as much as possible, almost never speaks of his Jewishness and even tries to reduce it. The non-Jew of good-will who does not attribute to the Jew the gloomy stigmata of a mythical being, also fails to acknowledge the suffering and misfortune that are fostered by outward hostility. Jean-Paul Sartre, to whom I spoke of his book, *Reflections on the Jewish Question*, explains why he thought the Jew was nothing but a negativity: that was the only way in which all his Jewish friends seemed Jewish to him.

"When," he wrote in *Situations II*, "I tried to define the situation of the Jew, I found only this: The Jew is a man whom other men consider a Jew and who is obliged to make decisions starting from the situation in which he is placed. For there are qualities we acquire solely through the judgment of others."

Later he acknowledged that he was greatly surprised on reading certain Jewish authors, to discover that the Jew had another existence. And I am convinced that if the eminent author were to re-write his book, he would develop those positive aspects more fully. In any case, it is in that perspective, generous but mutilated, that we must place Sartre's concept of the Jew as the pure expression of non-Jews, a view that was so popular after World War II. It is a friendly concept, eager to help, to save the Jew, but not enough to take account of the reality of Jewish existence.

For the Jew, as for his friends, the rejection of Jewishness is a defense mechanism. It is a question of presenting the smallest possible grounds for the accusation, of making the Jew invisible. The non-Jew of good will is thus a victim of his own good intentions. To save the Jew from the accusation, he denies him; in order not to hand him over to his assailants, he claims he has never met a real Jew. The anti-Semite accuses the Jew of numerous machinations and attributes horrible characteristics to him. A methodical examination of those traits shows that they are non-specific, contradictory or outrageously exaggerated. The anti-Semite's portrait of a Jew is nothing but an accusation: it exists only in the mind of the anti-Semite. Far from enlightening us about the Jew, it shows up the psychology of the anti-Semite. The Jew is thus the plaything of the stupidity and the injustice of other men; his situation arises from a social and spiritual disgrace.

All that, as we have seen, is perfectly true. But the demonstration is only half valid. What does the Jew become through this experience? Nothing, or practically nothing; nothing as a Jew, certainly. As a man, I am like other men, neither more nor less. Cleansed of the accusing mud, I am of the same metal—gold or copper—as all humanity. Despite the efforts of recent philosophies, at bottom one finds the noble but abstract ambitions of traditional humanism. In their benevolent desire to defend the colonized, my colleagues among the professors in Tunisia denied sharply that they had the defects the colonizer imputed to them. That was laudable; but carried away by their zeal and, perhaps, in fear of being disturbed in their turn, they also denied the special qualities of the colonized. This resulted in a strange reaction some time later: when the colonized began to assert themselves, to demand the right to live according to their own customs and traditions, they also disconcerted their naïve defenders, who often turned against them. In short, a man is not just a piece of abstract humanity. The Jew is also and above all, a mass of special qualities, questionable qualities if you wish, admirable or detestable, positive and negative. It is my opinion, I repeat, that in some ways certain aspects of the accusation are true. I am not good solely because I am a Jew, just as the proletarian is not virtuous and honest because he is a proletarian.

If only such defensive measures actually saved the Jew! But instead of making him invisible or homogeneous to other men, they emphasize the absurdity of his fate: if he is so volatile, so like other men, why such a destiny? Why does that destiny irritate other men to such a degree? Far from making him invisible, it makes him more opaque and incomprehensible. In *Doctor Zhivago*, Boris Pasternak sees in the Jewish fate, in spite of several allusive notations, only an immense and poignant negativity, a point of view that called down on him the anger of all Jewish critics with cries of "Shameful Jew! Cheat!" I do not think it is so simple. Pasternak's hero, probably Pasternak himself, is sincerely helpless: he asks himself in despair: Why does the Jew continue to exist, if he is nothing, if he is only negation? Why should such an accusation and such suffering be attached to a nothing? Because he has failed to consider both the positive and the negative aspects, the Jew is no longer a man: he is an abstraction. If Jewishness is only a tissue of lies and misunderstandings, with that defamatory placard removed from his back, the Jew, in short, no longer exists.

TWO

When Jean-Paul Sartre's book appeared, I was still a student and enthusiastic about the new theories of this philosopher who represented us to a degree. But his book so disturbed me that I immediately picked up my pen. I tried to explain that he was mistaken, that he had not gone far enough. At that time, I did not dare to send him my manuscript, but I believe that my immediate and youthful reaction did reflect my somewhat vague but dominating feeling about Jewish reality. I remember that I ended my letter with the words: "Now, believe me, the Jew does exist, Jewishness survives!"

I am not just the accused, ostracized and persecuted creature whom I have tried to describe so far. Intent on disclosing the various aspects of my oppression, I have concluded that the shadows of Jewish life are as important as the lights; the Jew is as much what he is not, as what he is. But it is time to remember that the Jew exists in the fullest and most positive sense. I do not exist solely in connection with others and the accusation; to a large extent, I admit to a description independent of the obstacles of my life. It is true that my whole history, my whole being, my entire conduct, is warped by my situation in the midst of other men; but my life is not limited to those disturbances and those reactions. On the contrary, my reactions to other men, the choice I make constantly of my own free will, the continuity which, in spite of everything, I persist in giving my life, depend upon other factors which far exceed that negativity. The Jew is not just the man who is looked upon as a Jew, nor even the man who reacts to that idea. There is another side to him: he lives a Jewishness and a Judaism that are completely positive. And in large measure he accepts and confirms that Jewishness. I am well aware that not all Jews have had my experience of the Jewish tradition and of the ghetto; among the majority of my friends it was even more often fleeting, incomplete, an experience they hardly know, and something they partially rejected. But after all, it is a fact that they have remained Jews, that they continue to live this experience directly or indirectly. To a certain degree, which changes of course under various guises, and by sometimes long and tortuous detours, the Jew acknowledges himself, accepts himself and wants to be a Jew. I must add that he cannot do other than acknowledge himself, and whether he wants to or not, approve of himself.

I say first of all that there is a Jewish will to live in spite of doubts, hesitations, impatiences, disguises and rejections. I find it in myself and I find it around me in other individuals of the Jewish group. One can argue about it, be surprised at it, minimize or magnify it, but first we must recognize the fact that this people has stubbornly persisted in remaining alive throughout so many centuries, with an astonishing continuity which makes other men recognize them and makes them recognize themselves. This is not, I insist, a concession to historical and mystical explanations: I am merely noting an established and commonplace fact, verifiable by anyone, and from which one must start as the basis of any exegesis. It is starting from this fact, and in the interpretation of it, that sentimentality and irrationality can take over completely. But it is impossible for me not to mention it. I did not even need to think about it or make any inquiries to discover it; it was well-known and obvious in every Jewish concentration of any importance; it was a simple, global reality, in which we steeped ourselves in Tunisia. If I have cast a doubt on it, tried to test its soundness and simplicity, it was merely a secondary impulse.

I know too that that affirmation of self, that continued confirmation, that sometimes veiled or deceitful persistence often provokes among the most humanistic and the most universalist of non-Jews a kind of annoyed astonishment. It seems to come from blindness or from stupidity, if not from historical impudence: how can the Jew still care about himself if he is so undesirable, so miserable, so maltreated by men and by history? By suggesting that he become other than he is, by permitting him to become part of other men, do they not give him a magnificent present? How can he hesitate a second to accept it?

Now not only does he hesitate, he usually ends by refusing it. The inhabitants of the ghetto and even our bourgeoisie, settled for generations in the European community, had no deep desire to become Moslems or Catholics. They wanted, at the most, to forget their encumbering Jewishness. They spoke of it as little as possible to other men, and when they were obliged to do so, they minimized it, softened it, or even pretended to treat it with disdain. But from that to becoming something else! What a catastrophe, what a sudden, uncontrolled upheaval in those so-called progressive families when one of their daughters, carrying the process of assimilation to extremes, decided to turn Catholic! Moreover, one had only to note the extraordinary failure of all those Christian missions on the soil of Africa, hovering vainly around ghettos. In spite of their wonderful promises and their real efforts to improve the lives of the new converts, they succeeded only in detaching a few adolescents going through a mystical crisis. For my part, in any case, no matter how much I examined myself, I was never seriously tempted to accept the famous gift. To be sure, it has often happened and it still happens, that I reveal that impatient refusal of myself, in everyday matters, in my behavior and in my thoughts. But in a way this is in spite of that will to live, and at the same time as I reveal the deep-seated affirmation.

THREE

Were I asked to explain that will to live, I confess that I would be embarrassed to have to do so. Why that mistrust of other men and that persistence in living, in persevering in oneself? Perhaps simply because the gift is poisoned or it is far from being as free as it seems to be. Another time I shall show the price one pays as far as conversion is concerned. Is it advantageous for the Jew to keep on living? One can argue the point; in any case, the Jew does live. One can attempt all possible explanations of this fact: a metaphysical idea, a socio-historical complex, a mass of mental attitudes, an extraordinary gift of a people who are always vital in spite of so many miseries, or instinctive defense on the other hand of a group of men always on the alert, or historical chance which has made these people survive, alone among so many others? The fact remains.

We have also tried, as we know, to get to the bottom of this fact, to reduce it to its opposite: in that case, far from possessing such a vital will to live, the Jew would be afflicted with a stubborn will to destroy himself. If the Jew persists in living, it is out of masochism, they say, because he wants to nurture his own misfortune. One of my faculty colleagues told me:

"I have never seen such self-executioners as my Jewish friends!" Some one has recently invented a new term to designate this ancient idea and even a new branch of instruction; victimology, which would study victimation: the Jew suffers from victimation and that is why he is a victim! In the same way, we were also told that if the colonized native has been colonized . . . it is because he was fit for colonization. Fine logic indeed: if the Jew is a victim it is because he could be victimized. But all joking aside, I grant that there is some masochism in most Jews.

However, it is most often a fear of misfortune and not any particular desire for suffering. Perhaps also, sometimes a sort of vertigo in the face of approaching and inevitable catastrophe. To put an end to it, to terminate the anguish that precedes the crisis, the victim ends by calling for it, by unleashing it himself in order to get it over. I told about a waiting period of this sort in one of my books, before a pogrom that never came to anything. But believe me, we did not feel cheated because it did not come off! In any case, this masochism, or this victimation, this profound Jewish anxiety, which is indisputable and which is, above all, fear and resignation in the face of a terrible fate, does not in the least exclude the will to live. Far from weakening it, on the contrary, it would prove its existence by the violence and vitality of its conflicts. Far from allowing himself to die, far from dying out through weakness like so many other groups, the Jew continues to live through horrible convulsions; which would prove, if there were need, that he is not tired of living and that he has never renounced it. I do not deny the anxiety, the suffering, the tempting neurosis, but that is not all there is. Besides, would it not be paradoxical that, beset with such rage for self-destruction the Jew has succeeded in preserving himself so long? Must we not think, on the contrary, that he was endowed with an uncommon will to survive to have withstood such violence, his own and that of other men?

As you see, I do not persist in discovering the exact genesis of this will to live. And I confess that, however interesting the problem may be, it does not seem essential to me, nor certainly, easy to solve: we probably find ourselves again before a logical circle. It can be claimed that this will to live would have disappeared if the Jew had not been so greatly persecuted. The immediate retort is: if the Jew has aroused such persecution, it is because that very vitality is still intact from being renewed throughout the ages and now his neck is too tough to be broken permanently. I am convinced that the two propositions go hand in hand: that will of the Jew to live, that tenacity in continuing to exist, has been forged for him by misfortunes; and inversely, that indomitable and irritating presence attracts and perpetuates that misfortune. The wisest thing, I believe, is to start from this will to live as a fundamental fact and to try to describe it in its varied manifestations, rather than to argue about its problematical genesis. I would gladly say, moreover, that this will to live must be considered as a prime and fundamental fact of all existence in individuals and in groups. From the psycho-analytical viewpoint: the human being goes on living as long as the life instinct is stronger than the death instinct. We can obviously still insist on going beyond this fact and seeking a deeper and more radical explanatory hypothesis: why does the human being live instead of die? Why is the life instinct stronger, at least temporarily, than the death instinct? But for the moment, we cannot go beyond the limits we have set.

And finally, there is the objection which crops up every time this inexhaustible Jewish problem is discussed. Let us admit this will to live: but why does it express itself in a non-Jewish will to live? Why is the Jew not content to live? Why does he cling to his Jewishness which he thus helps to perpetuate and which perpetuates him as a Jew —and unhappy?

Here we have the same question and the same sophism again. I do not know whether there is a will to live of man in general and a will of individual man. Man lives spontaneously in a certain manner: by asserting himself he makes himself felt through his emotions, his thoughts and his values. When the Negro asserts himself, he asserts himself as a Negro. The Jew, striving to survive, strives to live as a Jew. Like everyone else I have sometimes tried to distinguish between the man I am and my peculiarities, between the man and the Jew in me. In short, I have tried to fight against my Jewishness. Far from being natural and basic, the operation is at best harrowing and painful. The basic fact, on the contrary, is that synthesis which has already been made, which is my existence, which I find in me and before me, already sketched and full of meaning. And the basic and moreover happy impulse is to accept myself. It is only afterwards that I question myself and that the difficulties begin. Basically I cannot live without a minimal acceptance of my own fate.

The contrary attitude would be surprising, unusual, subtle and paradoxical. And frightening, too; in that constant suspicion, that corrosive challenging of my being, I cannot give up my positivity completely. Surrounded by a hostile universe, what else could we do in those helpless ghettos, but cling to each other? Far from being historical arrogance, that obstinacy was the only escape from, the only parry to annihilation. That positivity, even partial, toned down, or ignorant of itself, was the sole inner refuge against total despair.

Solidarity

ONE

Periodically, the newspapers of our community submitted a ritual discussion to us: is there a Jewish solidarity? Last winter, an Algerian newspaper took up the same question again; it is indeed the perfect kind of fascinating journalistic inquiry for a Jewish newspaper and one that never misses its goal. It is not a question, however, of simple astuteness: the question corresponds to one of the classic motives of the accusation: a close community of interests unites the Jews, the anti-Semite always declares, and that solidarity increases their terrible efficiency against non-Jews. Vance Packard has confirmed the persistence of the accusation in America; and before World War II, the French philosopher, Gabriel Marcel, made one of his Jewish characters say:

"Our people stand together: no sooner does one of them reach the top than he turns and holds out his hand to the others. In that lies a contradiction they will never recognize. They want to be considered Frenchmen like all the others and at the same time they treat each other as though they were members of a freemasonry." (*Le signe de la croix,* quoted by Aubry, *op. cit.,* p. 229.)

That is why the Jewish reader generally replies indignantly: "No! There is no such thing as Jewish solidarity!" The journalist on the Algerian weekly did not fail to come to the same conclusion, stating bitterly that he has never had the benefit of the slightest aid from his co-religionists. Well, I can only say that, on the contrary, I believe there *is* a Jewish solidarity and it would be most surprising if there were not. I have the pleasure of knowing that journalist who made the statement. He earns his living by giving lectures to Jewish audiences and by publishing articles in essentially Jewish newspapers. What does he call solidarity? Bernard Lazare, the author of the first serious study on anti-Semitism, definitely recognized its existence.

That this solidarity may be very effective or directed against non-Jews is another matter. In Tunis, as I have said, I had an opportunity to see at close hand the responsible members of our community in a dramatic moment of our history. I saw only wretched, panic-stricken men, who did not know which way to turn. There was no special emissary, no appeal to any mysterious authority, no secret and formidable conspiracy; only a terrified surrender to an incomprehensible fate. International Jewry, the Jewish-Masonic, Jewish Bolshevik or Jewish capitalist plutocracy, the famous Sages of Zion, are nothing but sinister rumors. In my naïvité, I tried later to find out whether there was any secret organization, any leading representative of Jews. I found nothing. There is not even a general, centralized will, for the grave events in our lives that would have called for a single strong decision. Read the story of the beginnings of Zionism: it shows an incredible indifference, followed by a surprising disper-

sion of efforts. The pioneers of the national Jewish rebirth obtained only with difficulty, the ear of responsible
Jews who then changed their minds several times. What
the anti-Semites write of Jewish solidarity generally results from the crassest stupidity. In my deference toward
culture and the printed word, as a once-poor man from
the East, it took me some time to admit to myself that
people who write, teach and speak in public, could be
such vain and stupid liars. And the public who listens to
them, who buys their books and their newspapers, has
the masters it deserves. How could Jewish solidarity be so
efficacious against non-Jews when it is frequently so un-
decided, so derisive toward the Jews themselves?

And yet, that solidarity does exist. But its necessary
existence is clarified when it is viewed in the light of that
Jewish will to live. Here, as always, we must distinguish
between the real basis of the accusation and a frenzy that
has no connection with reality. Jewish solidarity is much
more commonplace and more intelligible than the gloomy
machinations of the Jewish myth: Jewish solidarity exists
because the Jew exists. It is one of the attributes, both
negative and positive, reactionary and permanent, of the
Jewish group in so far as it exists as a group. It is one of
the manifestations of the Jew's existence among non-Jews.

In the presence of the black Jews of Ethiopia, the Falla-
chas, or the mystics of Central Europe, the Naturai-Karta,
my first reaction was a feeling of intense strangeness. I
did not recognize myself among those "flutterers" and that
fanaticism or in that black primitiveness. At first I saw
only strange men and did not recognize them as Jews.
And yet, once past that first impression, even in the presence of those Jews so different from mine, I discovered in
myself another emotion, a certain complicity, a fellow-
feeling greater than I would have felt before another
segment of humanity: the intuition of a certain similarity of destiny, displaced in time, lived differently but sev-

eral landmarks of which remained the same. First of all, of course, the community of risks. In the isolation, the extraordinary vulnerability, of those Jewish families I met in Southern Algeria, I could not help seeing my own situation carried to the extreme—the situation of a man helpless in a world of unpredictable hostility. Their relations with their neighbors were not necessarily bad, but the lives of those four or five Jewish families, lost in the midst of a Moslem conglomeration in the heart of the desert, depended so completely on the will, the mood of the neighborhood, that I felt a familiar anguish for them. They represented, in a nutshell, the whole Jewish fate. Whatever the distance that separates me from a certain part of Jewry in the world, I know that we are living a similar experience. What touches them, what affects them, may one day touch and affect me. They must suffer the same apprehensions I do, the same expectations, the same ordeals.

And frequently, the danger lies not so much in a potential fate, as in the geographical position of a real present-day community. The germ of the plague or the grippe crosses all frontiers: tracts printed in Belgium come to France to rekindle the hatred of French anti-Semites. So that when Jews are persecuted anywhere in the world, it is time for me to begin to worry: there is no certainty that the awakening of the disease in Belgium or in Germany will not this time be an epidemic that will end by affecting me in my turn. Do not tell me that all men are equally interdependent in the face of illness and death: the germ here is selective, it strikes only the circumcised or those who are presumed to be circumcised.

TWO

That minimal, almost negative, solidarity is, as I well know, merely the expression of Jewish negativity. But though it is the most definite expression, it never exists alone. I sympathized with the Jews of Saharian Mzab or with the Jews of Djerba first because we were aware of the same basic vulnerability, the same dangers and the same fears. But our relations were not limited to their strange and touching attentions towards me the moment they recognized me, that partnership that they immediately invented with me in the midst of all those Moslems —the men's happy winks and the women's stifled laughter. They were determined to make me visit the old synagogue and if I did not offer too much resistance, they led me to their homes. There they showed me the name of God above their doorways and their huge and very ancient book of Hebrew; and if this happened to be the festival season, as it frequently was during my trips, they made me attend the ceremony, and there I suddenly found again, beyond the Mzab and the desert, Arab garments and the special inflections of their language, our common background. And while we rested we talked of the Talmud and of Israel: they quoted Hebrew proverbs I vaguely understood, mentioned famous rabbis of whom I had vaguely heard. Then they questioned me about modern Israel. Had I been in *Eretz*-Israel, in the blessed land of our people? How fortunate I was! It must surely be a marvelous land: the Bible says so again and again. Was it true that . . . ? We had, therefore, a common past which they felt more intensely than I did, and I could give them information about a possible common future. Jewish solidarity is both negative and positive: completely positive because it is founded on the existence and the reality of Jewish fate: always positive in some way even though oblivious of or unconcerned about itself.

But more than that, Jewish solidarity does not exhaust itself in passive positivity; it contains more than that. It does not confine itself to discovering other Jews, to a more or less vigorous approval of Jewishness. Most of the time it acts. And that action is not only a defensive reaction to a negative destiny, it is also its positive reverse, a reassuring basic principle, auxiliary to the life of the Jew.

Confronted with the open or secret hostility of other men, I am at first inclined to try to disarm them. I can multiply my grimaces and protestations, I can, less frequently, try threats and firmness. All these practices are, in any case, unnatural and exhausting—assuming, moreover, that they may be effective. Why, in the long run, would I not simply withdraw as frequently as possible from such trying relationships? This explains those gatherings of Jews better than any mysterious calculations I know. Is it not the most natural, the most economical reaction to find oneself among Jews, "among ourselves?" To live the important part of one's leisure hours or even one's working hours among Jews? Or where Jews are in the majority, which comes to the same thing, since there hostility becomes impossible? Why deny it? Where you find one Jew, you are sure to find others. Jews have a tendency to gather in groups. In primary school, in high school, we preferred to have Jewish friends. My friends among the professors have often confirmed that. The partitions are fortunately not tight, but in general young Jews tend to go together. Later on I saw many a proof of this: a Jewish bourgeois "salon," even the most enlightened, the most "progressive" is by a large majority Jewish. It is not altogether intentional, of course, but happens with remarkable frequency. In Tunisia it was even simpler: each group lived to itself with a few guests of honor; even the voluntary gatherings, political, social or cultural, had one dominating note. The Communist milieu boasted of being the most open, which was true; but it was predominantly Jewish, and Jews could indeed feel at home there.

From that to crying Machiavellianism and permanent

conspiracy, the temptation is strong. What goes on in those gatherings of Jews? And why such gatherings? Is it not a sort of Freemasonry as the good Christian philosopher, Gabriel Marcel, wrote? An inventory is always taken —and with what triumph—of the co-workers of each Jewish minister of state, or of important Jews in the business world. The result is not always satisfactory and the anti-Semite then has no choice but to keep quiet. Many Jews, I am well aware, make a point of indignantly rejecting any idea of solidarity. I have seen Jewish faculty professors carefully turn down any Jewish colleague. But their very efforts are significant: they are trying to ward off the accusation. They reject that solidarity precisely because other Jews expect it of them and non-Jews suspect them of it. For the most part they systematically practice a solidarity in reverse. It is useless to add how inglorious I find that attitude.

Do I even dare say what follows without shocking my reader? The only normal attitude, the healthiest, in any case the most common, would be to bring into the group whoever around him had the required qualities. The automatic, the most spontaneous result would be, perhaps, to surround oneself with colleagues of one's own side. I do not say it is the fairest or the most desirable conduct, but that is neither unusual conduct nor is it done with intent to harm others. The contrary, I think, would imply a preliminary and deliberate line of action. I tried to show this in regard to economy; it is first of all a semimechanical concentration without any definite intention; in any case it is not directed against anyone in particular. An administrator, a politician who needs a colleague, looks around spontaneously. He naturally sees young men he knows, who have already approached him or have been recommended to him. The probabilities are he will find himself engaging men in his own circle, among his own relatives. This is nepotism and nepotism is by no means specifically Jewish. Who knows the number of sons-in-law and nephews, not to mention sons, who owe their careers to their birth or their connections? Why should the Jews be the only ones to refuse to employ their own people?

A friend of mine explained the mechanism very simply. "One of my young brothers," he told me, "comes to Paris. Can I help him to find work? I immediately think of our uncle, who has a drygoods shop on the rue de Clery. But at the same time I hold my tongue, I say nothing to the boy. Nor does he either, though I am sure he has thought of our uncle. I give him some vague advice: 'You should try this or that . . .' Time passes and, of course, the boy does not find anything suitable. He digs up a little job which folds after several days; he tries to place I don't know what sort of unsaleable gadgets. At last he comes back to me; thin, collar open, unshaven . . . Then of course I send him to our uncle. The uncle groans, but why not this boy instead of some unknown employee? Besides, the young man is not stupid and after all perhaps it might be an advantage to have his own nephew among his employees. In short, he takes the boy. The boy, as I told you, is not a fool; and the uncle is really very fond of him. Six months later, he is a sort of confidential adviser to the house and later . . . In any case, this is why the du Sentier quarter, the quarter of Jewish merchants—it is perfectly true—has a majority of Jewish employees."

Can one go any further? The ground becomes more slippery and yet one has to press on. Does a Jewish solidarity sometimes try to intervene in politics for example? There is talk from time to time of pressure being brought to bear by American Jews or American policy or of a campaign by the consistory of French Jews. Strictly speaking there is no Jewish policy. I have noted also how timid, hesitant and even fearful those interventions are when they do occur. They may even be contradictory or harmful; the leading adversary of the Jews at the 1918 Peace Conference, which had to decide the fate of the future Jewish state, was a Jew, Sylvain Levi, representative of the French Jewish bourgeoisie. The most rabid against the global interests of Jewish groups are often Communist Jews. But I have already said how much I regretted it; far from deploring those fragmentary and hesitant attempts, I would have preferred an open and more concentrated affirmation.

Why do Jews not make an effort to defend themselves, even to a small degree, as Jews? Why does not a group, living in its own special fashion (and why wouldn't it live in a special fashion since it exists? it is different and so considered) react in its own way to protect its life? What is so surprising or illegal in that? The truth is that people are so accustomed to seeing the Jew not defend himself, that his practically unorganized resistance seems to be a shocking provocation. Far from apologizing, I am humiliated that we have not been able to return the blows; that we cannot still return them in the majority of cases. How dare the philosopher, Gabriel Marcel, a Christian and a member of that formidable organization the Catholic Church, talk of Freemasonry in the face of the derisive efforts of the Jews!

THREE

I believe, in short, that every living group is interdependent. Jewish solidarity is in the first place one example of the vast solidarity of all oppressed persons, a defense reaction of a particularly vulnerable group. On these grounds mutual aid and active intervention are not peculiar to Jews. One finds them mentioned frequently in the works of Negro novelists or of North African writers at the same time as one finds other clearly contradictory manifestations. Certain passages in *The Apple*

Blossom Queen, the novel by the American, Chester Himes, reminded me strikingly of the memoirs of la Medina of Tunis: that miraculous cart that appears in the nick of time to save the hero; the way the Negroes ganged up against the white police. Against such determination the oppressor is helpless; for he is the one who arouses that solidarity; it is useless to get angry at a reply to his own aggression.

But solidarity includes more than cases of stated oppressions. It is also the way all isolated peoples, all minorities, defend themselves against solitude and danger. It is a means of reassuring oneself and of confirming oneself when outnumbered or when confronted with money, political power or simply a hostile geography. The other day I was amused to discover that a certain Paris editor, a Protestant, born in Switzerland, was surrounded chiefly by Protestant and Swiss employees. He did not pay them more than the normal rate and they did not work longer hours; but both employer and employees felt more at ease working together. Corsican solidarity was famous in Tunisia and I know dozens of stories on that subject. Alsatian newspapers carefully report every accident in which Alsatians are killed. It is, moreover, amusing to note that those very people who deny that there is a Jewish solidarity are ready to proclaim the existence of a universal solidarity in which I also believe. It is solidarity that gives such extraordinary value to a word, a human presence, in the threatening solitude of the desert. My wife and I had a surprising reception one evening in a little town in Sicily where we arrived late at night. That poor little village lost in the mountain seemed to us an unhoped-for haven of warmth and brotherliness which saved us from the agony of the chill night. The Sicilians from that little mountain village, who voted the Communist ticket, thought, from my name, that I was an Italian writer from Tunisia and a writer of the Left as well. I am convinced, though I do not deplore it, that universal solidarity is the extension of a narrower, simpler and more commonplace sentiment; the attraction of like for like, and not the reverse.

In a general sense, solidarity is a matter of establishing or of re-establishing communication with other men. Now the Jew's communication with other men is too often difficult or endangered or simply mistrustful. For several years I directed a center of psycho-pedagogical councils in Tunisia. Our non-Tunisian colleagues who were neither Jews nor Moslems, certainly brought an equal devotion and enthusiasm to bear on our common task. But I realized that that was obviously not always enough. How hopefully the Jewish consultants asked me: "Are you a Jew? Do you speak the dialect?" Did they hope to get additional favors from me? Yes, of course. For solidarity is undeniably active. One expects something from it. It is first of all recognition. The consultant is lost in a new setting which he finds menacing in a more or less strange and painful situation. Then he recognizes someone and is recognized by him: This man is one of his own people, he will understand him, and with him he will be able to talk freely. Communication thus established, he feels that he is a human being again, he begins to live as an interrogator and as a man. This phenomenon, I repeat, is not even specifically Jewish. Dr. Leguillant, chief physician in the psychiatric hospitals of Paris, and a Breton by birth, told me that patients of Breton origin were transformed when they learned that their doctor came from the same part of France. Their eyes lighted up and they began at last to talk . . . in the Breton dialect. I believe simply that recognition is stronger where existence is more confined, more in danger: which explains why solidarity is stronger among Jews than among non-Jews, stronger among the working classes than among the bourgeoisie.

My Jewish consultants were not satisfied to be treated as men in general, that is to say as men in the abstract. They wanted to be recognized as individuals with their own particularities. Then only did they feel reassured; they were no longer repressed, they literally blossomed out in all directions, in all their dimensions. They could allude by swift but sure references to their past, their culture, to everything they were. They could speak their mother tongue, dialect or slang, they knew they would be understood. They could put aside their paralyzing modesty, they knew in advance they would meet neither malevolence nor irony since their language, their past, their culture, their poverty, their oddities or their absurdities were the same as those of the man who questioned them. The words Talmud, Bible, Moses, Ghetto, Yom Kippur do not have the same importance on my lips nor the same savor when I speak them in the presence of a Jew or of a non-Jew. Moreover, I do not use them in the same way; you do not throw a ball at the same angle or with the same force at a wall or in the air or in the water. In a world that is too often stifling and restrictive, Jewish solidarity allows Jews that release of self, that resonance. To be sure, one can often call the signals without obtaining the reply; the communication is not established if the Jew refuses. Or rather: the appeal may embarrass or annoy him for very simple reasons: a reminder of his Jewishness may call forth that rejection of self that slumbers in every Jew. I remember having been curtly and firmly sent away by a Jewish professor at the Sorbonne of whom I had been mistakenly told that he did not deny being a Jew. All I asked of him was to listen while I told him briefly how uprooted I felt in a world too new to me. But I was his student and that was already too much. That conversation would have established a slight connection between us, and this he did not want. Now, years later, I realize that I vaguely expected it. Solidarity is, in short, expectation and complicity; an expectation more or less satisfied, more or less disillusioned.

That is why, after all, it appears to be an actual duty, which one expects to see realized. Such, in any event, has been my experience. In spite of periods of detachment, impatience or even rejection, I have almost always felt actively responsible for other Jews. I can, of course, refuse that responsibility and not respect the duties it entails as do many Jews. But how can I close my ears to the claims of my people and how can I prevent their surprised resentment? I confess that I cannot help feeling terribly guilty for what may happen to them.

Solidarity answers a demand and a need, a demand both negative and positive: "How can you do that to a Jew?" is a current expression among some people. Jews who deny the existence of a Jewish solidarity do so most often in such anger and show such resentment at that charge of insolvency, that in spite of themselves, they prove the contrary, that they expected the criticism and found it quite natural. People complain that Jewish organizations have not done this or that, that they have not done enough—which means, of course, that they ought to do something. When the French Jews were reproached for not having sufficiently aided German or Polish refugees, it was an implicit admission that they should have aided them.

And why not say so after all? As a matter of fact, this duty is widely and concretely met throughout the greater part of Jewry. One may cast aspersions on it and find it insufficient, one may propose a total reorganization of the community and of the social order; but the mutual aid of the Jewish community is one of the most remarkable in the world. Within a given Jewish community no Jews are allowed to die of hunger. The Jew is never completely forsaken by the community to which he belongs; frequently he is not forsaken even by communities which he joins by accident. It is obvious that he must present himself as a Jew! In other words he recognizes other Jews in order to be recognized by them. When I arrived in Algiers to begin my studies there, I did not have a single possession to my name. I was saved from an ugly experience thanks only to the Jews of that city. But before I found them, I had appealed to a Catholic priest to whom I had been recommended for a small job. The pitiable comedy he played with me, his hopes and the price I was to pay for his aid, were so transparent that I had either to comply or deceive him, which to me, in the intransigeance of my nineteen years, seemed equally impossible. The Jews asked nothing in exchange. Knocking automatically at their door, I introduced myself as a Jew and reminded them that they too were Jews. I was not called upon to smirk, make promises or to change my skin; on the contrary, all I had to do was to be myself or what they supposed me to be. With one stroke I confirmed their existence, our relations and their duties towards me.

The Heritage

I fear that I have placed too much emphasis on the voluntary aspect of solidarity; and the expression "the will to live" is, basically, fairly ambiguous. I recall a time when I, too, repeated arrogantly to anyone who would listen: "To be a Jew is a choice!" By that I meant: "Admire my courage; against wind and tide and, without being forced to, I have made up my mind to be a Jew!" Like most young animals, I believed for a long time that I had, to begin with, a great and marvelous freedom at my disposal. When I discovered that the Jewish fate was restrictive, curbed, I began to rebel. I hesitated between a systematic revolt and an impassioned claim; I fluctuated between not being a Jew at all or being one insolently and provocatively. With the result that I maintained whatever role I chose and, apparently, my freedom.

Now all that was fairly false. That puerile pride was based on an optical illusion.

Neither the Jewish will to live, nor solidarity, nor belonging to Jewry, are the results of a free choice. A man is not a Jew because he decides to be one: he discovers that he is a Jew, then he either consents or refuses . . . without ceasing to be one. Of course he is a Jew in a different way depending upon his refusal or his approval, but in any case he is still a Jew. It is a matter of age, perhaps. Since those days I have discovered, rightly or wrongly and even before those impassioned decisions, that the important thing was to take stock of what I really was in relation to the world and to other Jews. Only then, after I had admitted the essential facts, made up my mind and recognized my duties towards my own people and towards other men, would I perhaps be able to find a moderate if not a definitive peace.

Now it is clear that one always feels a close kinship with one's own people, even if they repel you, even if they irritate you. Even several years ago I was surprised to find that when I was in a strange city, I was glad to meet other Jews. It reassures me, I suppose, makes the city seem more homelike to me. Most Jews acknowledge this more or less tardy experience, this obvious awareness of their firm ties with other Jews—and not only when they are in trouble either. But that admission is not enough. In presenting solidarity or the will to live as inner experiences, as struggles of conscience, sharp though they may be, I run the risk of failing to show clearly that there is an objective side to them. Even when one insists on the reactive aspect of solidarity or of the will to live, one cannot deny that objectivity and that exteriority. The oppressed person is, to be sure, interdependent in his reaction to oppression, but after all, in the crucial moment he is sure to find at his service the help of other oppressed persons; the hiding-place in the Casbah, the helping hand of other proletarians. He discovers a collective fact that serves him and is greater than he is and to which, some day, he contributes in his turn, thus carrying on the great collective gesture. I would almost say that the subjective aspects of Jewishness are, in the end, the least restrictive. To a certain extent I can decide to remain apart from the life of the community, I can ultimately free myself of all responsibility towards it. Nevertheless, the community in which I live, the entire Jewry, offer themselves to me, thrust themselves upon me as exterior and objective facts. I can uphold them or deny them; neither my blindness nor my voluntary deafness will rob them of existence or suppress those very real, very objective and very menacing problems that every Jewish life in the world encounters, mine included.

In fact, the farther I have advanced in taking stock of my Jewishness, the more I have confirmed the resistance to it, a flexible insistence on it. The problems of recognition, of approval or disapproval of my people and of myself, have certainly been of great concern to me, as they have to the majority of young Jews. That is one of the characteristics of our problem. But so much passion was obviously based on a firm foundation. I can recognize myself as a Jew or pretend to forget it, I can seek to develop myself as a Jew, or attenuate or hide my Jewish characteristics. But in a certain way, I am already outside of myself; in a certain way the Jew is above all a Jew. Jewishness is first of all a collection of facts, conduct, customs which I find in myself, but especially outside of myself, throughout my entire life. Before they become the object of my choice, a decision of my will, these are, in short, social facts. Their confirmation or their uncertainty, important as they may be, are supplementary steps.

I should say that to misunderstand this fact or to carelessly forget it is characteristic only of Western Jews and more particularly of their bourgeoisies. And, for this, the anonymity and dispersion of large European cities are perhaps equally to blame. In every Jewish concentration of any importance one notes, on the other hand, the persistence, at least formal, of Jewish traditions, values and institutions, even those that are disputed and scorned by Jews themselves. I come from a country where rabbis still had the power to put a Jew in prison! They would certainly not have dared to intervene in a quarrel unless both parties were willing; but as recently as 1958, there were enough inhabitants in the ghetto requesting that arbitration to fill a rabbinical court. Family life and its organic solidarity, religion and the synagogue, the community and its procession of poor people, the successive rituals that mark the life of any Jew: circumcisions, the Bar-Mitzvah (first Communion), the obligatory religious marriage, death and the private cemetery—made any doubt of Jewish positivity such as exists in Europe, utterly ridiculous. Our liabilities were to be sure greatly criticized. Our life was passed within narrow bounds; we had hardly any share in the conduct of public affairs in the city; we were not even citizens in the eyes of the law. But, after all, very few people were and that did not seem to us so harsh because we lived tightly among ourselves. That warmth, that collective presence was unconsciously our whole world. I did not fully understand that until later when I discovered the ill-balanced negativity of the Jews in Europe, and my own surprising nostalgia for the vast lost community which was to all of us a kind of common soul.

I know the prompt objection certain of my friends will offer: "Not I! We did not celebrate many festivals in my parents' home." One man adds: "Look! I was not even married in a religious ceremony!" And another, the most daring, declares: "I did not have my son circumcised!" Such boldness: their voices, their eyes proclaim it even as they announce it proudly, thus belying their assurance and revealing, in spite of themselves, the vitality of Jewish rites. Then I ask the man who was not married by religious ceremony: "But have you had your son circumcised?" And to the man who did not have his son circumcised, I say: "But were you married by religious ceremony?" The replies to both questions are generally, "Yes, yes!" How often, in talking with a Jewish revolutionary, a Communist, for instance, who seems completely free of all Jewish ties or any anxiety about the Jewish destiny, or even better, who openly fights any separate consideration of that destiny, have I discovered that he had an acknowledged Jewish past. He received a religious education, was at first part of a Youth Movement or had been a Zionist. And immediately I discover that that apparent lack of positive Jewishness is of recent origin, deliberate and a matter of strategy. Most often the accuser is misled by a political and cerebral position which is very superficial for understanding many intellectual or bourgeois Jews.

But here we must leave the personal point of view or at least go far beyond it. In these matters we are too much the heir of philosophic individualism, which barely expresses the present human reality. Whether I myself am married by religious ceremony or not, my brothers and my sisters as well as my cousins and the majority of my friends, have obeyed the rites. I may, or I may not, decide to have my son circumcised, but almost all of my nephews have been. I no longer celebrate Passover, but every year I am urgently invited to celebrate it in my parents' home. My mother never fails to inform me of the approach of all the festivals. Every year, after the fast of Yom Kippur, I go to embrace my father and my mother; and even though I have not fasted, this does not prevent them from offering me the first glass of lemonade with which we break the fast, and which I accept with a smile. The Jew who denies Jewish positivity is guilty of immodesty; Jewish positivity does not depend upon him: he is the one who depends upon it. Even were he to reject it, to doubt everything, even to dispensing with the collective customs of his people completely, he would still be powerless to change all that world about him in which he has his place, those ties of family, marriage, connections, that thread of traditional meanings, both cultural and historical, which he thinks he can deny, but which sustain him and give him his real physiognomy.

TWO

For, after all, it is not the same thing to have had a long history, a rich, cultural tradition, and not to have had one. As a Jew, I am heir to a powerful tradition and culture. Traditionalists are right to speak of a "Legacy of Israel": as Jews we are rich heirs.

I can fail to recognize the extent of the lands of that heritage, the number of horses, the geography and the importance of the wells; the invader has often ridden roughshod over the frontiers, carried off cattle, uprooted trees. But I know that the heritage is great and almost inexhaustible; and above all that it is there, within reach of my hand. That has not prevented me, and very often, from rebelling frequently against the supremacy of the Tribe, from mocking the words of the ancients. Would I even say that, in my opinion, it is the best way to live a culture? The other way, that scrupulous and obedient submission to detail, is a way of embalming. But in discussing the teaching of my fathers, in debating against the written and the oral word, I nevertheless am nourished by it. I can even reject completely the riches of my people, give it away, dissect their teaching bit by bit, exorcise it of all false prestige Explained, rationalized, humanized, restored to its place in the perspective of all the cultures in the world, it still occupies a considerable space. And it is always mine in some fashion, since at least it once was mine: "It is always on me," as they used to say in the ghetto. Goetz von Berlichingen, Sartre's hero in *The Devil and the Good Lord*, discovers it is one thing to be poor after having been rich, and another never to have known riches. At least I have been rich: it is not true that one can forget that.

I am not even sure that I seriously wish to forget it. If my people had not had so much trouble in other respects, why would it have occurred to me to forget who I am, I who am so rich with such ancient riches? And when, in a burst of pride, I try to remember who I am, I turn instinctively to that heritage. After all, I say to myself, it is a fabulous heritage! The next moment, it is true, I laugh at myself for that proprietary reflex, the reflex of the prodigal son, tempted to go back home, to receive his father's blessing and the advantages of life in a community. But though I can make fun of details, at heart I do not find it ridiculous to belong to the "People of the Book," as they all call themselves; my people and non-Jews in agreement on this point. And in moments of distress, too, why not admit it? I know that this at least is left me: that culture and that tradition, that extraordinary age-old refuge of all Jews that stands unscathed through so many storms and all the firmer because they themselves have strengthened it against the tempests. That refuge is still surprisingly habitable precisely because they themselves have fashioned it throughout the ages with their own bones which history has gathered, burned and pulverized; with their own ingenuity, with their own spirit which is always on guard. All his life my Uncle Khailou, a poor silk weaver, never failed to gather all his friends together every Saturday. Bending over their huge books from the midday coffee till the first stars shone out, they sought, with marvelous confidence, the answer to all problems, the most commonplace and the most metaphysical, their own problems and the problems of their families, of the community and of the world. They argued, examining line for line, word for word; and if the text did not seem to give them the answers they needed, they added their own commentaries so vividly that they made it vibrant with their own life.

"In exile," writes David Ben-Gurion, the President of the Israelian Council, "we have continued to live, in heart and mind, within our Biblical heritage." ("Ethics, Science and the Pioneer Sp_rit," speech made at Boston University.)

Let us set aside at least for the moment a philosophical examination of those Jewish values or even the question of their compatibility with the world in which we live. Not that I have nothing to say on this subject; nor that I am intimidated by postures of respect or a guilty and paralyzing modesty. I have shown that enough, I hope. But I must make it clear that the problem is greater than an ideological discussion. At the level of the experience lived, a cultural tradition is not only a culture in the bookish sense of the word, a concatenation of ideas or even a coherent system of truths that one can shrug off after proving that it contains serious errors, prejudices and even lies. A cultural tradition is also a sum total of ways of living, of mental attitudes, of confused riches in which the best, the mediocre and the worst rub elbows with the marvelous and the striking, with solid virtues and vulgar waste, the whole so well blended, assimilated and incorporated that it constitutes a collective way of being which, as a matter of fact, is transmitted by inheritance. One can, of course, try to carry the analysis farther and I have suggested elsewhere distinguishing sanctuary values and defensive institutions in the heritage. By those words which have since had some success, I meant all that ideological social machinery slowly constructed by the Jewish will to live to preserve the Jew during the terrible vicissitudes of his history. But institutions, like family or religion, like ethical, religious or social values, apparently all tend towards the same end: the Jew's heritage is also a concrete organization of his life and of his relations with other people in the world. Whence probably their extraordinary perenniality, both positive and negative, coercive and protective, so rigid and yet supple enough to persist throughout so many vicissitudes.

I mean, in short, that my heritage as a man and as a Jew is essential to me, above any discussion, above any problematical issues. More precisely, it embraces and comprises those problematical issues and that reflection as a part of itself. No doubt that my hesitations, my misgivings, my revolt, my shifts, stem directly from my uneasy attachment to that Jewish heritage. When I would launch into a long, critical, detailed and impassioned examination of a certain point of doctrine, my Uncle Khailou would listen to me indulgently and conclude: "I have hopes for you: you argue well."

That is why, paradoxically, no matter how helpful Jewish values may be in gaining a true understanding of Jewishness, those values would themselves seem mystifying and even incomprehensible if they were viewed in complete isolation, apart from the concept of Jewishness. In any case, if I may venture to say so, the lot of the Jew would not be fundamentally altered by his Jewish values, as these fail to account for his destiny. It is that specific Jewish destiny which must be first accounted for and comprehended before we reconsider those values in the light of that destiny as a whole.

THREE

The above statement can be easily proved in the case of religion. Religion is certainly the most notable and the most effective defense institution of the Jew, as it is among colonized peoples—which is not accidental. I have gone to some length to point out exactly what concerns the religion of my people and perhaps I have not quite finished. I thought I had practically disposed of religious magic; I rejected the irrational and mythical opportunities that systems of religious thought offer. My case was not exceptional for that matter; a great many, if not most young Jews showed the same mistrust. And yet, in that respect, my dealings with the Jewish religious fact were based on an ambiguity. Because the dogmatic content of Judaism did not seem to us on a par with modern science and philosophy, which we held henceforth to be the sole truth, we wanted to believe that the Jewish religious factor no longer interfered in any way with our lives. Because traditional religious attitudes no longer seemed to us compatible with our professions, our ambitions, our desire to be integrated in the non-Jewish city, we pretended to believe that those attitudes belonged to a sort of familial museum, which we visited from time to time but which did not influence to any extent our daily conduct, our spirits and our thoughts.

Then one day we had to admit that this religious factor, a complex mixture of beliefs more or less quiescent, of diffused values, of traditions more or less supple, of institutions more or less altered, continued surprisingly to govern our lives either directly or indirectly. More or less inwardly perhaps, often in opposition to it, but we lived it constantly; our every action was conditioned by it. Whether we decided to fast or not to fast on the Day of Atonement, we had to stop our activities out of respect for the tradition; whether we ate properly or not at Passover, whether we organized or refused to organize a certain ceremony. Was it necessary or not to have the prayer for the dead said at our uncle's funeral or in memory of our father? Was it necessary or not to send for the rabbi, accept or reject his presence at the birth of our children?

We decided first one way, then the other. But, in any case, we took into account that fact which cropped up insistently on every solemn occasion in Jewish existence, and which was rarely altogether absent from that existence. In short, I have long confounded a philosophic doubt with a practical void, a doctrinal decision with the actual absence of a social fact and a behavior pattern which, more or less impatiently, more or less willingly, I have continued to live.

Besides, I now see clearly that this practical divorce has never been as complete and as virulent with me as my theoretical impatience sometimes was. Perhaps because they did not seem to me so closely connected. In agreeing to sing the Haggadah at Passover or to celebrate Purim, I did not think that I was confirming the existence of God or the miracle of the Red Sea or of the fall of Haman. Simply, I was returning to my own people, to my father, my mother, my brothers and sisters, and to the ghetto, in a half-serious, half-childish collective game which either irritated or amused me according to my mood; an almost obligatory game, however, if I wanted to be one with them again or merely not to hurt them. The truth or the falsity of the traditional dogmas, the post-reasonings of apologists as to the presence of God or the rejection of God which by the very violence of my refusal would confirm it, and other theological jugglings, had truly nothing to do with it. This hiatus must also have contributed to that mistake in perspective I mentioned farther back among well-meaning non-Jewish authors. Their Jewish friends have often declared—and sincerely I believe—that they do not know if they themselves can be called Jews. Traditional beliefs had no theoretical value for them or rather they scarcely knew them; they had never read a line of the great Jewish books, the Talmud for example, and sometimes not even the Bible! Are not those authors therefore right in concluding that there are Jews without Judaism and without Jewishness? And, going a step farther, that Jews are perhaps nothing but a word? In fact we would have had to study the actual conduct of those same Jews, their total behavior. Beyond their declarations, their scholarly affirmations, or rather their lack of knowledge, we would have to discover their real relations with Jewry and Judaism even though those relations might appear to be very lax and negligent; disregarding the fact that, in these matters, deep sentiments, strong emotions are infinitely more revealing than the thin layer of declared ideas even when they are presented in a coherent doctrine. The man who states clearly that he has no religion and yet has been married in a religious ceremony, explains his action with a certain condescending irony. "It was to please my parents!" But after all, he did it; and the potential displeasure he might have caused his parents was strong enough to do violence to his philosophical convictions. The other man had his son circumcised, at the insistence of his parents-in-law or because his wife would be upset. And almost all of them have themselves buried in a Jewish cemetery, thus obliging their descendants to go to separate cemeteries to make their annual pilgrimages.

This matter cannot be considered solely on the plane of language. It is always that same idealistic mistake that unfolds the drama on the level of words, whereas that drama affects all of life. I have said that we should not believe the non-Jew on his statements alone, on what he affirms or denies about the Jew, but should rather consider what sort of life he has made for the Jew: the actual, concrete relationship that has been set up between them. Nor must the Jew's statements about himself be taken literally. We cannot characterize a man merely by what he thinks of himself, nor by what he thinks he believes, but by what he does: that, moreover, is what reveals his real thought and his real beliefs. For a long time I have not believed myself on the basis of words and I do not expect it from others. My own behavior, my unexpected emotions, have shown me that I am much more sensitive than I thought to signs of recognition from my native group. On that point, of course, one has to correct oneself, choose, keep and reject. But, after all, to consider the Jewish religious fact only as the religious ideology of the Jews would be a false and idealistic attitude which ends by losing sight of the fact. Now there is a Jewish religious fact, more or less coercive, more or less approved, but tenaciously lived by the vast majority of Jews. Once we have said this, that tenacity, that survival of a Jewish religious positivity is neither incomprehensible nor mysterious: it is constantly nourished by the whole Jewish fate. Family, religion, and the various Jewish institutions have given Jewry its historic character. But inversely they themselves have been slowly secreted and fashioned by that stubborn will to live. The Jewish body, fighting for its very existence, has known how to discover and to forge painfully the instruments of its survival.

Basically, all Jews are at least in some way aware of this. That is why attacks by unbelieving Jews against the Jewish religion have never been effective. It has been said, and quite truly, that when a Jew condemns religion and priests he is thinking especially of the Christian religion and its priests, and not of the synagogue and its rabbis. There are two very different reasons for this: the real clerical power, which is politically and philosophically dangerous, is obviously not the Jewish, but the Christian religion. A war against the synagogue and the rabbinate would indeed be ridiculous and unjustified; they have trouble enough in keeping their place in a non-Jewish society. The second reason is that there is no real Jewish anti-clerical tradition; for example, there is no atheism among Jews as violent, as aggressive as that of the Catholic's. Not that there are no Jewish atheists. I have met atheists more frequently among Jews than in any other group, but theirs is a more discreet atheism and, surprisingly enough among masochists, in a way less directed against itself. Why? Because when a Catholic attacks his religion, he does not feel that he is endangering the entire social structure. On the contrary, the anticlerical Christian has good intentions; he wants to defend society against an institution and traditions he considers harmful. Among Jews it is not so easy to consider religion apart from Jewry. The Jewish religion is so closely bound up with it that any attack against it rebounds heavily, whether the Jew wishes or not, on the whole Jewish society. Now Jewish society is already so threatened, so weak, that any additional attack, especially from within, would be really intolerable. In the midst of non-Jews an attack by a Jew against Jewry and Judaism cannot fail to look like pure treason not only to other Jews, but surely also to himself. That is why the renegade (I use this word attenuating as much as possible its pejorative connotation) quickly loses his head. If the community has not resolutely excluded him, he generally excludes himself. Historically, Jews who have given in to a fairly systematic attack on the Jewish religion, have almost always ceased to belong to Jewry. And this is obviously true where Jews are scattered among various nations. It is not unthinkable that, in the bosom of a recovered Jewish national organism it may be possible to criticize religion without appearing to betray it or to question the entire Jewish destiny. But that is another story. As long as the Jew was lost in the midst of hostile people, he could not permit himself to add his attack to the attacks of non-Jews, even from other motives, an attack on one of the rare pillars that support the common household.

"If you want to know, I myself have lost faith in God. If you want to know, I am a Marxist, but nevertheless I believe I am part of the community of Israel. No one can live without his family name . . . The God of Israel is absent, undoubtedly He does not exist, and yet He is the rallying point of our dispersion. One day a year men and women from New York to Helsinki, from Paris to Tashkent, from Johannesburg to Buenos Aires can commune in the same thought, can bear witness to their fundamental communion of destiny with the aid of an identical mask formed by hunger. In speaking to their God-Symbol, they are speaking to one another no matter what the diversity of their tongues and of their language." (A. Mandel, *The Burnt Vessel*.)

The religion of the oppressed person is not only a religion: it is a cement and a dike, an opportunity and a powerful means of reunion. Whence that fact, paradoxical only in appearance, that in those transition periods in which the oppressed person begins to free himself, in which he tries to go forward and to leave his accursed past behind, he reverts to his old rites, the most ancient and sometimes the most hidebound in which he has ceased to believe for a long time.

My students among the colonized, who had often affirmed their atheism, used to fast on the day of Ramadan. When I would ask them why, they would answer, "To be with the people who believe in it and who fast." In the same way, when we were young Zionists, we organized demonstrations to explain to the still skeptical ghetto the meaning of Zionism, the need to guarantee our collective future, we took care to make use of our common past and the traditional solemnities. We organized meetings on Purim, excursions on Passover, and the sale of lapel buttons for pilgrimages. Of course, we gave all this a new meaning, we minimized the mystical dimensions, we made fun of ourselves a bit, but in the end we had reaped the heritage.

The Burden
of the Heritage

ONE

I will not dwell further on the positive aspect of Jewish life. And may certain of my readers spare me a useless argument. I am convinced that one could give a detailed and interesting description of the Jewish heritage. But such was obviously not my intention. I have not in any way attempted to make an exhaustive study of Jewish institutions, customs, rites, beliefs, etc.; I merely wanted to offer a true and adequate picture of the Jewish fate: and it is sufficient for me to have shown that the components of that fate are very real and not merely reactive. Of course, much Jewish behavior is only a reaction to threats: many features of the Jew's physiognomy are merely lines slowly chiseled there throughout the centuries. But there again the genetic explanation is one thing and the real fact, as it actually happened, is another. To uncover the origin of a fact, a custom, does not in the least impair its soundness. Recently I listened to a recording of Jewish-Tunisian songs of circumcision, joyous and grave, wonderfully tender towards the mother and the newborn babe. At least that is the way they sounded to me as I heard them again. On thinking it over, I suspect that in the beginning they were meant to praise and reassure the young mother, to combat the general fear of such an appalling rite, to disguise and extol a barbarous custom that would be unbearable were it not encouraged and imposed by general acclaim. As I listened to that record, I felt a real sense of jubilation, a sort of nostalgic happiness caused, I suppose, by the memory of our collective observances, of the touching sense of communion on days of circumcision or of amusing ritual songs the evening before. And in spite of her fear, her frequent sobs at the crucial moment, the young mother is visibly happy through her tears, proud of her importance, of the gift she is giving to God and to the community of men. The men, whatever the harshness of the bargain concluded with God or with our history, appeared to be relieved at having once again reaffirmed the great chain that links us to life and to each other. Like most cultural symbols, any rite is, fundamentally, largely positive and above all experienced as such. For me Jewish positivity, I repeat, is an obvious fact.

Having said this I must add, however, that nothing can altogether escape the profound evil that undermines the entire Jewish fate. At the very heart of Jewish positivity, we still find again the same poison at work. To throw light on the shadowy figure was, in truth, too simple a procedure. Such is the negativity of the Jew's life and history that everything about him, even those things that are apparently the most solid, still bears traces of his defeat and his humiliation. The survival of his religion is certainly an astonishing victory of the Jew over time. But the terrible problem of his existence in the midst of others has undoubtedly governed that religion and given it its particular aspect, demanding, coercive, both omnipresent and hypercritical. For that age-old and greatly threatened religion is the least comfortable religion there is: it is unquestionably more formal and more ceremonial than the religion of most of the peoples among whom the Jew lives. Catholic priests often make that perfidious remark in boastful contrast to the rich and deeply moving vitality of their own religion. One must admit, however, that they are not completely wrong. It was Nahum Goldmann, the President of the World Zionist Organization, speaking before the XXVth Zionist Congress in January, 1961, who said:

"Judaism is not an easy religion. It is a very exacting and demanding religion, not satisfied with a confession of faith and a recital of prayers but trying to shape, to influence and dominate the life of the individual Jew in all its spheres."

I have frequently had occasion to write this about the Jews of North Africa, and I have been able to confirm it in Europe. In spite of a recent effort by the rabbis to revive religion, it is true that the European synagogue and its servants remain, in general, astonishingly hidebound. In Tunisia we had a fairly ambiguous attitude towards religion and the rabbinate, a kind of affectionate contempt, a more or less amused complicity which, by sterilizing any revolt, kept us from breaking away altogether. In our case, it is true, the spectacle of a vanquished religion, of wretched priests belonging to past ages, could scarcely arouse anything but indifference or derision. But the situation in Europe is not very encouraging either. There the Jewish religion is as far as possible from that triumphant flowering, that simple security that stems from a healthy vitality. It is almost always narrow, mistrustful, fiercely opposed to any innovation. To contract a mixed marriage, for example, which may be advantageous to the community because it brings in new blood, you almost have to bribe a rabbi—even if the young wife agrees to be converted! For some time now, young liberal rabbis have been trying to get around a number of prohibitions, more social and traditional than strictly religious, but they are literally detested by the majority of their colleagues.

Now those restrictions, that formalism, that watchful and stifling intolerance is found in the institutions of many oppressed persons. As if those restrictions and that intolerance were the condition itself, the price paid for their survival. Religious formalism is, moreover, only one of the aspects of a more general formalism, which is also seen in the behavior of colonized natives. It is a spontaneous reaction of self-defense, a means of safeguarding the collective conscience, without which a people rapidly disappears. Under conditions of dependency or oppression, the collapse of religion, like the breaking up of the family, certainly entails the grave risk of extinction of a group of people. I have already shown my impatience and where my philosophic sympathies lie; but I must admit that if the Jewish religion had been unstable and obliging, it would have been diluted and drowned out and the Jew with it. Its mission, fixed at an early stage, was to protect the Jew, and in order to maintain himself the Jew has had to maintain his religion intact.

The result, however, is a social and historical catalepsy, a kind of cyst in which the group is enclosed and hardened, reducing its vitality in order to save itself. The institution-refuge is thus armor and corset: it protects and stifles; it sustains but at the same time it prevents any development. Which explains the ambiguity, the hesitant approaches of the Jew and of all oppressed peoples with respect to their institutions and their traditions. The Jew appears to scorn them and to hide from them and at the same time to cling to them in despair. As young Jews, we generally began by applying our irony and aggressiveness to them. It is a fact: Heritage is a burden for us at first. We wanted to leave everything behind us, to have a wider scope, a complete freedom of movement. Then, the defeats becoming almost inevitable, the world's hostility triumphant, we usually fell back on the past, on the old collective customs, weak and hardened as they might be, but, at least, definite landmarks in our lives, solid bastions as long as oppression lasts, for they are constantly strengthened by it.

TWO

Another defensive institution essential to the existence of the Jew is the family. Non-Jewish authors have often noted it.

"Take all that you have asked," said he, "Sir Knight —take ten times more—reduce me to ruin and to beggary, if thou wilt,—nay, pierce me with thy poniard, broil me on that furnace, but spare my daughter, deliver her in safety and honour!—As thou art born of woman, spare the honour of a helpless maiden—She is the image of my deceased Rachael, she is the last of six pledges of her love—Will you deprive a widowed husband of his sole remaining comfort?—Will you reduce a father to wish that his only living child were laid beside her dead mother, in the tomb of our fathers?"

"I would," said the Norman, somewhat relenting, "that I had known of this before. I thought your race had loved nothing save their money-bags."

"Think not so vilely of us, Jews though we be," said Isaac, eager to improve the moment of apparent sympathy: "the hunted fox, the tortured wild-cat loves its young —the despised and persecuted race of Abraham love their children!" (Sir Walter Scott, *Ivanhoe*).

The Jews have sometimes denied this, but to tell the truth, weakly. The importance of the Jewish family is too obvious. The family suggests family spirit and family spirit means solidarity . . . and here we are back again at a familiar theme. It would do no good to retort that in our bourgeois societies the family is considered the basis of society, the social unit *par excellence,* the hearth at which communal virtues, the personalities of children are developed, etc. People seem to forget this when they speak of the Jew. Far from paying him a compliment, they vituperate against Jewish clannishness which isolates him from, and hinders the functioning of, the life of the community. So true is it that there is no virtue in itself, that like a disastrous catalysis the oppressed person's good qualities change significance in the context of his own nature. But I have already said enough on this subject and I have ended it with the accusation. I shall confine myself to noting a fact which I consider obvious: like religion, the Jewish family is an undeniable factor in the life of the Jew, a factor of an organization and a solidity seldom found elsewhere.

Why? That is obviously no more incomprehensible than the extraordinary survival of religion. With his participation in the collectivity in which he lives, in the nation and in history questioned, what can the Jew fall back on? One quickly discovers, if one thinks it over, that the outlets are not unlimited: family and religion, profession sometimes, even humanity as a whole. Within the national collectivity or outside of it, in short, where the Jew cannot be challenged, where the will of others has not reacted seriously against him. Of course, the accuser also disparages the Jew's family and is suspicious of his strange love for humanity; if he could, he would even deny the Jew any human characteristics. De-humanization is the extreme but logical method of most oppressions. Even in the case of woman, man frankly monopolizes the entire human species (Simone de Beauvoir), of which woman is but a variant, a little rib as we know.

But after all, in spite of a certain anxiety, the Jew does not believe in his own inhumanity. If forced to, he would acknowledge a few blemishes, several weaknesses in his biology and in his psychology, but at the same time he insists on his own humanity, on his universality. In his opinion, they are unusally excellent; on this point there is undeniable Jewish pride. But more than that: the accuser can do nothing about it; his will-power is not strong enough. Even if he can actually prevent the Jew from participating fully in the life of the nation, how could he prevent him from being a part of humanity? It is true that the Nazis tried to—but their efforts worked against them and succeeded in casting doubt on their own humanity. In short, the Jew takes refuge in the most restricted groups—the family, and in the broadest groups—humanity; in the most concrete and the most abstract. Certain other groups have been able to welcome Jews, certain political parties, for example; and almost always when they were trying to measure up to the dimensions of the world and universality. The day when there is a chauvinist reaction, when people start to become "nationals," they get rid of their Jews who, for that matter, leave of their own accord.

Those outlets do not really save the Jew from misfortune, though they permit him to survive. They even foster the misfortune in the same way that an appeasement preserves a bad situation instead of letting it deteriorate and die. In every case, the Jew remains socially cut off. He can live only with the closest of his own people or in the anonymity of a great crowd, that is, in the abstract. He lives with an idea of men, not with flesh and blood men. How can he do otherwise? I have related how, smothered in the overwhelming and perpetual supervision of my family (in the broader sense of the word: uncles, aunts, cousins, relatives!) I reacted violently in my first novel against all family life. That rejection of the family aroused angry disgust on the part of the entire community of my native town. Was it a simple reaction of defense? No, not entirely: in the discussions that followed I discovered that most of the members of my group had a genuine appreciation of the Jewish family. They cited all those uncles who pay for their nephews' education, oldest sons who spontaneously assume responsibility for the entire family and do not marry until they have settled the lives of their sisters; brothers who contribute to the maintenance of their less fortunate sisters' households, etc . . . And all that was true; I have since verified it often. For a moment, I was baffled.

My malaise, however, persisted and I did not understand it till later on when I studied the family of the colonized native. One finds there, as a matter of fact, the same dialectic of the negative and the positive in the same institution. Rejected by non-Jewish society (or by the colonizers), the Jew like the colonized can take refuge only in his family. But he will unfortunately pay very dearly for it. The family is both sanctuary and flight, the protecting wall and the prison, riches and poverty. The Jew is protected and subjugated by it. That extraordinary protection of each member by all the members is, at the same time, the demand of all on each. That proffered gift, given permanently, authorizes a constant claim which had become intolerable to me, at least during my adolescence.

Moreover, I felt obscurely that this extraordinary warmth was cloying, that it dangerously weakened all our energies, new to begin with. When I returned from my trips and found myself again in the bosom of my family, it seemed to me that my energy slackened. At first, on edge and mistrustful, the sense of exile and anonymity I still felt on the station platform quickly left me, vanished like a bad dream. There was no longer any need to put on armor, parry, calculate and take precautions in that trusting unity, in the warmth and noise of the little room where we were all crowded in together. There everything was permitted, everything would be forgiven, nothing serious could happen. But still I held back a little, mindful of old and petty grievances and perhaps, too, out of pride. Then, with a vague regret and making fun of myself somewhat, I let myself go, I gave myself up to that immense peace and quiet I had finally found again.

There is worse. The Jewish mother is admirable in her tenderness and devotion, the father is everything to his children who are brooded over, protected, preserved as much as possible from the hostile world. But the child will have an unreal picture of this world of non-Jews, which is infinitely harsher than the life within the tribe; and which he will think he can disarm with kindness, reasoning or by appealing to emotions. All his views of this world are falsified. For a long time I thought, and at heart I have never completely rid myself of the idea, that I could always keep on good terms with other men by saying to them: "Let's forget for a moment conventions, prejudices, distrusts and get to the heart of our common humanity. There we are surely going to find a common meeting-ground!" Basically, I had a tendency to seek a possible relative in every man. In everything that has happened to me since, I have always felt a childish and painful astonishment when confronted with the incomprehensible cruelty of non-Jews. I would probably still have to restrain myself from saying to the police or to the enemy's soldiers: "But how can you treat me like this?" The Jewish family, a defensive institution for the Jew against the world, shields him, from his childhood on, from the reality of that world.

On the other hand, he is inevitably hurt by the world because he is not prepared for the struggle; and because, in every way, the struggle is too harsh and too unfair to him, the Jew turns back to the family, re-enforces it and supports it with ever new contributions. The child, the adolescent Jew, is the hope, the most precious investment of the father, the mother and all the adults who are vindicated and live on in him. But the father is strengthened by his sons, recognized as the indisputable leader of that tiny, ridiculous and touching society. This is one of the possible interpretations of the famous dictum: on Friday evening, every Jew is a prince in Israel . . . he is a prince in the bosom of his family. It is through that miracle that the Jew, so often miserable, defeated and humiliated in the outside world, becomes in the midst of his own people, a majestic patriarch. It is a just revenge, acknowledged and consolidated by his people. Through such a paradox the Jewish father may appear even today to be one of the most terrible, he who is socially so weak— which is why the works of Jewish authors almost always resound with the conflict of the father. Look at the works of Kafka, of Wassermann. In a certain way the Jewish family and the Jewish father are the symbol of the only social reality the Jew directly experiences. I repeat: the Jew does not only lose by his isolation, he also gains by having a warm, benignant, indispensable life in common with his own people, a life he cannot seriously have with others. He cannot be spontaneously a complete citizen like the others. But does that matter? He will be an undisputed member of his family, more and more convinced himself, as he grows older, of that family which gave him birth because he, in his turn, will father a child. Is he not a part of history? Is he not a part of the city? He will be a son while waiting to become the father of numerous children, then a grandfather and a patriarch in his turn. He gains and he loses, and what he loses, he brings back to the family which is more assured than ever, strengthened and, always generous and protective, is ready to welcome his successors. And because the family is generous and protective it is of necessity encroaching, coercive and emasculating. That is also why the revolt of the Jewish child fails so often. Against whom shall he revolt? Against non-Jews? They are too numerous, too powerful and too legally organized—let us not forget that. There is no hope of changing their course in his favor. Shall he revolt against his own people? An absurd rebellion; and above all, as he quickly discovers, they are his sole support, his last recourse; inevitably he comes back to the family one day, resigned, mocking and confident. But once again the revolt has miscarried and the heritage becomes more burdensome, more terribly paralyzing. The Jewish religion is perpetuated intact, the Jewish family continues, since neither that revolt nor that family can actually end in a social order in which the Jew, rediscovering his full measure as a man, would cease to cling to the family that clings to him.

THREE

The Jew, in short, adapts himself in a certain measure to his misfortune. He ends by perfecting a chain of patient strategies, defensive measures against others and against himself: as for instance the famous Jewish humor, a marvelous exorcism for anguish and guilt, or certain professional choices, such as medicine. One can easily make the same analysis of numerous other characteristics: the number of children, undeniably greater in the average Jewish family, the importance of family ceremonies, a certain appetence for living (which the anti-Semite dubs vulgarity), an unquestionable intellectual passion (which is denounced as "intellectual voracity"), etc. . . . All that is very well inscribed and is linked in that perspective. Is it necessary to find the beginning of the chain? It really makes little difference. Does the number of children make the family important, or the reverse? Is this the sign of the greatest vitality or of the greatest anxiety? Both, I think.

The same thing holds good for the importance of food: oral compensation, sublimation, an outlet for anxiety, the psychoanalyst would say, and it may be so. One must take care, however, to attribute that revenge and anxiety to that social defeat; that impossibility of really becoming part of the world of other men. When a man is not recognized by other men, he must strengthen himself among his own people.

These little tricks of survival are found among the majority of oppressed peoples; oppression has only to last long enough for the oppressed person to discover the responses best adapted to his particular oppression. But if the oppression becomes manageable in the long run, it becomes imbedded, marking its victim more profoundly, more definitely. Thus the oppression of women seems the most benign and the most elegant: I consider it the most difficult to combat because it is the most ancient. I am convinced that colonization is not so harsh because it is relatively recent. The oppression of the Jew falls between the two: it is ancient enough to be tractable in appearance, but at the same time it is deeper-rooted than the oppression of the colonized native. The longer oppression lasts and the more the responses become precise, and are shaded, the more institutions of defense are reinforced and consolidated, the more the positive and negative aspects are inextricably intermingled. Solidarity is thus an unquestionably positive aspect of Jewish life. It is a social fact, which the Jew finds before him, an integral part of the collective behavior of his own people towards him and which calls forth a spontaneous response on his part. But how can he fail to discover an equally menacing dialectic? Solidarity is an answer to threat and heterogeneity, but it confirms that heterogeneity and keeps alive that threat as much as it tends to mitigate it. I remember one of those interminable and impassioned discussions of our adolescence. Is Jewish clannishness the cause of our exclusion from the world of non-Jews, or does exclusion force us to be clannish? Has Zionism created the animosities of nationalists toward the Jews, or has the animosity of nationalists given that national aspect to Jewish demands? All that, of course, is true at one and the same time. Solidarity, necessary, called forth and strengthened by mistrust and threat, in its turn, feeds mistrust and threat because it insists on heterogeneity and makes it definitely more noticeable. Thus even the replies to oppression become suspect to the oppressor and he is able to use them again as fresh accusations.

Where conditions of oppression exist, everything has a tendency to become negative. Negativity attacks everything, corrodes everything. It is not enough to say that there is as much negative as positive in the Jewish fate, as much malaise and hostility as there are will to live and institutions. The contagion of misfortune penetrates even the most positive aspects. As if Jewish positivity, partial fruit of a harmful situation, must engender of itself a certain harmfulness. It appears, moreover, literally as disgrace and confusion to others. We can therefore suggest an additional interpretation of the myth of the scapegoat: the Jew is a real disgrace, an intolerable disharmony in a non-Jewish society. The scapegoat is charged with confusing the world and is sacrificed in order to find again the lost order. Once he is dead, the confusion must end and order reappear. It is understood that the Jew could be chosen to embody this terrible role. Indeed, he embodies in part social and metaphysical confusion. He is not only non-Jewish; he is not satisfied not to be what he must be; he is something else. Not only does he not go to the same church as everyone else, but he goes to a different temple. Not only does he not have the collective habits of everyone, but he has different customs. It is plain to be seen how unusual and even irritating Jewish life is when the social milieu is less polished and in moments when collective life is intensely vital.

"You cannot understand from the outside what the

feast of Easter means in our countries," a friend, a native of a village in the East, said to me one day. "The people are at a white heat; Christ has just been arrested and led before Caiphus. They stick pins in his forehead. The priest prostrates himself on the ground . . . literally. And there is real fasting, too, for the people are actually starving! Fiction and privations intermingle; people are tired, exasperated by real penances for imaginary motives, but which become as real as the privations . . . Now who is responsible for all that? Who are the guilty? The Jews! The priests repeat it all the time, all through Easter week especially and long before . . ." He added, "And may I say this, too? The trouble is that during that period the Jews, too, are in an unusual state: they are celebrating their own Passover; they bustle around, they are serious, they are preparing something mysterious . . . You must admit that this custom of painting a bloody hand on their doors is really sinister! All the same it has something to do with the anxiety of the others. . . ."

I was astonished. I had never looked at the question from that angle.

"In Tunisia," I said, "not so long ago, we still put the mark of the famous bloody hand on our doors . . . You know, I hope, that it is sheep's blood, the sheep from which we cut the meat we eat that same evening . . . I assure you there was nothing sinister about it, nor even solemn. It was a rather amusing ceremony; besides, every Jewish Passover is relatively gay. It is a feast of freedom . . ."

"For you, perhaps! We don't see it in that light. Christian Easters are generally austere; they forbade us to sing, we meditated on the martyrdom of Christ . . . Perhaps you have seen some of those processions in Italy, in Sicily, in Spain, those people with their heads covered with black hoods, carrying a corpse the color of wax, of bloodless flesh, and pierced through with bleeding wounds. That is Easter for our populations. That sadness, those privations, that corpse which represents them all, unjustly, ignobly immolated! That is Easter . . . Don't be surprised after that, that at the slightest pretext—which they furnish themselves—they fall furiously, even joyously, upon the people they consider guilty!"

"All the Jew asks is to live!" I protested. "It's insanity!"

"Perhaps . . . or, rather, it is the meeting of two insanities. A meeting in which you are the underdog, because you are the weakest. The Christian Easter is, in one sense, the feast of resentment; from resentment to vengeance is only a step. That pretext is easy to find, I grant you. It might be the blood of the Pascal lamb with which the Jews smear their doors to commemorate the famous sign to God's messenger: to Christians it might become human blood, the blood of any Christian child who has disappeared during that period . . ."

At the time of that conversation I was struck by that interpretation of the Easter celebrations, Jewish and Christian, but I was not convinced. It seemed to me too theatrical, too paradoxical. Since then I am certain that my friend was fundamentally right, more right even than he knew. Setting aside spectacular crises, I am convinced that Jewish existence as a whole is unusual, and not only Passover, the bloody hand, or kosher food. If the Jew exists, that is, if he exists ever so little in his own way, he cannot fail to clash with others and as a result suffer and sometimes die. And we have to admit that the Jew's heritage and all his positive aspects which, to be sure, help him to live, nevertheless lead to shame and provocation. There is, of course, no certainty that, once all Jews are expelled, reduced to absolute invisibility and exterminated, harmony, order and happiness would be restored, but I admit that a certain shame will have disappeared.

conclusion

THE OPPRESSED

"To talk of despair is to conquer it. Despairing literature is a contradiction in terms."

ALBERT CAMUS (THE REBEL)

"For as often as I speak, I cry out, I cry: 'Violence and spoil'; Because the word of the Lord is made a reproach unto me, and a derision, all the day."

JEREMIAH 20:8

The Oppressed

Before closing this evaluation of my life, I have one final hesitation; have I not painted too gloomy a picture? Have I not exaggerated the importance of the Jewish misfortune?

No, sincerely, this is just the way I have lived it; everything I have written has almost always seemed obvious to me. I would like to tone down the intensity, the fever and the furor with which I have often fought against my destiny as a Jew; but not the ultimate significance, the general appearance, the sequence and the principal points of my evaluation. I admit that a man of a colder temperament than mine, one less given to impatience, one who had lived in another country, under other institutions, in less troubled circumstances, might tell his story more calmly. That is why I warned from the beginning (and I remind you of it again), that this was a portrait of myself and only by extension the portrait of other

Jews. But I still think that every Jew, if he forces himself, must describe the same processes and the same restrictions on his life, in some ways more or less obvious, of course, and more or less acknowledged. The pathetic note I have perhaps injected into my narrative and which I have often tried to moderate, has perhaps only dramatized a little more a condition that I have lived as fundamentally dramatic.

I believe, in short, that there is a Jewish fate, a specific Jewish fate. This fate makes the Jew a minority being; different; separated both from himself and from others; a being abused in his culture and in his history, in his past and in his daily life—in the end, an abstract being. What have I done up to this point but sketch the principal traits of a figure of oppression? Yes, as a Jew, I am above all an oppressed person and the Jewish fate is essentially a condition of oppression. I have by now verified this often enough: in this perspective, my figure resembles astonishingly that of many others: to be precise, of other oppressed peoples.

If it is not always clear that the Jew is an oppressed person, it is because oppression does not always have the same appearance. It can be obvious as in the case of the proletariat, an oppression of class against class within the same nation; or as in the case of the colonized where it is an oppression of people against people, nation against nation. The oppression of the Jew stands midway between the two: it is within the same nation without being involved in the class struggle. The oppression of the American Negro is still more complex; it includes at the same time economic, cultural and political pressure. The oppression of woman is probably the most artful, being tempered and disguised by eroticism and maternity. I said, at the beginning of this book, that I would one day try to bring together in a single picture the similarities and differences of all these contemporary oppressed peoples. But did I need to wait till then to discover that though each has his own special characteristics, we are all brothers in suffering and bitterness, that we are all burdened with negativity and that our positivity is gravely threatened?

Why not say so, after all? As a Jew I am a man of deficiencies. Those deficiencies are actual defects in my existence; I am not only suspected and accused, I am bullied, restricted, curtailed in my daily life, in my development as a man. These objective deficiencies, often institutional, involve true restriction, ever serious destructions of the soul of the Jew. For the most serious element, perhaps, the one most difficult to admit, is that the Jewish fate is a degrading fate.

This is a bitter truth, and I realize it is a provocative one. Let those who would dispute it, however, think it over further. If oppression were not so disastrous, so productive of deficiencies and of actual destructions in the oppressed persons, why would it revolt us? Why would we fight against it? The sad reality, unfortunately, is that all oppression debases and ruins the oppressed. Our weak reaction to aggression, for example, and our resignation before catastrophe are not a sign of a certain obscure metaphysical grandeur, or the proof of an intransigent moral will, as we like to say. They are the symptoms of a terrible usury, of an accumulated historical lassitude. An overwhelming and many-shaped myth plus numerous and perfectly concrete deficiencies are united to bring about this beautiful result.

As if it were possible that such a situation, such a mythical rejection and such a persistent exclusion, a degrading pressure so difficult to bear, could fail to leave any traces, any chronic scars in the soul and figure of the oppressed. The longer the oppression lasts, the more it profoundly affects him. It ends by becoming so familiar to him that he believes it is part of his own constitution, that he accepts it and could not imagine his recovery from it. This acceptance is the crowning point of oppression. If oppression lasts for even a short time, the majority of the oppressed end by being equally oppressed inwardly.

"Our inner putrefaction," explained the contemporary Jewish philosopher, Hahad Aam, ". . . all the blemishes that devour the Jewish soul." To which Albert Einstein, in *The World As I See It,* echoed, "I saw worthy Jews basely caricatured, and the sight made my heart bleed. I saw how schools, comic papers, and innumerable other forces of the Gentile majority undermined the confidence even of the best of my fellow-Jews. . . ."

I am well aware that the Jew's defenders often maintain that he is an ideal human being, just as the proletarian is supposed to be essentially virtuous and the colonized always innocent. I must confess that I do not believe it. No doubt special qualities develop as the direct result of misfortune. In the case of the Jew, a greater respect for human life, perhaps, and a sharper understanding of the suffering of other people. But those are usually the reverse side of a more serious deformation and they are too dearly paid for. That aloofness from human beings and events, for example, that we have acquired, may be, it is true, the cause of a strength, an irony and a greater freedom. The two men who have done most to reveal the working of society are Jews: Marx and Freud. The former discovered the economic scope, the foundation of the pyramid, the latter the motor of the wish motive behind alibis and ideologies. Perhaps to accomplish that they had to be Jews: they had to be able to look at that society both from within and from without. Common values and popular idols, considered with our detachment, our troubled mistrust, often crumble, revealing what they are: temporary and fragile, and not sacred. But this lucidity, born of aloofness, is paid for in advance. It is the complement of our solitude and of our abandonment by others. Moreover, not all Jews become a Marx or a Freud, not all Jews turn the hostilities of others and their restlessness into intuitions of genius. But almost all Jews are oppressed, anxious and ostracized, with no control over their destiny and in doubt as to their future. Almost all Jews are afraid, and it is not good for a man to be afraid for such a long time, from father to son. All Jews are at grips with the fate which is imposed upon them, and they must try to respond to the problems which this fate poses for them.

I definitely do not want to shock my Jewish readers with exaggerations, especially since this is neither a question of a definitive moral decay, nor of a natural constitution, nor, of course, of a diabolical trick as the anti-Semites and all racists suggest. What history has done, history can undo. Every time the Jew is treated as a complete man, he behaves like other men, not to say better than they. The events in Israel have largely confirmed this. And, in every way, it is untrue that the Jew pays less dearly for his participation in the life of the city. On the contrary, the oppressor always makes him pay more for a smaller share of the common life. Contrary to prejudices, statistics show us that the Jew contributes more liberally than his fellow citizens to miliary obligations, even though he is coldly abandoned when the triumphant enemy demands it. That is equally evident in the colonial situation and in employer-employee relationships. Thus this evaluation in no way strengthens our accusers. I know, however, that such confessions will trouble the reserve of my people—how would I not know it?—but isn't it even more injurious for us to hide from ourselves our wounds and infirmities, of which we must surely be cured someday?

I even dare to hope I will not shock my non-Jewish readers unduly. Will they believe me if I tell them that this book has taught me, in some ways, to temper my resentment? It is true that I am convinced that there are more anti-Semites than people who are indifferent. But it is because the misfortune of the Jew involves, beyond the accusation, a myth and a language, in an ensemble of concrete relationships which link the Jew to the non-Jew, which the two partners find, discover and live from birth to death. That is why it has seemed to me false to isolate any particular traits, as is often done, to account for the existence of the Jew. The Jew is not explained by his religious, economic or political situation alone, nor by his psychology alone, nor by the pathology of the anti-Semite. It was necessary to evaluate an entire life, mine under the circumstances, all the successive discoveries, this long, complex and coherent itinerary, to understand each detail of this existence. Finally, in some ways I recognize a certain amount of fatalism in the fate imposed upon the Jews or, more exactly, in the social and cultural facts that are so heavy and so coercive that they are equally imposed on the non-Jews; I recognize that it is necessary to make a great effort to escape them and that one must be among the best to succeed.

I must add that I have made as great an effort as possible to write in the past tense, as if all this belonged to the past; and, in fact, I believe it does in part, and I say this not merely to avoid arguments. The rebirth of a sovereign Jewish state, the still fresh memory of a terrible war in which Jews paid so dearly for being Jews, in which nearly the whole world connected anti-Semitism with a government of shame, have made an open expression of hatred of the Jew difficult, at least for the present time. It is even possible that we may have entered upon a wholly new period of history, one that would see at last the progressive liquidation of that oppression the Jews have suffered for so long. But aside from the fact that a regression is always possible, that process of liberation is only just beginning. For that matter, it has begun several times already, and though each time the life of the Jew has been improved, it has never been on his own terms. Let us hope that this time it will succeed.

But meanwhile a tremendous negativity continues to limit, stifle, and cut off the life of every Jew. Except for some devotees anxious to show others and to prove to themselves that Jewishness is a gift from heaven and a garden of delights, and Judaism a pure and permanent positivity, except for a few liberals, whose modesty is so delicate that they prefer to deny a persecution that everyone recognizes, I am naïve enough to think that no one can quarrel seriously with me on this point. As I write these lines, two scandals, significant though of no great consequence, have broken out: the leading literary prize, the Prix Goncourt, has been awarded to a former pro-Nazi and notorious anti-Semite; the beneficiary of France's second literary prize, the Prix Femina, is suspected, rightly or wrongly, of latent anti-Semitism. Without entering into an esthetic or moral controversy, how can one fail to notice, at least, that it is still possible in France to be an anti-Semite and yet be held up to the admiration of crowds and to glory? A purely esthetic admiration and glory, we will be told. As if it were possible to separate those feelings from the meaning of a work . . . Well, so be it! In any case, it seems that hatred of the Jew can still be considered an admissible, bearable, almost normal fact. The members of those committees, it is true, defended themselves with an indignation which I believe to be sincere. Had they not, the previous year, given the prize to the work of a Jew which was one long outcry, a litany of Jewish sufferings? They also called our attention to the fact that their protests, and even all the commotion that surrounded the incident, were a good sign; and that again is true. Today this would not be so readily permitted, and the Jew has indeed been given an established place in the distribution of laurels. But, after all, it was as though they had fêted in succession the victim and his aggressor. In spite of themselves, those honest literary men had cast light on the ever present drama of the fate of the Jew. The weights of the scale move, it is true, the complete liberation of the Jew has perhaps begun, but as long as history hesitates, the calling to account goes on.